Critical Approaches to Fie

In *Critical Approaches to Fieldwork* Gavin Lucas provides a fundamental examination of the historical and conceptual framework within which archaeology is practised today. Drawing on the development of the discipline since the nineteenth century, the relation between theoretical paradigms and everyday archaeological practice is critically explored.

This work takes as its starting point the role of fieldwork and how this has changed over the past 150 years. The author argues against progressive accounts of fieldwork and instead places it in its broader intellectual context. From this, a number of key structural changes are identified in archaeological practice which correlate interestingly with the emergence of sub-divisions within the discipline, such as finds specialisms, area/period research and theoretical/methodological specialities. It is argued that such structural divisions within archaeology have major theoretical consequences which need to be addressed. This work contributes greatly to this emerging discussion.

In providing a much-needed historical and critical evaluation of current practice in archaeology, this book opens up a topic of debate which affects all archaeologists, whatever their particular interests. This will be essential reading for all current and future archaeologists.

Gavin Lucas is currently working for the Cambridge Archaeological Unit involved in directing excavation and post-excavation programmes.

Critical Approaches to Fieldwork

Contemporary and historical archaeological practice

Gavin Lucas

London and New York

First published 2001 by Routledge
11 New Fetter Lane, London EC4P 4EE

Simultaneously published in the USA and Canada
by Routledge
29 West 35th Street, New York, NY 10001

Routledge is an imprint of the Taylor & Francis Group

© 2001 Gavin Lucas

Typeset in Goudy by Florence Production Ltd,
Stoodleigh, Devon
Printed and bound in Great Britain by St Edmundsbury Press, Bury St Edmunds,
Suffolk

British Library Cataloguing in Publication Data
A catalogue record for this book is available from the British Library

Library of Congress Cataloging in Publication Data
Lucas, Gavin, 1965-
   Critical approaches to fieldwork : contemporary and historical
   archaeological practice /
   Gavin Lucas.
   p. cm.
   Includes bibliographical references and index.
   1. Archaeology. 2. Archaeology—field work. I. Title.

CC75 .L78 2000
930.1—dc21
                                     00-032213

ISBN 0–415–23534–0 (pbk)
ISBN 0–415–23533–2 (hbk)

Contents

Figures

Tables

Acknowledgements

This book first took form in 1997 and has since been modified quite substantially due to the helpful advice of a number of people. In particular, its direction and coherence has benefited immeasurably through this feedback. I would like to thank many people for their help and support: Ian Hodder who read various drafts and provided much support, particularly in the initial stages of writing; my friends and colleagues in Cambridge and from Çatalhöyük (1996–7), among whom I had the best possible environment to learn what it means to do archaeology; and in particular those who read and commented on various drafts or parts of this book – Craig Cessford, Adrian Chadwick, Jenny Bredenberg, Victor Buchli, Chris Evans, Carolyn Hamilton, Mark Knight, Lesley McFadyen and Roddy Regan. My thanks also go to Vicki Peters at Routledge for pushing the book through with encouragement and sound advice, and to Polly Osborn for taking it through its final stages; and finally to Randy McGuire, Bob Preucel and two anonymous readers for providing much needed criticism and comment.

Several figures in this book have been drawn from other publications and I would like to thank the following for permission to reproduce them: Academic Press Ltd (Figure 7), Institute of Archaeology (UCL) (Figures 14 and 16), Orion Publishing Group (Figure 4), Oxford University Press (Figure 5), the Prehistoric Society (Figure 22), Salisbury and South Wiltshire Museum (Figure 1) and the Society of Antiquaries (Figures 3 and 22). In addition, I would like to thank the Salisbury and South Wiltshire Museum for providing the photograph reproduced as Figure 1, the National Monuments Record for supplying the photograph in Figure 3 and Fornleifastofnun Íslands for providing the photographs used in Figure 20.

This book is dedicated to my mother and late father.

Gavin Lucas
Cambridge

Chapter 1

Introduction
Archaeology and the field

Not so long ago I was working on a small trial excavation in the village of Castor in eastern England; it involved cutting a narrow trench into a beautiful old orchard garden backing on to a churchyard in order to find evidence for a Roman palace which once occupied almost the whole village. In the end, we did find the remains of Roman buildings on a terrace, as well as a great deal of subsequent occupation which ceased sometime in the twelfth or thirteenth century when the area became part of the church-yard. The process of excavation involved using a machine to strip off the garden soil, followed by hand digging with mattocks, spades, shovels and trowels. In the process, we sought to identify separate deposits marked by differences in their composition, deposits such as slopewash, floor layers, pit fills, walls and so on. Each of these was described on separate record sheets accompanied by measured drawings to scale, and identified by a unique number; any artefacts or other remains such as animal bones or shells were bagged and labelled according to the deposit they came from. Critical to the whole process was understanding both what any deposit represented and what its relationship was to other deposits, i.e. earlier, later or contemporary.

After excavation, all the finds and records were taken back, put in order and checked through; the different finds – the pottery, the animal bones, the coins, etc. – were sent for study to different specialists, each of whom analysed the material in certain ways and produced a report. For example, the ceramicist sorted out all the sherds into different types of vessel based on their fabric and form, quantified this information and at the end was able to say what kind of vessels were represented from the site, what period they dated from, and where they were made. On this site, most of the pottery came from local kilns, but some came from other places such as France, and most could be dated to the latter part of the Roman period. This and the other specialist information was then integrated with the records made on site to produce a narrative which aimed to establish the sequence and nature of events which left their trace under that old orchard garden about 1,500 years ago.

I have just described very approximately what happens on innumerable archaeological sites in Britain and all over the world; the precise procedures might differ, but basically they share similar goals. How is it that we use these procedures? Why do we do it in this way rather than in any other? I ask these questions because I think there has been a notable lack of concern for them in the recent wider theoretical debates about archaeology, in particular with the development of post-processual approaches in the past ten to fifteen years. While one can point to changes in practice which New Archaeology effected – from field survey and sampling techniques to statistical representations of data – can post-processualism be said to have had such an impact on everyday practice? This may seem a harsh statement, since post-processualism is certainly not a purely theoretical, armchair exercise (as some might believe) and its studies are as data-driven as any processual work. But this is not the point. How much has post-processual theory actually altered the everyday practice of archaeology? When I consider the investigation of the Roman palace described above, I cannot think of any way in which post-processualism has effected the process, yet there are numerous ways in which New Archaeology has. To me, this points to a serious lapse in critical thinking about what we do. Why has this occurred? I am not the first to raise this issue of course (Tilley 1989; Hodder 1989b, 1997; Richards 1995), but one of the aims of this book is to bring the issue to greater prominence through an examination of the historical and conceptual framework within which archaeology is practised today.

I want to begin by asking, perhaps strangely, why do we even go into the field at all? This may seem rather paradoxical, but the very idea of fieldwork is not necessarily synonymous with archaeology as Chris Tilley has argued – 'digging as a pathology of archaeology' (Tilley 1989: 275). However, Tilley's main point is not so much directed towards excavation itself as to the purpose behind it and he believes this should shift from being 'a process whereby the material traces of the past are recovered and "rescued" to being an exercise in a very different kind of production: the manner in which interpretive experience is produced' (Tilley 1989: 278). His work with Barbara Bender and Sue Hamilton on Bodmin Moor exemplifies this (Bender et al. 1997), and recent work by Ian Hodder at Çatalhöyük addresses similar issues in terms of a reflexive methodology (Hodder 1997). Both these projects are innovative, positive moves towards reconceiving fieldwork and are discussed further below. But what is the historical context of their reaction? Why do we go into the field, how do we decide what constitutes fieldwork and post-fieldwork, and why do we do things in certain ways in or out of the field?

The 'field' in archaeology

The significance of the field

In the paper referred to above, Tilley remarked that much emphasis is given to methods in textbooks, but less on what the end-product is supposed to be (Tilley 1989: 275). What is the status of the 'field' in archaeology? We might say that without fieldwork, there would be no material to work on, and therefore no archaeology – it is the bread and butter of all archaeologists, even those who do not go into the field themselves. Whether studying transistor radios or palaeolithic hand axes, archaeologists need fieldwork to sustain what they do, to produce the very material or 'data' on which to work. And yet this is perhaps rather too simple. Fieldwork does not just mean the recovery of objects; fieldwork is, as Tilley is at pains to point out, an interpretive exercise, an experience. There is a whole unwritten mythology about the nature of fieldwork.

Fieldwork, as part of a professional practice performed by the scientists themselves, emerged in the later nineteenth century primarily among naturalists and geologists but also among archaeologists and, slightly later, anthropologists (Kuklick 1997: 48). Earlier, most researchers had relied heavily on material brought back by travellers or specially commissioned collectors; going into the field was not regarded as the proper activity of a gentleman, aspects of both class and commodification being implicated in this. This, however, was determined by the proximity of the material. In terms of exotica (whether plants, people or artefacts), reliance on others was largely the case, but with specimens closer to home there was a great tradition of gentleman scholars going into the field. In Britain, for example there was the antiquarian topographic work of William Camden, John Aubrey and William Stukeley followed by that of Cunnington and Colt Hoare, for whom surveying was seen as part of the culture of a 'gentleman' (Piggott 1976: 111; also see Ashbee 1972).[1] Different European countries had their own differing emphases, but most (except France) had a history of antiquarians who went into the field (Malina and Vašíček 1990: 27; Schnapp 1993: 154). However, it is questionable how far one can call the work of these antiquarians fieldwork in the sense of modern archaeology.

It is interesting to see that, particularly in the seventeenth and eighteenth centuries, antiquarian researches were frequently part of the wider study of natural history, and archaeological remains are discussed alongside flora, fauna, and other aspects of the environment (Schnapp 1993: 198). For example the antiquarian Robert Plot's works were entitled *The Natural History of Oxford-shire* (1677) and *The Natural History of Stafford-shire* (1686), and many of the early local society journals were similarly ecumenical in their coverage and entitlement. This idea of a regional approach, based on a topographic and environmental framework became particularly a hallmark of the British antiquarian tradition – the work of Cunnington and Colt Hoare in the late eighteenth/early nineteenth centuries was founded on the same basic approach as that of Stukeley: topographic survey. Excavation was supplemental, merely an exercise in the recovery of artefacts, and ultimately, without written records, such things were often considered mute (Trigger 1989: 70). There was no real consideration of how to engage with the material – it was merely there, attesting to an incomprehensible antiquity. The association between antiquarian studies and natural history, however, was perhaps most marked with prehistoric remains; historical and classical antiquarianism was much more closely linked to art history and was perhaps a stronger theme in early field research in mainland Europe than in Britain (Malina and Vašíček 1990: 27). The eighteenth- and early nineteenth-century excavations in Pompeii and Herculaneum or in Mesopotamia and Egypt are obvious examples.

The real advances were made, not by those who did go into the field, but by those who largely stayed at home and examined material collected by others, whether this came from abroad or closer to home. The major later nineteenth-century archaeologists such as Daniel Wilson, John Lubbock and John Evans did not really conduct fieldwork but relied on collections, and when they did go into the 'field' this was rarely to initiate controlled excavation but rather to visit sites and monuments. Typology more than fieldwork characterises the emergence of archaeology as an academic discipline. There are exceptions to this mode of work however – palaeolithic archaeology on the one hand which, from being closely allied to geology, did engage in fieldwork to a greater degree, and, on the other, individuals such as J. J. A. Worsaae in Denmark or those working in the Near East such as Paul-Emile Botta and Austen Layard, or Heinrich Schliemann in Greece and Turkey. However, these exceptions need to be qualified.

Thus palaeolithic archaeology either involved observations of sections already cut, as with Boucher de Perthes' work in the Somme Valley, or purposive investigation as with William Pengelly at Brixham Cave. Yet, ironically, the sites in the Somme valley only gained academic credence after they had been visited by a stream of famous British scientists including John Evans, John Prestwich and Charles Lyell in 1859. The Académie des Sciences, when first presented with de Perthes' results in 1846, rejected them (Trigger 1989: 93–4; Schnapp 1993: 311–14). A remarkably similar scenario occurred with the question of palaeolithic occupation in North America, where investigations at the Trenton Gravels were subject to a visit by most of the principal figures in American archaeology. However, in contrast to Europe, the findings were much more equivocal and, in the end, were rejected (Meltzer 1985: 254–5). The situation with other nineteenth-century fieldworkers is more complex. I discuss this in more detail in the next chapter, but Schliemann and Worsaae, despite their more careful techniques and records, have in common the central focus of

artefacts and the retrieval of a 'collection' which places them in close align-
ment to that 'father' of field archaeology, General Pitt Rivers.

What emerges from this, though, is a division between the fieldworkers
and the intellectual elite, which more or less reproduces the same division
between the person who collected the material and the museum or individual who commissioned the expedition. In Britain, much of the fieldwork
in the latter part of the nineteenth century was conducted on prehistoric
burial mounds, and major fieldworkers such as William Greenwell, Thomas
Bateman and John Mortimer are not known for their interpretive contribution to archaeology – indeed in most histories they may get only a passing
mention in comparison to figures such as Daniel Wilson and John Lubbock.
Indeed, both Greenwell and Bateman commissioned other people to excavate barrows for them (the most famous of whom was James Ruddock) as
well as paying locals to collect surface flints. In the US, the American
Bureau of Ethnology and the Peabody Museum were the major sponsors of
fieldwork. Although Putnam at the Peabody is renowned for his own fieldwork, both he and John Wesley Powell frequently commissioned others to
conduct fieldwork for them (Hinsley 1974, 1985).

Part of this division relates to the fact that archaeology was part of the
wider discipline of the science of man, or anthropology, not only in
the USA but also in Britain. The idea of a distinct profession of archaeologists was not fully developed, and fieldwork was highly variable because
of the people doing it – all were effectively amateurs, though towards the
end of the century there was an increasing concern for professionalisation
(Hinsley 1974; Levine 1986: 31, 87). Fieldwork thus played an ambiguous
part in archaeology in the middle of the nineteenth century – if there was
anything in common in archaeological practice, it was the 'collection' rather
than the 'field', and more particularly the association between the collections and museums and systems of classification (Cole 1974; Chapman 1989;
Jacknis 1985). The defining feature of archaeological work before the 1870s
was this focus on collections rather than the observation of material *in situ*
(Kehoe 1998: 34), and, even when this did occur, it was, as with geology,
from a desire to answer questions posed by these collections. Most archaeologists, as well as naturalists, stayed at home or at the academy waiting
for the material to come to them.

It is even debatable how much the growth in fieldwork after the 1870s
was not still very much in the same mode – I develop this point further
in the next chapter. Someone such as the so-called father of archaeological fieldwork, Pitt Rivers, may not have been quite as we paint him. It
could be argued that fieldwork as we understand it today has more in
common with the work of Mortimer Wheeler in Britain or Alfred Kidder
in the USA and with developments in the early decades of the twentieth
century, especially when we consider how it was only at this time that
ethnographic fieldwork took on its modern character through the mythic

figure of Bronislaw Malinowski (Stocking 1983). One could argue that the dominant concern with universalising classification and evolution meant that fieldwork was still viewed primarily as a means of enhancing the collection rather than an interest in the site itself, and only when the idea of culture as particularistic emerged – that is, culture history or culture groups/areas – did fieldwork become more relevant. The very concern for particularity meant that presence on the site and the site's own particularity became important too. As long as one views culture as a universal concept, the best place to appraise it is perhaps the armchair – going into the field potentially achieves nothing (Gupta and Ferguson 1997: 8).

Franz Boas's early involvement in museum work in the USA is a good example of this shift in thinking – he attempted to restructure the way collections were organised at the American Museum, an approach which epitomises the Boasian revolution in American anthropology (Jacknis 1985: 77–83; also see McVicker 1992). In contrast to Otis Mason's or William Henry Holmes's method of organisation which placed objects in typological groups, Boas argued for objects to be arranged according to tribal or cultural criteria; for example, instead of showing different examples of rattles together, he suggested each should be placed alongside other objects from the same tribal group. It was not that Mason or Holmes did not see the relevance of this approach, but rather that they gave precedence to the typological one, arguing that it told much more about the objects that any cultural grouping (Jacknis 1985). Boas's approach eventually led him to see museums and collections in general as of limited value, in that they restrict the dimensions of cultural life available for study. It ultimately led to the development of a new kind of fieldwork, one based not on simply enhancing collections but on a concern with a more contextual understanding of cultural lifeways. One can easily see how this is translated into fieldwork, with a greater concern for the specific spatial and temporal contexts of objects. The primary locus of research necessarily shifts from museums and studies to the field (Boone 1993: 330).

The politics of the field

When scientific fieldwork first developed in the later nineteenth century, the broader cultural background certainly fostered its development. Owning or studying collections was often a way of increasing one's social status (Levine 1986: 11) and, in terms of fieldwork, the idea of travel as part of personal – more specifically masculine – growth encouraged scientists to acquire their own collections (Kuklick 1997). Even for the archaeologist who worked at home rather than abroad (never such a romantic figure), the 'Field' remains an arena of personal development with definite machismo undertones. Even if there are no dangerous animals or tribes, it is, at the very least, awful weather. Of course a touch of irony is intended here, but in the early days of archaeology the element of personality was prominent in those texts dealing with fieldwork, and the definition of masculinity came to be implicated in fieldwork practices. J. P. Droop's small book *Archaeological Excavation* (1915) contains the infamous epilogue on 'women on site', in which he states that 'mixed excavations' are a bad idea, but that if women have to be present they ought to be kept separate (Droop 1915: 63–4).

The issue of gender in fieldwork is deeply implicated in the wider acceptance of women into archaeology. Before the issuing of formal degrees, fieldwork was the crucial step towards a career in archaeology, and there was much opposition to women going into 'the field' (Díaz-Andreu and Stig Sørensen 1997: 8; also see Dincauze 1992). There were, however, women who did go – women such as the Swede Hanna Rydh or the American Harriet Boyd Hawkins early in the twentieth century and, later, British Kathleen Kenyon. There were also the less visible wives (Hilda Petrie, Tessa Wheeler and Madeleine Kidder) of famous male archaeologists. In fact, wives of archaeologists were often expected to accompany their spouses into the field, though often to deal with finds rather than help with excavation (Reyman 1992: 74). The extension of the exclusion of women from the field was the rejection of any 'feminine' characteristics in those men intending to work in archaeology. Flinders Petrie's *Methods and Aims in Archaeology* (1904), perhaps the first manual on fieldwork in English, begins with a chapter on the character of the archaeologist, with attention to bodily appearance:

> his readiness [to dig] should be shown by the shortness of his fingernails and the toughness of his skin . . . one might as well try to play the violin in a pair of gloves as proffer to excavate with clean fingers and a pretty skin.
>
> (Petrie 1904: 6–7)

This whole chapter of his book reads very much like a colonial handbook on how to deal with 'natives', and while Petrie's work was mostly in Egypt, Wheeler makes similar allusions to the masculinity of the discipline half a century later in his main book on fieldwork which he regarded as 'an earthly book, inapt to clerkly hands' (Wheeler 1954: v).

In the USA, John Rowe in his paper on 'Archaeology as a career' similarly notes that archaeology requires special characteristics, such as the ability 'to withstand a considerable amount of physical discomfort without it interfering with his work or making him excessively irritable . . .' (Rowe 1954, reprinted in Heizer's *Guide to Archaeological Field Methods* (1958: 154). One also recalls the phrase attributed to Alfred Kidder distinguishing archaeologists with hairy chests from those with hairy chins, assuming, of course, that all archaeologists were male anyway. Perhaps the most outspoken example, though, comes from Noel Hume's advice on women on site:

Digging is, after all, a masculine occupation, and while more women than men are likely to do well in the pot-washing shed or in the laboratory, shovel-wielding females are not everyday sights in Western society. If they are to be useful on site (and the right women can be splendid excavators), they must be prepared to be accepted as men, eschewing the traditional rights of their sex. It is vastly time-consuming for men working in one area to be constantly hopping up and down to push barrows for women working in another.

(Noel Hume 1969: 60)

This is undoubtedly an extreme view (though not perhaps for its time), and few could point to such blatant sexism today. Nevertheless, there is still a tendency for male archaeologists to work in the field and for female archaeologists to work in the laboratory or finds room (Gero 1985); and it is not extreme in the slightest to argue that the field remains heavily inscribed as a masculine space – something which has been raised before in other disciplines (for example, see Sparke 1996).

More broadly, the striking feature of many fieldwork texts up to the middle of the twentieth century was their focus on the properly disciplined individual. In Britain, after the 1960s, there was a shift from concern with the 'character' of the individual archaeologist to concern with site 'discipline'. Of course the focus on site discipline has always been there – throughout the earlier part of the twentieth century there was frequent use of military analogies, with references to 'campaigns' of fieldwork (Wheeler 1954: 1; Webster 1965: 63; Noel Hume 1969: 54). However, the issue became much more significant as the workforce changed from primarily unskilled labourers to students and skilled professionals. Fieldwork manuals are no longer written for the site director but the excavator. The development of new recording methods and excavation practices in the 1960s, required 'great site discipline and well-trained workers'(Biddle and Kjølbye-Biddle 1969: 213). The same point is made in what is perhaps the most popular book on fieldwork in Britain today, Barker's *Techniques of Archaeological Excavation*, where a section on site discipline argues for 'a careful balance of that which is self-imposed and that imposed from above; where all the members of the excavation do what they are told or required because they understand what they are doing' (Barker 1982: 110).

Currently, each excavator (or 'site assistant' as they are often called) can be responsible for the whole process from digging to recording a feature on a site and the director/supervisor merely co-ordinates; this gives the impression of democratic digging – yet the excavator's focus is very narrow and the level of interpretation minimal (for example, 'this is a pit'). This is not to denigrate the skill involved, but it is an illusion to think that the average excavator of today has necessarily any more *power* on a site than had the labourer of a century ago. In the end, the supervisor/director, the one who writes the report, determines the interpretation of the site not only by being in possession of the 'wider picture', but by selecting *where* and *what* the site assistant excavates. In many ways, site assistants are completely inter-changeable – he or she is not a person but a digging machine and although some assistants may be more efficient than others, their 'local knowledge' or personality is often ignored and certainly never mentioned in any contem-porary manuals on fieldwork.

Although Barker reiterates the importance of a hierarchy and this indeed remain a key element of the organisation of fieldworkers, since the 1960s the channels of discipline and power on site have been much more concealed and dispersed. Instead of simply having an overall director who monitors and controls the workforce – which still of course occurs to some extent, especially in non-Western contexts – control is articulated through *pro forma* context sheets and other records which can proliferate excessively, and which are used to constantly check the quality and quantity of work. It is critical that all records are signed and dated, and many records have boxes headed 'checked by . . .', to be filled in by the supervisor. There is a clear inscription of surveillance in modern record-keeping which is directly linked to these hierarchies. It is argued, of course, that such a system is to provide a standardised and 'objective' record of the excavation, but in fact it controls not only the record, but also the bodies who produce it.

Thus, while there may have been a shift from the disciplined individual to the disciplined workforce, there is clearly a continuous sense in which the 'Field' is an area in which proper discipline is essential, as part of scien-tific rigour. These disciplines and controls were all linked in with the issue of trust, which was such a major part of nineteenth-century fieldwork. It is as if the credibility and reliability of any material generated through field-work takes its validity directly from the command of self/personnel on site. And this returns us again to the issue of gender politics, where 'male' prac-tices frequently have a higher value than 'female' practices, because they generally exhibit those attributes of certainty, authority and dichotomous thinking which science values (Gero 1996: 276). Moreover, the very fact of who is credited as an archaeologist largely depends on other archaeolo-gists and, as a result, many women in the history of archaeology have not merely been silenced, they have not even been recognised as archaeolo-gists because of a masculine valuation of what constitutes an archaeologist (Mason 1992: 93). As Joan Gero says in her critique of gender bias in field-work, much of this links back into the current model employed in archaeology about how knowledge is produced, exemplified by that (by now) old diagram showing the relation between theory and data as a cycle or feedback loop (Gero 1996: 254).

The place of the field

This often cited relation between theory and data has come to be almost the standard position on the relation between archaeologists and the phenomena they study. It states that the archaeologist will always have an effect on the phenomena under study but that the phenomena still exist in a real sense and are not a figment of the archaeologist's mind. Thus, in so far as archaeologists will *select* what aspects to investigate, based on what at the time is considered relevant, they construct the data. This of course changes as new questions, new theoretical perspectives guide the investigative process – examples might include anything from the development of new techniques (e.g. soil micromorphology) to new analytical questions (e.g. structural oppositions in artefact patterning). Conversely, there must be *something* there to select from, something which is beyond/independent of our conception of it and which can accommodate or conflict with our expectations of it. Practice is, in effect, this process or relationship between theory and data.

This sounds very reasonable and it seems to have become almost a point of agreement or convergence among many of the different theoretical schools, in particular the processualists and post-processualists (Wylie 1992). But, as Gero says of this theory–data interdependence model, 'it misrepresents the complex historical and sociopolitical interactions that condition every stage of archaeological research, from the naming and classifying of archaeological data through the writing of interpretive explanations' (Gero 1996: 254). These are issues of critical importance, issues which highlight the importance of archaeology as a practice, of the process of archaeology rather than just the final product. How might we re-envisage practice? I think it helps to look a little deeper at how practice is articulated, because in many ways the old model of theory/data referred to above masks a much wider politics of fieldwork and archaeology, one which in some respects contradicts the initial impetus for fieldwork. When, by the 1870s, fieldwork had become an established component of archaeology, it presented experience, presence in the field, as a critical guarantor of scientific validity. As Kuklick says of the wider scientific establishment of fieldwork, 'when naturalists made experience in the field a defining property of membership in their disciplinary communities, they were setting fundamental standards of scientific craft' (Kuklick 1997: 48–9). Now while this may still be believed to be the case, it can also be argued that fieldwork has become quite widely separated from broader interpretive practices. This is exemplified by a paradox which has developed over the past thirty years and which closely relates to the development of a group of professional fieldworkers, archaeologists whose specialism is fieldwork itself: contract archaeologists.

Before I address the paradox, it is useful to elaborate a little further on how this split of fieldwork from interpretation has been conceived. A commonly held view of archaeology, chiefly in the USA and especially during the earlier half of the twentieth century, was that it was primarily a method of data retrieval. Walter Taylor, for example, wrote that 'Archaeology *per se* is no more than a method and a set of specialised techniques for the gathering of cultural information. The archaeologist, as archaeologist, is really nothing but a technician' (Taylor 1948: 43). More recently, the most vocal exponent of this view is Irving Rouse, who has written in numerous places on what he sees as a basic distinction between archaeology and prehistory: archaeology is essentially a method, a technique for data retrieval, while the interpretation of that data belongs to the prehistorian or any other interested academic, such as the historian, the sociologist, or the anthropologist (Rouse 1968; 1972). Rouse is not saying that an archaeologist cannot also be a prehistorian, but the two roles must be made quite distinct. Both Taylor and Rouse produced similar systematic outlines for archaeology's position within the wider study of culture which they call anthropology. In this scheme archaeology is quite emphatically at the base (Taylor 1948: ch. 6; Rouse 1972).

Many have of course disagreed with his approach, including Willey and Phillips (1958), Chang (1968), Deetz (1971) and Clarke (1973), and since the 1960s the status of archaeology as more than mere fieldwork, or data retrieval, has been widely accepted. This difference, however, may have been more virtual than real – it was after all the same Gordon Willey and Phillip Phillips who proclaimed that 'American archaeology is anthropology or it is nothing' (Willey and Phillips 1958: 2). By this they meant that archaeology, as much as any other branch of anthropology, should concern itself with explanation and not be merely descriptive – and yet in their scheme, steps similar to those given by Taylor and later Rouse are presented, with clear divisions between fieldwork (observation), integration (description) and explanation (interpretation) (ibid.: 4). The difference really seems to be that Taylor and Rouse reserved the term 'archaeology' for the data collection and analysis stage of any investigation or research.

Now I want to quote a portentous statement made by Rouse in 1968, who foresaw

> that the people interested in archaeology as technology will eventually become sufficiently numerous and specialised to be recognised as a separate profession, bearing the same relationship to interpretive archaeologists that engineers and applied scientists bear to pure scientists.
>
> (Rouse 1968: 12)

This returns us to contract archaeologists, and indeed others who effectively work full time in the 'field', whether this is on site or in the laboratory. From one perspective, such archaeologists might be viewed as specialists, akin to zooarchaeologists or micromorphologists; from another, however, they are merely technicians, collecting and processing data for the 'real' scientists. Thus to a large extent Rouse's prediction has come true, for while we are all still called archaeologists, this may serve only to mask the different modes of scientific production in operation in archaeology today (Shanks and McGuire 1996: 82). Shanks and McGuire indeed talk about 'archaeological engineers' and how a hierarchy is in place with 'those of us who manage and sit on committees, synthesise, generalise and theorise and those of us who sort, dig and identify' (ibid.). Indeed, since the rise of contract archaeology and the amassing of large quantities of data, there have been cries for this material to be incorporated and integrated much more into research agendas. But the question is, who will do this?

I suspect that in many cases it will *not* be the people who dig it up, but the academics. Is there a danger that we may return to the pre-1870s situation (with often the same class implications too) where one group of people go out and do fieldwork while the 'real' archaeologists stay in their armchairs? Probably not, but there can be no question that there is a very large group of anonymous and silent archaeologists engaging in fieldwork in Britain and elsewhere today, who have no voice. This is the result not only of a lack of a platform but of an ideology founded on the assumption that data collection is independent of interpretation; that excavation, as Tilley says, is merely an exercise in retrieval rather than in interpretation. This is not to suggest that anyone who claims to be an archaeologist should conduct their own fieldwork and only draw on the product of their own labour – no one can confine themselves solely to writing about what they themselves have excavated, and a value which privileges first-hand experience should be contested. But this is not really the issue here – rather it is about a politics of archaeological practice which separates fieldwork from interpretation, which sees the production of archaeological knowledge as akin to factory production rather than, as Shanks and McGuire (1996) suggest, as a craft.

The paradox is, then, that fieldwork became established as the basis of the discipline in the nineteenth century, as the guarantee of its scientific validity, because it was done by the same people who interpreted the material gathered from that fieldwork. It was this fact which defined archaeology and a host of other disciplines as scientific enterprises. And yet, over the course of a century, it is as if the whole situation has been turned upside down – archaeologists are now no longer required to go into the field themselves; indeed, a whole group of specialist fieldworkers has emerged, albeit under development-led conditions, who can collect much of the data archaeologists need. And yet perhaps this paradox was always there, for the very construction of the 'field' was established in opposition to 'home', to the library, study or academy (Gupta and Ferguson 1997: 12–15). Fieldwork in archaeology, as with anthropology and other disciplines, always has had its counterpart in the 'writing up' – post-excavation, post-survey, etc. Each practice has its own texts, its own tropes and materials (ibid.; Table 1).

Table I Discourse and the field

Fieldwork	Post-fieldwork
field	library, laboratory, academy
fieldnotes	monograph, paper
fragmentary	coherent
raw data, description	analysis, interpretation

One does wonder, however, how widely this opposition is experienced. For many contract excavators, there is no post-excavation work – the field is all they know, the field is work. Indeed, the issue of the invisibility of the bulk of an excavation team in post-excavation work has been sharply highlighted in a joint project at a Bronze Age ring-ditch in Cambridgeshire (McFadyen 1997; McFadyen *et al.* 1997):

> In terms of the excavation work that we carry out, we cannot find the words, and this is literally speaking, to describe to you how painful the process of cutting ourselves out of an archaeological imagination is? Or describe what a dangerous shattering of subjectivity there is in drawing and interpreting where you and others made something, but without you? And yet everything else is sectioned, planned and given a context. Do you know what it is like to always focus the camera in the shadows that reside after you deliberately push a colleague out of the frame, making them wipe out their footprints and pick up their work tools in the process of leaving. What kind of archaeology are these forced experiences for and who is it for? Why are we so professional about creating an archaeology devoid of us?
>
> (McFadyen *et al.* 1997)

Archaeology is a practice we do with others, perhaps in fieldwork particularly, and there is a violence which accompanies this when people are silenced in the name of representation, the production of knowledge.

The over-riding conception of the relation between fieldwork and its sequel is one of transformation, of fieldnotes into the monograph, fragments into a whole, raw data into interpretations – and, by implication, the change from engineer to thinker. Who and what gets lost in this process is usually neglected, however; indeed this neglect is probably compounded by the fact that, as Clifford says of anthropological fieldwork, the fieldnotes serve to reify and naturalise a place called 'the field', kept separate from the operations of theorising and writing up (Clifford 1990: 66). And yet, this model is more than just the single movement from field to study. It should recognise feedback between these two poles and consequently a certain movement, a hermeneutic. In the next section, I want to look in a little more detail at some recent attempts to explore this relationship, which try to break down the distance between the field and the academy.

Alternative fieldworks

More reflexive approaches to archaeological fieldwork have been presented recently, in particular the work directed by Ian Hodder at Çatalhöyük (Hodder 1997) and Barbara Bender, Sue Hamilton and Chris Tilley on Bodmin Moor (Bender *et al.* 1997). Hodder's argument is in many ways merely an inevitable and long overdue extension of post-processual ideas into the realm of fieldwork (Hodder 1989b, 1997). He identifies what he calls a contradiction within British fieldwork in that it recognises there is interpretation prior to, or embedded in, the process of excavation and yet in practice it continues to pretend that this primary data collection was prior to interpretation; that description can be separated from interpretation. Hodder is probably correct in this observation and he argues that we should take a more reflexive approach to fieldwork methodology. This involves, perhaps most critically, enabling the relationship between finds analyses (e.g. faunal remains, lithics, pottery, seeds) and the determination of stratigraphic events/contexts to be more interactive, facilitated through increased personal interaction between excavators and specialists and a relational computer database. The traditional approach is that such analyses are done *after* the excavation, not only temporally but conceptually. It is as if data collection was factory production (see Shanks and McGuire above), the process marked by various stages: excavation → finds processing → analysis → synthesis. This indeed is the premise of English Heritage's Management of Archaeological Projects (MAP 2) which is the model for most contract fieldwork today in Britain.

The general point is that this process is almost seen as uni-directional, whereas in fact a reflexive methodology encourages constant feedback. Of course, in practice, finds analysis often might change the in-field interpretation of a site, but this is an *ad hoc* process which is not explicitly encouraged in the literature or in general attitudes. Frequently, for example, pottery specialists are not given stratigraphic information in case it biases their dating (or is it a test of their ability?), the point being, I suppose, to have independent checks between stratigraphy and dating. But this seriously misunderstands the nature of pottery as a dating tool; it is not like having a stopped clock. The deposition of pottery and the types of pottery which get deposited are not necessarily independent from the formation of that deposit, and it is often crucial to know something about the context in understanding the pottery. Object and context are not independent and should not be treated as if they were. It remains to be seen how widely Hodder's approach at Çatalhöyük could be adopted, but the issue certainly becomes sharply focused through the relationships between the excavators and various specialists (Hamilton 1996) and, particularly in contract archaeology, this is a major obstacle.

Tilley's work in many ways expresses the same concerns as those of Hodder, although his approach is somewhat different (Tilley 1989; Bender et al. 1997). Tilley, and later Bender and Hamilton, are perhaps less concerned with fostering new methodologies as with focusing simply on the process of fieldwork, the movement of interpretation which is usually left behind in the presentation of a final or finished product. They see the whole fieldwork enterprise as part of the process of interpretation, not simply as primary data collection, and thus its reportage should be as much a part of the published site report. The same general issues which concern Hodder concern them: excavation as interpretation, reflexivity, multivocality – the fluidity of interpretation, but in a much more informal way. They achieved this in their first publication of fieldwork through a juxtaposition of feature descriptions, diary entries and narrative discussion. What they have achieved is questionable, because the context descriptions are still there, and there is a sense that we have not necessarily learned anything by having the process of the excavation charted and narrated. However, in attempting alternative approaches, there is no doubt that the project represents an important innovation.

What seems to be missing from both the above projects is any concern for reflecting on the actual nature of the encounter as an experience – rather the authors appear more concerned with the process and the structures established in moving from fieldwork to text or how data are created. Michael Shanks has discussed the experiental aspect of archaeology, but most of his work focuses on objects and monuments rather than the act of excavation (Shanks 1992a; e.g. see pp. 68–9). Another recent paper has focused more on this particular aspect, with a call to 're-discover the act of discovery' (Edgeworth 1990). But this in a way takes the reflexive methodology almost back to its point of origin, the discussion presented very much revolving around the same issues; while Edgeworth writes about the embodiment of the act, his concern is very much with the practical knowledge archaeologists bring to fieldwork in identifying and interpreting what they find. This kind of implicit, embodied knowledge is really only the other side of the formal explicit structures which Hodder is concerned with and is ultimately a call for a kind of ethnomethodology or anthropology of fieldwork. Not that this is uninteresting, but all the time we are reminded that the encounter is almost one-sided, that it is a subject encounter with an object. Even though Edgeworth argues that the objects are the products of other humans, this is precisely where the problem lies, I feel; by viewing what we excavate as products, our relationship is put at a distance.

In 1997 Victor Buchli and I 'excavated' an abandoned English state housing property (Buchli and Lucas, forthcoming). The project arose through an interest in exploring the dual themes of the alienation of late twentieth-century individuals and the way we, as archaeologists alienate our material, our data through the act of fieldwork. We spent two intense days recording the contents of a house recently abandoned by a single mother with two children, the results of which can be found in our published paper. A version of the paper was also presented at a Heritage seminar in Cambridge in 1998, causing distress among some of the audience who thought we had gone too far in invading someone's privacy. Needless to say, there was some debate about how far this is ordinarily done, both in archaeology and anthropology. I want to quote from a diary entry I made at the time of the fieldwork, because both it and the response which the paper received at the seminar, illustrate, I think, something deeply central to the act of the archaeological encounter.

> Many broader issues come out of this, particularly issues of privacy and invasion; there were occasions when it did feel like we were invading H—'s privacy, particularly in those things which were closer to the body. The erotic lingerie to some extent, but no more than some of the other items. In particular the things in the bin seemed most 'of the body' – tampons, K-Y jelly, used tissues, cotton buds. It's the things which are *intentionally* thrown away, which seem to bear the marks of privacy the most – those things which are not meant to be seen but to be destroyed, put out of sight. Of course not all the rubbish can be characterised like this but there is an element which can. More generally, why is it that we feel we are invading someone's privacy in doing this but not when doing 'normal' archaeology? I think familiarity obviously plays a strong part – the more familiar, the closer one can draw the boundaries over privacy, whereas in an unfamiliar context – archaeology, but more generally anthropology, the limits seem to be set much further back in the name of understanding – making a connection with the Other. One could imagine limits in anthropology still, however, but in archaeology? This is very rare indeed and usually it is still when the archaeology is still 'wet' – e.g. graves of our or another's recent dead.

(GML, 22 July 1997; extract)

From the response at the seminar, we had clearly found other limits. I think this question of limits is critical because it tells us so much about the nature of the archaeological encounter, things which we can perhaps only discover *at* the limits and not in the safety of, say, a prehistoric settlement.

It also highlights an important point about the nature of much archaeology – that it is an *encounter*, not just observation, albeit active or interpretive observation. We are not simply *observers* of the traces left behind by people. These traces are not merely impassive objects separated from us as subjects which we must interpret to get to the *other* subject behind, invisible, absent, gone. We encounter these traces materially and physically, they are alive, they are real. A group of people excavating a site are immersed in this material culture as well as bringing things with them of their own time (trowels, pens, texts, cameras); these intermesh with things of the past (ditches, dirt, pot sherds, bones) and an encounter is created which is unique. But it is an *encounter* and one which is always lost in the aftermath of excavation in the name of representation. The twentieth-century objects are erased or backgrounded as are the people and the relationships between people – the *politics* of fieldwork (see above). Indeed, this is perhaps the crucial meaning of the term 'trace' – rather than being an object of interpretation, a foil for the subject, it rather mediates the hermeneutic, and provides the possibility of archaeological discourse through its materiality, its presence (see Ricoeur 1988: 119–26; also Levinas 1996: 59–64).

I will return to the issue of materiality in archaeological practice at the end of this book, and in particular to how it might help us re-think the nature of the archaeological process; for now, however, I would like to establish the main themes I will be discussing. First let me say that this book will cover primarily the European (with a bias towards Britain) and North American scene. One of my regrets is that it could not be wider in its coverage – especially, for example, to include the way European archaeology was transplanted through colonialism but subsequently developed differently in other parts of the world. I can only say that the topic is so large that, had I done so, this book might have lost out in coherence and perhaps persuasiveness. Initially, I will explore the first side of Clifford's equation – development of fieldwork in archaeology – in order to pull out major shifts in the way it has been practised and how this relates to broader conceptual changes within archaeology. These shifts produce foci for discussion in the subsequent chapters, all of which in one way or another also relate to major disciplinary divisions which fall on the other side of the equation, the post-fieldwork realm. These divisions include the emergence of finds specialists, area/period specialists and, ultimately, archaeology as a specialism. By focusing on the issue of specialisms and how these are articulated historically and theoretically within the discipline, I hope to reveal some major faultlines in archaeology, but, at the same time, areas of great potential.

Chapter 2

Finding the past

On 17 June 1873, in the third year of his excavations at Hissarlik, Heinrich Schliemann discovered what he regarded as the ultimate proof that the site he was digging was the famous Troy of Homer's *Iliad*:

> In excavating this [city] wall further and directly by the side of the Palace of King Priam, I came upon a large copper article of the most remarkable form, which attracted my attention all the more as I thought I saw gold behind it. . . . In order to withdraw the treasure from the greed of my workmen, and to save it for archaeology, I had to be most expeditious, and although it was not yet time for breakfast, I immediately had 'paidos' called. . . .
>
> While the men were eating and resting, I cut out the treasure with a large knife, which it was impossible to do without the very greatest exertion and the most fearful risk of my life, for the great fortification-wall, beneath which I had to dig, threatened every moment to fall down upon me. But the sight of so many objects, every one of which is of inestimable value to archaeology, made me foolhardy, and I never thought of any danger. It would however, have been impossible for me to have removed the treasure without the help of my dear wife, who stood by me ready to pack the things which I cut out in her shawl and to carry them away.
>
> (Quoted in Deuel 1978: 205)

Much of the public perception of archaeology lies in the excitement of discovery, of buried treasure, of the find (Biddle 1994). We tend to downplay this aspect in academic archaeology, almost as an emotional reaction to what should be a dispassionate, scientific exercise. However, there is clearly a tension involved here, of the thrill of discovery, a hasty scrabbling in the earth, and at the same time a certain pride in meticulous, restrained excavation. It is not that the two are contradictory – we can all unearth wonderful finds in what might appear a greedy way and yet maintain the standards of observation and recording required by contemporary practice. Yet in any text you might pick up on field archaeology today, while the emotive thrill may be alluded to, it is the stress on a controlled encounter with the archaeological record that is maintained.

And yet in the quote above from Schliemann, he clearly describes the moment of discovery and links it into the archaeological value of the objects; in his narrative, the two aspects seamlessly interweave. We may deride Schliemann as a treasure hunter, even see some hypocrisy in his allusion to the greed of the workmen and his own secretive removal of the finds, but he was working in a very different intellectual climate and it is too easy to dismiss his archaeology as a primitive version of today's progressive techniques. What did it mean at the end of the nineteenth century to excavate – and how different was that from today? This is the question I want to address in this chapter – it is not simply a history of field techniques, but of how what we today call the archaeological record has been conceived in the past century or so since the discipline became properly established.

Cultural evolution and the object (1880–1920)

Pitt Rivers and the total archaeological record

A few years before Schliemann began his Trojan excavations, Lieutenant-General Pitt Rivers had begun his excavation career in Ireland and then later in England (Bowden 1991). When we think of these two figures of archaeology, they stand at quite opposite poles – Schliemann the romantic, the treasure-hunter, and Pitt Rivers the field archaeologist, the scientist. But how differently did they see the archaeology they – or rather their workmen – unearthed? Pitt Rivers has gone down in all the history books as the father of British field archaeology in that he introduced detailed and systematic excavation and recording techniques, perfected over many seasons of fieldwork on his estates at Cranborne Chase. But what exactly did this involve, and how different was it from the work of his forebears and contemporaries? Pitt Rivers himself summed it up thus in his preface to the first volume of *Excavations in Cranborne Chase*:

> It will, perhaps, be thought by some that I have recorded the excavations of this village and the finds that have been made in it with unnecessary fulness, and I am aware that I have done it in greater detail than has been customary, but my experience as an excavator has led me to think that investigations of this nature are not generally sufficiently searching and that much valuable evidence is lost by omitting to record them carefully. That this has been so in the present instance is proved by the fact that this village had before been examined and reported upon in the XXIVth volume of the *Journal of the Anthropological*

Institute, and not a single pit or skeleton had been found; whilst I have discovered 95 pits and 15 skeletons.

(Pitt Rivers 1887: xvi–xvii)

These comments on a previous investigator, Austin, highlight two key points which Pitt Rivers saw as crucial to fieldwork: a 'sufficient search' and 'careful recording'. These are undoubtedly the aspects of his work which make him stand out. His accounts in the four volumes of his excavations make it quite clear that his investigations were extensive, frequently included open-area trenching and were detailed in the recording. For example, regarding the 'sufficient search', during the excavation of the Romano-British village at Rushmore Park (to which the above quote also alludes), he not only cleared out major sections of ditch circuits, but also opened up inside the enclosure by

placing the men in line at working distance apart, digging down everywhere through the surface mould until the chalk beneath was reached, and noticing carefully any irregularity in the latter. Where the mould went deeper it was dug out, and in this way pits, hearths, ditches, and irregularities of all kinds were cleared out and exposed.

(Pitt Rivers 1887: 10)

It is unlikely, however, that a whole area was stripped in one pull but rather that he used the technique known as 'strip-digging', by which the ground was cleared in a series of successive parallel trenches, the spoil from one being used to backfill the last (Barrett *et al.* 1983: 196). This was a common nineteenth- and early twentieth-century method in shallow quarrying and therefore probably one the workmen were familiar with. The consequences of this for not identifying features or finds has been remarked upon (Barrett *et al.* 1991: 13; Bowden 1991: 156). When not excavating like this, he tended to run single trenches across earthworks such as dykes, or into the centre of barrows. For example, at Wor Barrow he began in a fairly conventional way, running a trench north to south through the mound, even leaving standing blocks at certain points as references for find location (Figure 1; Pitt Rivers 1898: 64, and plate 255). In many ways this is similar to what other mound diggers had done, including Canon Greenwell, under whom Pitt Rivers had excavated and whom he acknowledges as his first teacher (Pitt Rivers 1887: xix). However, unlike Greenwell, Pitt Rivers then removed the rest of the mound, exposing the whole plan of the barrow including the mortuary enclosure. It is this aspect of trying to achieve total excavation which really separated him from others, something which H. St George Gray highlights in his memoir, illustrated by the excavation of South Lodge Camp where total excavation was carried on, even after nothing was found in the first three sections (Gray 1905: xvii).

Figure 1 Excavation of Wor Barrow by Pitt Rivers

The point Gray makes is that Pitt Rivers was not after treasure but after history. Gray was one of Pitt Rivers' supervisors in the later years of the Cranborne Chase excavations, and was trained by Pitt Rivers to conduct most of the actual fieldwork and post-excavation analysis. This second innovation, 'careful recording', is enshrined in the oft-quoted paragraph of the preface to Volume I of *Excavations*:

> Excavators, as a rule, record only those things which appear to them important at the time, but fresh problems in Archaeology and Anthropology are constantly arising, and it can hardly fail to have escaped the notice of anthropologists, especially those who, like myself, have been concerned with the morphology of art, that, on turning back to old accounts in search of evidence, the points which would have been most valuable have been passed over from being thought uninteresting at the time. Every detail should, therefore, be recorded in the manner most conducive to facility of reference, and it ought at all times to be the chief object of an excavator to reduce his own personal equation to a minimum.
>
> (Pitt Rivers 1887: xvii)

Pitt Rivers' military background probably strongly influenced his ability and desire for systematic recording (Bradley 1983: 3); he trained up assistants in surveying and draughting who carried out the actual fieldwork and, increasingly, the post-excavation analysis for the Cranborne Chase excavations. Of course Pitt Rivers had supervised fieldwork himself and one cannot accuse him of being an armchair archaeologist, although by the time he began work at Cranborne Chase, this is what in effect he was:

> The work of superintending the digging – though I never allowed it be carried on in my absence, always visiting the excavations at least three times a day, and arranging to be sent for whenever anything of importance was found – was more than I could undertake single-handed, with the management of the property and other social duties to attend to, and I had by ample experience been taught that no excavation ought ever to be permitted except under the immediate eye of a responsible and trustworthy superintendant.
>
> (Pitt Rivers 1887: xvii)

To this end, a whole string of archaeologists learnt their fieldwork through him, and it is probably this as much as anything which helped perpetuate his image as the father of British field archaeology. Pitt Rivers' concern for 'total excavation' comes out in his reports where equal emphasis is placed on plans and sections. Comparing *Excavations in Cranborne Chase* with his teacher Greenwell's major work, *British Barrows* (published only ten years before

Volume I of *Excavations*), the difference in the graphic record is startling. Greenwell mostly showed artefacts, site figures rarely, and when the barrows were illustrated, it was usually as a section (Greenwell 1877). In contrast, Pitt-Rivers' volumes are in effect read through the illustrations, each portion of text entitled as a description of plate such-and-such. The plans are measured, showing contours of the surface and the location of all features after excavation, while the sections are schematic, although with some representational elements, but again measured. In addition, tabulated summaries (his 'Relic Tables' which were first used at Mount Caburn and Caesar's Camp in the late 1870s) appear at the end and give details of each feature, including dimensions and quantities and types of finds. In many respects, this structure is still used today, with topographic introduction, presentation of excavated features, followed by finds reports which include not just artefacts but faunal and botanical remains in many cases too.

Pitt Rivers' actual reports, then, very much live up to the standards he preached in his preface. In everything I have said here it sounds as if he was indeed the revolutionary figure he has been painted. But I think we need to qualify this and try and place his innovations in some kind of context. In the first place, we noted in his excavation of Wor Barrow how he started in an almost conventional manner with a linear trench and only then opened up the rest. This is quite revealing, because his actual *methods of excavation* were in many ways no different from those of Greenwell or other contemporaries – he merely applied them on a more extensive scale (Bowden 1991: 154–5). While he was not working on very deeply stratified sites – although in many cases they were certainly multi-phase – he rarely mentions stratigraphy or raises issues of stratigraphically phasing a site (e.g. looking at ditch junctions/cuts, etc.). Bowden, in his detailed study of Pitt Rivers, sums this up very well:

> His recording was meticulous but his physical digging methods let him down. Though recognising the importance of stratigraphy and the interrelationship of features he failed to excavate in such a way as to be able to see them clearly. He dug in spits and not by layers, a technique which he was to retain until the end of his life.
>
> (Bowden 1991: 94; also see pp. 155–6)

The same lack of originality could be said of his recording; the sections look little different from those of the better excavators of the time, and locating all finds by vertical position as well as contextual location was nothing new – he merely applied the same technique more exhaustively than did others (see Bowden 1991: 154–5). More significant, however, is that towards the end of his Cranborne Chase excavations he gave up even these sections in favour of 'average sections' which he continued to use thereafter (Bowden 1991: 128); these were simply generalised profiles with the finds location plotted on (e.g. see Pitt Rivers 1898). This suggests very strongly that his main interest was not in stratigraphy but in sequencing finds, and he clearly felt that a simple vertical position was sufficient to do this. This comes out very clearly in a paragraph on how to excavate a ditch in Volume IV of Cranborne Chase (1898), where he argues for horizontal excavation in spits, against the usual method of digging down to the bottom in one spot and then working the face vertically along the length of the ditch (Pitt Rivers 1898: 26). His reasoning for this is simply in terms of finds control. In summary, to quote Bradley:

> Recent work in Cranborne Chase suggests that it is an over-simplifi-
> cation to see Pitt Rivers as the advocate of a purely empirical school
> of archaeology. His reluctance to interpret the structural sequence on
> his sites did not result entirely from scholarly restraint; the General
> had quite different objectives.
>
> (Bradley 1983: 8)

The key point, I believe, to Pitt Rivers' innovation was not that he invented field archaeology or new methods of excavation and recording, but that he applied the standard techniques of the day in a much more totalising and exhaustive manner – he wanted a *total record* of what was in the ground. While he may have been among the first to excavate non-barrow sites (most of his contemporaries, such as Greenwell, were almost all barrow-diggers – see Marsden 1974), his interest was in the recovery of a wider range of everyday finds rather than in the site itself. I think this comes out very clearly in the first quote we gave above, where he opens with an apology for the 'unnecessary fulness' of his account. We may still applaud this as no mean achievement, but it is to be questioned whether such a thing as a total record is possible. Carver discusses this aspect in relation to two schools of field archaeology, one stemming from Pitt Rivers and the idea of the total record, and the other from Petrie and Wheeler who argued that one always selects what to record (Carver 1990: 45–7). Petrie, writing four years after the death of Pitt Rivers, said:

> In recording, the first difficulty is to know what to record. To state
> every fact about everything found would be useless, as no one could
> wade through the mass of statements. . . . The old saying that a man
> finds what he looks for in a subject is too true; or, if he has not enough
> insight to ensure finding what he looks for, it is at least sadly true that
> he does not find anything he does not look for.
>
> (Petrie 1904: 49)

If we accept that the real force behind Pitt Rivers' approach was the idea of a 'total record', it means that this is what we should focus on rather than any mythical revolution in field methods or techniques. I think in this respect it is extremely productive to mention Pitt Rivers' other major contribution to archaeology, evolutionary typology. It is possible to believe that Pitt Rivers' intellectual faculties were applied with much greater force to classification and an evolutionary conception of material culture than they were to excavation (for example, see Pitt Rivers 1906; also Bradley 1983; Bowden 1991: 161). Moreover, one could argue that typology is in its very nature, an exercise in totalising objects; it brings them under a single system by placing them in relation to other objects and in this way, every object is connected in a structured chain – which in the case of evolutionary typology, is ordered by the criterion of complexity. I will not go into Pitt Rivers' concept of evolutionary typology here as I touch on it in more detail later, but for the moment I think it is important to recognise the link between a totalising classification and a totalising excavation. The reason Pitt Rivers pushed the conventional field methodologies to a much greater extent than anyone had done previously is because of his desire for totalisation; it was his intellectual background in classification and desire for a total record which drove his innovations in the field.

If there is a link at the conceptual level between Pitt Rivers' excavation methods and evolutionary typology, is there a more practical link? This can be answered by posing a further question: why, despite all his detailed recording and the presentation of the site through plans, sections, photographs, text and even model reconstructions, does Pitt Rivers never really discuss the way a site 'works' or functions? What is really glaringly marked by its absence in his accounts of Cranborne Chase, is any sense of phasing (Barrett et al. 1991: 13). Why this lack? He clearly had a sense of the importance of the site as opposed to just artefacts or objects – he was after all the first Inspector of Ancient Monuments. But what value did he put on these sites? That is the question that surely needs answering. I think the answer relates to the observation we made earlier about his interests in evolutionary typology. What really matters to him in the archaeological record are objects and how they reflect upon human history. While his concern for detailed recording may have been motivated in general by a desire for totalisation, his particular aims were dominated by the need to provide a secure context for objects, to establish their proper place in the evolutionary scheme of culture. Bradley has even suggested that his main motivation in early excavations was to recover material purely to illustrate his typological sequences – not in the sense of testing but merely as a physical addition to a collection (Bradley 1983: 4; also Barrett et al. 1991: 13).

I think that this motivation perhaps never left him. Indeed, as Bradley points out, at the end of Volume IV of Excavations there is an essay on the evolution of chevron-decorated pottery. In concluding this section, Pitt Rivers re-asserts the importance of recording the proper levels of finds in order to help answer these questions (Pitt Rivers 1898: 238–9). Moreover, in commenting elsewhere on the need to recover all artefacts, not just the 'nice' pieces, his argument is based on the significance that common (i.e. frequently occurring) objects have for classification (ibid.: 27). I think this is crucial to appreciating how the archaeological record was conceived in the late nineteenth century and to contextualising Pitt Rivers' contributions to field archaeology. While he gives every *appearance* of concern for all those issues which are important today, such as the site plan and context, in actuality it is very hard to find in any of his writings, any real interest in interpreting the *site*, the meaning of features and so forth. This may seem something of a contradiction, but this relation does not really surface in Pitt Rivers' work, partly because his texts on archaeological excavations and those on anthropological issues of evolutionary typology, are quite separate. The same cannot be said of another major British figure in field archaeology, Flinders Petrie. Petrie provides an interesting study of the relation between the way in which the archaeological record was conceived and the prevailing concern for the evolution of material culture.

Flinders Petrie: the site and its finds

Flinders Petrie's *Methods and Aims in Archaeology* (1904) was perhaps the first archaeological field manual in English; although largely based upon and applied to work in Egypt, it can be read as a more general statement on a 'scientific archaeology'. In it he discusses a whole series of issues surrounding excavation, from the personality of the archaeologist to methods of recording and the ethics of fieldwork. I shall return to this text on later occasions but here I will focus on certain points only, chiefly the methods of excavating and recording sites. In terms of excavation, Petrie recommended two main types of trenching – open area and linear, depending on the nature of the site. The former was better for complex sites with deep stratigraphy, while simpler sites were best tested by a series of parallel trenches which could be extended according to the layout of structures (Petrie 1904: 41–2).

The concern for the *plan* of a site is clearly paramount in Petrie's discussion and indeed in his recording he focuses on how to plan large areas by means of a grid of squares identified by a letter (for the row) and number (for the column) (Petrie 1904: 48–54). In this he is clearly following on the innovation of Pitt Rivers who undoubtedly changed the graphic representation of archaeology through the use of plans – a point acknowledged by O. G. S. Crawford as being the 'one essential feature in every excavation' (Crawford 1921: 208). Petrie's method was still in use on some post-war sites in this country (e.g. Clark on Starr Carr). Moreover, Petrie's great criticism of earlier excavation reports was their lack of plans – he singles out as an example Greenwell's *British Barrows* (1877) which contained very few illustrations, yet most of the text of which could have easily been reduced to a series of plans (Petrie 1904: 114). Petrie's vision of a good archaeological report was clearly one dominated by its figures rather than its words – 'the text is to show the meaning and relation of the facts already expressed by form' (ibid.: 115). This visual sense of archaeological data was increased by the importance he attached to photographs, and more generally his whole attitude can again be seen as partly derived from Pitt Rivers. Indeed, Petrie had met Pitt Rivers in 1881 in rather comical circumstances when the latter was on a tour in Egypt (Burleigh and Clutton-Brock 1982).

The element of visual representation is one to which I shall return in the final chapter, but it is worth qualifying Petrie's focus on plans by his almost total disregard of sections which gets, by comparison, very little mention in the book. Why this should be so is curious, for Petrie was not unconcerned with the chronological development of a site. Mortimer Wheeler, who was a strong critic of Petrie, remarks on this: 'The almost complete absence of measured sections from Petrie's reports is the inevitable corollary of his "method"' (Wheeler 1954: 15). What Wheeler is referring to here is Petrie's lack of concern for stratigraphic relationships; a closer look shows that it was chiefly the *finds* which provided the site's chronology rather than stratigraphic analysis; in the chapter entitled 'Systematic archaeology' (ch. XI), he identifies two modes of work necessary for archaeology to become properly scientific: the 'complete definition of facts by means of a *corpus* of all known variety of objects', and the 'arrangement of material in its order of development by statistical methods and comparison, which bring out the original sequence of construction' (ibid.: 123).

Petrie's interest in typology is well known, especially his work on seriation, but we need to ask why typological sequences should be seen as defining the development of a site rather than stratigraphy. A few years later, his approach was to be criticised as relying on 'evidence from style rather than stratification', as being subjective rather than objective archaeology (Droop 1915: 8–10). One could put it down to 'bad archaeology' (as Droop and later Wheeler did), but given the evolutionary conception of culture which was dominant at the time, is it not surprising that sections at least should not have been seen as a greater resource? Petrie makes an interesting comment towards the end of the aforementioned chapter with regard to displaying objects in museums; he states that they should be displayed so as to demonstrate both their *development* and *context* (Petrie 1904: 132). This idea of the twofold character of an object is derived from the Scandinavian innovations in museum display by Thomsen and later Hildebrand, and it is worth exploring a little further as it helps to understand Petrie's focus on seriation and typology in providing the 'original sequence of construction' of a site.

Antiquarianism and archaeology in Northern Europe: redefining the object

It is all very well having stratigraphic sequences but the question arises whether there is any archaeological site in the world which has a 'full sequence' of deposits representing all prehistoric periods (forgetting for a moment the absurdity of this very conception). More commonly one has to link stratigraphically unrelated deposits or groups of stratified deposits across unconnected sites. The greater the lack of stratigraphic information, the more reliant one is upon typological methods – indeed in Sweden where typological studies were effectively developed, properly contexted finds were rare compared to Denmark. Where in Sweden most finds came as 'strays', in Denmark graves and hoards were far more common, offering a better basis for using find combination to construct chronologies (Almgren 1995: 27). This is well illustrated by the exhibition in the Museum of National Antiquities at Stockholm in 1866 which was modelled upon that of Thomsen at Copenhagen in 1819, for 'the exhibitions were arranged in two parallel running series, one arranged according to *types*, and the other according to *find location*' (ibid.: 27). The lack of closed finds, (e.g. graves, hoards) meant that type series came to have greater importance. B. E. Hildebrand, who directed the exhibition, employed an aesthetics of similarity, imitating an exhibition of modern mass-produced items of the same year (ibid.). Helping out at the exhibition was his son, Hans Hildebrand (who later published the first evolutionary typology, on Iron Age brooches), and the young Oscar Montelius (ibid.: 28–31).

The development of typology might then be said to have arisen out of a need to provide chronology in the face of poor stratigraphic information. A debate later emerged in the 1880s between Montelius and another archaeologist Sophus Müller about the relative priority of find combination (*fundsammenængen*) and typology in constructing prehistoric chronologies (Klindt-Jensen 1975: 84–96; Gräslund 1987). The basis of the find combination is that:

> A find consists of a number of artefacts within a common spatial framework, which indicates that they got into the soil on one and the same occasion or that they were accumulated during a definite and continuous period of time. Thus, a find indicates an absolutely simultaneous deposit or a relatively simultaneous accumulation in the soil.
>
> (Gräslund 1976: 70)

From this definition, it seems clear that the 'find' is conceived much as a 'context' or stratigraphic unit is, although in the same statement it is described both as the deposit and the finds defined by the deposit. Gräslund goes on to say that, in themselves, the deposit or associated finds offer no means of relative dating – it is only when the deposits in a group are compared in terms of the composition of their finds, e.g. through seriation, that a chronology can be constructed. Fundamental to this process is classification, in so far as one analyses what *type* of find one deposit has in common with another. Of course Gräslund is not saying that stratigraphy is irrelevant to the relative date of the deposits in a group but the chronological value of stratigraphy is conditioned by the type definability of the artefacts (Gräslund 1976: 74). The crucial point in all this, however, is that the find combination, whether it has any stratigraphic content or not (i.e. is open or closed), is primarily seen in terms of its relative date, its 'epochal' attribution (e.g. Iron Age). Stratigraphy as a concept is of little importance except in so far as it aids chronology via closed find-combination analogies. This is best demonstrated by the work of Worsaae, who succeeded Thomsen at the National Museum and who was the principal figure in Danish field archaeology in the late nineteenth century.

Worsaae is often cited as another pioneer of scientific field techniques, but his methods leave a lot to be desired. In the appendix to *Primeval Antiquities of Denmark* (1849), he discusses the methods used in excavating barrows: first one should make a proper, measured description, preferably with a drawing, and only then excavate (Worsaae 1849: 152–3). He recommends two techniques – first, trenching across the barrow, sometimes supplemented by another trench at right angles, and the second technique, digging a pit through the centre from above, again preferably supplemented by a trench leading to the barrow edge. What is interesting about the trenches is that he gives orientations – these are not arbitrary but run along specific alignments, which correspond to where satellite burials are predominantly located (ibid.). These trenches are not dug in order to understand barrow construction, but are geared to the location of burials and the recovery of artefacts. Indeed for the same reasons as Pitt Rivers, he argues for total recovery of all finds no matter how trivial, as it is usually the common objects which provide the means for comparison (Worsaae 1849: 156). Sites, like barrows, are treated as 'mines' for artefacts, albeit in a controlled manner, and he cites other good places where antiquities may be found, including peat bogs and quarries (ibid.: 155). No mention is made of stratigraphy beyond a passing mention of distinguishing interments at the top and base of barrows and nowhere in the book is stratigraphy used to argue for the dates of antiquities – he draws instead on general evolutionary assumptions. Even his later work on shell middens, which exhibited greater concern for stratigraphy, does not alter the fact that his main concern was the retrieval of artefacts.

Now perhaps we can appreciate why Petrie showed little concern for sections and the stratigraphy of the site; in itself it was deemed of little relevance to chronology except through seriation of closed find groups, and even then it was not strictly necessary as the same effect could be achieved though seriation of purely typological elements, that is, evolutionary typology. This attitude is strongly expressed in his paper 'Sequences in prehistoric remains' (1899); Petrie complained that although broad period divisions had been achieved, there was still a lack of finer resolution. To achieve this, he outlined five methods which he employed to resolve issues of chronology:

> 1st Actual superposition of graves and burials; but rarely found.
> 2nd Series of development or degradation of form; very valuable if unimpeachable.
> 3rd Statistical grouping by proportionate resemblance; the basis for clas-sifying large groups.
> 4th Grouping of similar types, and judgement by style; giving a more detailed arrangement of the result of the 3rd method.
> 5th Minimum dispersion of each type, concentrating the extreme examples.
>
> (Petrie 1899: 297)

The first, stratigraphic relationship, was for Petrie rarely of practical use but he does affirm its importance in the broadest periodisation and as a framework for the more refined sequences; moreover, it appears to be of quite a different order from the other four in that it uses direct character-istics of the contexts to sequence themselves rather than relying on comparisons of their objects. Of the other four, each has different aspects worthy of remark. The second method, essentially an evolutionary typology, is comparable to Pitt Rivers' method and, under one guise, that of Montelius. The third method is closest to what we call seriation, though it seriates the presence/absence or frequency of different types of objects rather than attributes of objects; this latter is closer to what Petrie describes as the fourth method which looks at the similarity/dissimilarity between objects, such as brooches, of a single type. The fifth method is more of a supple-ment to the others and is merely a kind of Occam's razor or law of parsimony which would see each different type in the sample as occupying the shortest possible duration.

From this, it is fairly clear what Petrie's priorities are; but more than that, they reveal that while stratigraphy may be relevant in understanding the constructional sequence of a site, neither it nor the sequence itself was the aim of field archaeology; rather these were simply means to an end, the end being understanding the evolution of material culture. A demon-stration of this is given quite clearly in the opening paragraphs of the same paper:

But it may be said that in dealing with ages before any written record of years no reference to time or dates is possible. In the narrowest sense this may be true. Yet the main value of dates is to show the sequence of events; and it would matter very little if the time from Augustus to Constantine had occupied six centuries instead of three, or if Alexander had lived only two centuries before Augustus. The order of events and the relation of one country to another is the main essential in history. Indeed, the tacit common-sense of historians agrees in treating the periods of great activity and production more fully than the arid ages of barbarism, and so substituting practically a scale of activity as the standard rather than a scale of years.

It would be, therefore, no fallacy to portion out the past by the ratio of events rather than by the seasons; and to measure history by the stages of thought and action of man rather than by inanimate celestial motions. In this truest sense, then, we may have a possibility of reducing the prehistoric ages to a historical sequence, and defining them as readily as historic times. If some scale and ratio of human activities can be adopted, we may measure the past by means of it definitely as we do by years B.C.

(Petrie 1899: 295)

One could argue that Petrie, as much as Pitt Rivers or Worsaae, was not really concerned to understand how a *site* worked or developed in itself – the site was merely the context for the *finds*. The epochal concept of culture provided the framework within which a context or stratigraphic event was primarily understood – as denoting a particular phase or period (*epoch*) within a *relative* chronology whose ultimate purpose was to place an object in the correct point of a sequence. This was its *primary cultural relevance*.

Despite the so-called innovations of Pitt Rivers, the differences between him and Greenwell are not differences in kind, but only of degree. Indeed, one might even suggest that Schliemann was as good as Pitt Rivers, especially when one considers the complexity of the sites he excavated, identifying building levels/layers in a Tell. In 1881 he also brought in an architect, Dörpfeld, to produce accurate plans (Cottrell 1953: 79, 85; Trigger 1989: 197). Similarly, Giuseppi Fiorelli at Pompeii in the later nineteenth century excavated in wide horizontal layers rather than the usual 'mine shafts', expressing a concern for controlled excavation (Malina and Vašíček 1990: 49). Petrie, who started excavating in Egypt around the same time, also produced work of an equal standard and was followed by George Reisner at the turn of the century who improved techniques even more (Trigger 1989: 197). We have not discussed Reisner's work here but it is significant to note that the American archaeologist Alfred Kidder, who is discussed below, had studied under him at Harvard (ibid.: 188).

What brings most of these archaeologists together is a similar conception of archaeological fieldwork as primarily one concerning the *retrieval* of artefacts. The actual precision used in such retrieval is in many ways irrelevant since the significance lies not in any stratigraphic context but in a find's relationship to other finds. This is clear for example in Pitt Rivers' adoption of average sections and the concern for three-dimensional recording rather than stratigraphic association. This is not to say that they were not interested in the features from which finds came, such as graves, buildings, ditches – but rather that these took second place to the finds. Schliemann's conception of the recovery of Priam's treasure shares the very same background as Pitt Rivers' recovery of Romano-British pottery from Rushmore Park; both archaeologists wanted to be sure of the context from which the finds came, but were not concerned for the context in itself, so much as for the find.

From this perspective, the proximity of late nineteenth-century archaeology to antiquarianism is much closer; what unites them is a focus on the object rather than the site. What separates them is a concern to place the finds in an evolutionary/historical rather than an aesthetic/speculative context. Schliemann's major intellectual concern was with the literal truth of Homer; Pitt Rivers' preoccupation was with the evolution of material culture. Both focused on the object to achieve this, and the methods they actually used to retrieve objects were not that dissimilar. It is interesting to turn and see how the same issue was dealt with in North America, because, despite differences, the same conceptions lie at the root of fieldwork conducted there at the end of the nineteenth century.

The development of field archaeology in North America

As in Europe, late nineteenth-century archaeological fieldwork in North America was highly variable in quality, being conducted by a mixture of peripatetic collectors such as Edward Palmer or people trained in other disciplines such as William Henry Holmes (art), Cyrus Thomas (entomology) and Frederic Ward Putnam (zoology) (Meltzer 1985: 251). Archaeology in North America was very much dominated and forged at this time by two institutions, the Bureau of American Ethnology (BAE) in Washington and the Peabody Museum, Harvard, both of which were concerned to develop a profession of 'real archaeologists' although with some differences of opinion (Hinsley 1974, 1985). The BAE certainly regarded itself as the leader of a new science, claiming it represented the 'New Archaeology' (Meltzer 1985: 252); on the other hand, it was perhaps Putnam who did more than anyone to train groups of students in careful excavation and recording and he was one of the few to talk publicly about his techniques (Putnam 1973 [1886]).

In an address to the Harvard University Archaeological Society in 1885, Putnam outlined the methods of investigation for burial mounds, settlements and cemeteries, all of which followed a similar procedure of trenching or slicing:

> For instance, in exploring a mound a trench is first dug at the base of the mound. A slight vertical wall is made thereby showing the contact of the edge of the mound with the earth upon which it rests. . . . This wall is the first section of the exploration, and its outline should be drawn or photographed and its measurements noted. For the latter purpose it is best to stretch two strings over the mound, one north and south and the other east and west, and to take all measurements from those. After this first section is made, the work is carried on by slicing; or cutting down a foot at a time, always keeping a vertical wall in front, the whole width of the mound. Each slice thus made is a section. . . . This method is continued until the whole mound has been dug away, and a thorough knowledge of its structure and contents obtained.
> (Putnam 1973 [1886]: 3)

This slice method was basically a way of progressing by means of a continuous vertical face, allowing constant check on the stratigraphy. It is important to recognise that while it is *not* stratigraphic excavation, it is still excavation which is *aware* of stratigraphy. This is an important point, because there is a great deal of disagreement over who conducted the first stratigraphic excavations in North America, and misunderstanding of this difference may lie at the base of many of these disputes (Browman and Givens 1996: 81). The 'stratigraphic revolution' is discussed later in this chapter, but it is worth looking at other fieldworkers in the late nineteenth century who used stratigraphy to interpret their sites.

Browman and Givens analyse several early claimants for stratigraphic excavation, including William Dall and Henry Holmes, both of whom, like Putnam, clearly observed stratigraphy in cross-sections, but this is not the same as excavating stratigraphically (ibid.: 82). However, others such as G. Nordenskiöld, Richard Wetherill and George Pepper have also been accredited with early stratigraphic excavation, and at least in the case of Pepper this seems incontrovertible, thanks to Reyman's study of his unpublished field notes (Reyman 1989). Pepper's work in the 1890s was certainly ahead of its time (if only by a decade or so) and not only because of his field methodology, but also because of his concern with chronological change – and the two are linked. His methods remained unpublished and were not taken up, perhaps because the discipline was still not quite ready for an interest in chronology.

Much the same point can be made of early stratigraphic excavations in

South America by Max Uhle which were more or less ignored in their own day. Uhle was born and trained in Germany, and in particular his early museum work in Europe would have made him attentive to issues of typological development. Moreover, he was familiar with Petrie's studies. His most influential work was conducted in Peru and Bolivia in the 1890s, and, after Petrie, he used seriation techniques on grave assemblages to create a highly successful chronology (Uhle 1902). Only rarely did he employ stratigraphic means to verify these, but during later excavations on a shell-mound in California he used the stratigraphy to suggest a sequence of cultural change. The reaction to this work is very interesting, because essentially the work was disputed and ultimately ignored; and yet the man responsible for this, Alfred Kroeber, was also responsible for later resurrecting Uhle's work and bringing the importance of seriation into archaeology (Willey and Sabloff 1993: 63–4; Browman and Givens 1996: 82).

While it is important to recognise Uhle's contribution to archaeological fieldwork, I think one must not lose sight of the fact that his use of stratigraphy was not common and, like Petrie, he preferred to use discrete graves to work on rather than stratified deposits such as middens. Where he perhaps differed from Petrie was that he was more concerned with specific regional/historical culture change than general evolutionary trends – a fact which also caused him to clash with prevailing views at the turn of the century in North America. The latter part of the nineteenth century in North America has been characterised as a period of formalisation for American archaeology, much as it was in Europe (Willey and Sabloff 1993). It was a time when a great deal of fieldwork was conducted, and sites described and classified; however, unlike in Europe, there was comparatively little concern for chronology which appears partly linked to the legacy of Evolutionism which saw non-Europeans as 'peoples without history'. This may be an over-simplification, however, especially if one looks at a work such as the Marquis de Nadaillac's *Pre-historic America* (1885), which distinguishes several periods 'from the shell-heap to the mound, from the mound to the pueblo, from the pueblo to the structures of Mexico, Central America and Peru' (de Nadaillac 1885: 534). However, it is telling that he was French, not American, and his book was an explicit copy of his earlier work on prehistoric Europe. Nevertheless, it might be noted that the book was edited (and its themes endorsed) by William Dall, a prominent North American archaeologist who made use of stratigraphic observation in his studies.

For North American archaeologists, the major issues in the latter part of the nineteenth century revolved around the antiquity of human occupation and the origin of numerous mounds in the Ohio and Mississippi valleys, which some claimed had been built by a 'lost race' rather than by ancestors of present-day North American Indians (Dixon 1913: 549; Meltzer 1985: 252). Through the efforts of the Bureau of American Ethnology under the guidance of Wesley Powell and later Cyrus Thomas, both issues were resolved, with most unanimity centred on the latter issue. Putnam, at the Peabody Museum, also contributed greatly to destroying the 'lost race' theory of the mound-builders but, in opposition to Powell, argued for a more ancient origin for the North American Indians. The important point here is that the only issue of chronological significance was over the very long term – between palaeolithic and present-day Indians – and when Powell's views eventually prevailed, North American prehistory became more or less a single period discipline. Part of this undoubtedly relates to the close association between archaeological and ethnographic work by the Bureau, and, while destroying the lost race hypothesis of mound-builders was an important development, the very premise of this association also underpinned the continuity perceived between contemporary and prehistoric North American Indians (Meltzer 1985: 255).

It is this lack of concern for chronology which accounts for the relative obscurity of those early stratigraphic excavations. Finding any published work on field methods for this period is hard – indeed much information undoubtedly lies in fieldnotes and manuscripts (Reyman 1989: 41–2). Yet this fact itself is instructive – in many ways, the issue of who conducted, and when, the first stratigraphic excavation is a red herring. The larger point is that there was no standardised or widely adopted approach to fieldwork in North America before the 1930s; indeed before 1900 there was little agreement over how to evaluate archaeological discoveries, except on a personal basis (Hinsley 1976; Meltzer 1985: 254). Putnam's address from which I quoted above ended with an appeal for all archaeologists to follow similar principles; at the heart of the drive for the professionalisation of archaeology was fieldwork which one could *trust*. Hinsley raises this issue both for Putnam at the Peabody and Powell at the BAE, in terms of their seeking people to conduct fieldwork for their respective institutions (Hinsley 1974: 41; 1985: 62). This essentially came down to the need for a full and proper record of the excavation, as Putnam's references to measured plans, sections and photographs intimate, and while articulated differently from Pitt Rivers' call for the total record, the basic issue of trust, i.e. reliable data, was the same.

The period between 1870 and 1900 was a period of major transition in many ways in North America, as in Europe, with, on the one hand, a fieldwork which was largely driven by the desire to build and enhance museum collections, and, on the other, one which also clearly recognised the importance of context. But, unlike Europe, the meaning of this context was quite different: in Europe, context was chronological due to the evolutionary interpretation of prehistory; in North America, context was far more ethnographic due to the anthropological perspective. This view, however, was soon to change, largely through the influential figure of Franz Boas. Within the second decade of the twentieth century, culture change became *the* issue, and it was largely articulated through a combination of stratigraphic excavations and seriation. But it was also mediated by a very different conception of culture which rejected evolutionism outright.

Culture history and the assemblage (1920–1960)

The Wheeler–Kenyon school and stratigraphy in Britain

It has been an often raised point that Pitt Rivers' exhaustive approach to fieldwork was almost ignored by his successors as few excavators reproduced his standards, at least in Britain (Petrie's fieldwork was in Egypt). Mortimer Wheeler clearly regarded Pitt Rivers as a model:

> Between 1880 and 1900 General Pitt Rivers in Cranborne Chase had brought archaeological digging and recording to a remarkable degree of perfection, and had presented his methods and results meticulously in several imposing volumes. Then what? Nothing. Nobody paid the slightest attention to the old man. One of his assistants had even proceeded to dig up a lake-village much as Schliemann had dug up Troy or St. John Hope Silchester: like potatoes.
>
> (Wheeler 1958: 55; also see Wheeler 1954: 13–14)

This assistant who dug a site 'like potatoes' was none other than H. St George Gray, the site being Glastonbury in Somerset (Bulleid and Gray 1911/1917). But how bad was this site in fact? Gray joined Arthur Bulleid in 1902 after the latter had already been excavating the site for several years in the 1890s; fresh from Cranborne Chase, Gray's contribution seems to have been predominantly on the finds rather than the excavated structures, and indeed Bulleid's excavation and recording appears to have been as good, if not even better than Pitt Rivers' – scale plans were drawn with most of the finds plotted on them, and full feature and finds descriptions are given in the final report (Barrett 1987: 412–13). In general, the only criticisms that can be made about the excavation are the same as those applicable to Pitt Rivers – namely lack of stratigraphic information, although perhaps the location of finds was not always as precise as with Pitt Rivers. Corroborating this picture was another site excavated by Gray between 1908 and 1913 – Maumbury Rings in Dorset, a multi-period site; this appears to have been done almost exactly following Pitt Rivers' methods, from trenching techniques to recording (Bradley 1975: 5–6).

Wheeler then is certainly wrong in describing the decades after Pitt Rivers as retrograde; rather, it appears that he has exaggerated the brilliance of Pitt Rivers. Wheeler himself gained one of his first experiences of field archaeology as a young student with Jocelyn Plunkett Bushe-Fox at the excavations of the Roman town at Wroxeter in 1913. Looking at this site report, one sees that it is very similar in layout to Pitt Rivers' *Excavations in Cranborne Chase*, with detailed discussion of the site followed by finds 'reports'. Measured plans and sections are shown and in all respects it is very difficult to say it is of a lower standard than Pitt Rivers' reports. What is clear is that Bushe-Fox was conscious of the importance of both plan and stratigraphy and the last site report of 1914 shows three phases of building development on the site (Bushe-Fox 1916; plates XXX–XXXII).

This is way ahead of anything Pitt Rivers did; what is significant, though, is that Bushe-Fox's concern for stratigraphy was partly in order to produce local Romano-British pottery sequences, as he highlights the importance of 'well-stratified deposits' in the discussions of coarse pottery (e.g. Bushe-Fox 1913: 68). It is no coincidence, then, to find he worked with Petrie in Egypt, nor that his excavations at Wroxeter were preceded by a study on dating Roman pottery from excavations at the Roman fort at Corbridge the previous year (Bushe-Fox 1912). It is also perhaps no coincidence that Mortimer Wheeler's first work was on Roman pottery, a work he began after the 1913 season at Wroxeter.

Through his experience at Wroxeter and on sites in Essex after the war, Wheeler developed his ideas on field methodology, particularly stratigraphy, and it was in Wales that these first crystallised at the Roman fort of Segontium in 1921–2 (Wheeler 1958: 60). He clearly saw the publication of Segontium as a key moment, drawing attention to a section of a cellar where, as he puts it, 'the whole bones of the matter are' (Wheeler 1956: 60; see Figure 2). Soon after, in 1927 in an address to the Royal Society of Arts, he pronounced stratification as the key principle of excavation, and through a number of examples, particularly of Roman sites, he

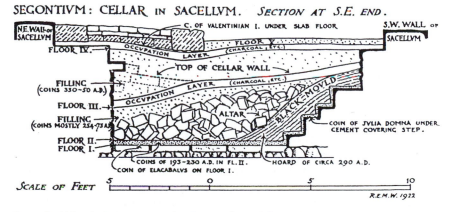

Figure 2 Wheeler's section at the Roman fort of Segontium

demonstrated how the basic geological concept can be applied on archaeological sites; natural stratification such as the lake bed clays of Sweden
illustrated 'the principle of definite chronological sequence represented by
the superposition of stratum over stratum in the soil. This principle lies at
the basis of all archaeological excavation' (Wheeler 1927: 817). His follower
Kathleen Kenyon affirmed the same principle: 'The science of excavation
is dependent on the interpretation of the stratification of a site, that is to
say the layers of soil associated with it' (Kenyon 1953: 69).

However, years before, J. P. Droop in his *Archaeological Excavation* (1915)
had preached the importance of stratigraphy and even gives an example of
stratigraphic interpretation rather similar to Wheeler's in his 1927 article
(Droop 1915: 75–7). It is Wheeler, however, who gives the classic example
– which he uses later in his book, *Archaeology from the Earth* – of what can
happen if stratigraphic excavation is not followed. A buried wall will cut
through certain layers, be contemporary with others, and sealed by still
more, 'yet the first instinct of the inexperienced excavator when he discovers
a buried wall is at once to cut alongside it in order to see where it goes!
Thereby destroying beyond amend just that evidence which might have
made his discovery a real and living addition to knowledge' (Wheeler 1927:
824; also see Wheeler 1954: 73–7; and Kenyon 1953: 90). Wheeler might
have been thinking of Petrie when he wrote this, for in his *Methods and
Aims in Archaeology* Petrie recommends just what Wheeler abhors: 'In the
case of tracing a building, trenches cut along the lines of the walls are a
good beginning; and then if more is wanted, the plan is clear and the rooms
can be emptied with foresight' (Petrie 1904: 41).

The importance of stratigraphic excavation is made clear in his criticism
of arbitrary digging, where the 'notion of peeling off the successive strata
in conformity with their proper bed-lines, and thus ensuring the accurate
isolation of structural phases and relevant artefacts, is not even considered'
(Wheeler 1954: 53–4). Throughout Wheeler's examples, the importance of
stratigraphy is usually referenced to its role in providing chronological information; this is ironic given that Petrie's concerns were practically the same.
How is it, though, that for Wheeler stratification came to take on so much
more significance than it did for Petrie? One may point to the fact that
Wheeler was working a great deal on deeply stratified sites (e.g. Roman
towns) – but while this may have played a part, it cannot be the whole
answer as Petrie too worked on such sites in Egypt. The answer must relate
to the changing concept of culture within which Wheeler was working; to
address this, it is worth examining the field techniques of Wheeler a little
more closely, along with those of his contemporaries, especially Kathleen
Kenyon.

It is quite clear from both Wheeler's and Kenyon's work that stratigraphy *was* the section; the two were inextricably linked and in this, perhaps,
we can see something of the same 'visual' sense of an excavation as Petrie

had in terms of finds and the plan. In a similar manner to Petrie, Wheeler identifies three basic methods of investigating a site: trial trenching (sondages), open area and substantive trenching (Wheeler 1954: 63). The first and last are rather similar in execution if not in strategy, involving limited cuttings – though in the former it is to test or attempt to uncover the archaeology, while in the latter it is directed at specific types of situation such as across an earthwork or to link up open areas. Wheeler's main method, as Petrie's, was the 'open area'. This term has different connotations, however, especially today when we often use the phrase 'open area' to denote absence of baulks, as distinct from Wheeler's 'box' system (see p. 52). For Wheeler, there were many ways to excavate an open area but only one satisfied all the necessary criteria for a proper, stratigraphic excavation: the box or grid method (ibid.: 64–8; also see Atkinson 1946: 41–3; Kenyon 1953: 94–5).

The method, first employed at Maiden Castle (Wheeler 1943), subdivided the area to be excavated into a series of squares on a grid (as Petrie recommended) but leaving baulks (i.e. standing sections) along the axes of the grid so that in effect the open area is divided into a series of 'boxes' within which excavation proceeds (Figure 3). In employing his method, Wheeler tended to use a control square (or, similarly, before opening an area, dig a trial trench or sondage) in order to establish the nature of the stratigraphy on the site. The control pit helped guide the progress of the excavation for 'stratification must, by its nature, always be controlled from the side, i.e. from the side of the control-pit, since it obviously cannot be controlled prophetically from the top: *vertical digging first, horizontal digging afterwards*, must be the rule' (Wheeler 1954: 66; emphasis in original). It is worth reiterating that phrase, 'stratification must, *by its nature*, always be controlled from the side'; stratification *is* the section. This, as we shall see, is not the way we view things today and the difference is quite telling.

Wheeler himself does not give much information on how one goes about correlating the different strata between the squares or even between sections within a square except to say that it must be continually done as excavation proceeds down (Wheeler 1954: 66–7). He was aware of the potential hazards of a section-based stratigraphy where layers may not 'follow through' (ibid.). His follower, Kathleen Kenyon, gave a more detailed example illustrating the procedure which it is instructive to follow for what it reveals about a section-based conception of stratigraphy (for a later, similar example, see Alexander 1970: 71–4). In her two examples (Kenyon 1953: 130–1; figures 13–14), one of a prehistoric site and another Roman, she shows how one lays out the different squares in adjacent columns, the different layers in each listed in rows, producing a sort of matrix (in the strict mathematical sense – which is ironic given the use of this word for the modern system developed by Harris; see p. 56). The layers are then placed on the same row if they either represent the same deposit or are contemporary, and

Figure 3 Wheeler's box-trench excavation at Maiden Castle

can be adjusted up or down according to their place in the sequence (i.e. later or earlier). Moreover, each row or a group of rows is collected under a periodisation or phasing, as we would say today. The Kenyon 'matrix' is indeed almost like a visual analogue of the section itself and stresses a simpler, unilinear sequence of layering (Figure 4).

Throughout Kenyon's and Wheeler's texts there is a very clear bias towards seeing stratification chiefly in terms of layers, which, as Harris has pointed out, is an overly geological conception of stratification (Harris 1989: 12–13). Wheeler himself in his 1927 paper begins his discussion of archae-ological stratigraphy by using the geological example of lake-bed clays (Wheeler 1927: 816–17). Pyddoke's whole book *Stratification for the Archaeologist* (1961) focuses very much on geomorphological processes. Today the debate is still alive about the geological conception of archae-ological stratigraphy, especially between Harris and proponents of archaeostratigraphic classification (Gasche and Tunca 1983; Farrand 1984; Stein 1987; Harris 1991; also see Chapter 5). However, the point to note here is the effect such a bias has on giving over-emphasis to the concept of a *layer* in archaeological stratigraphy.

Although Kenyon (1953: 69) affirmed that 'the term stratification may also be applied in the archaeological sense to things which are not strictly layers at all, but pits, banks, trenches, in fact any disturbance in the soil', there is still a real sense that the layer provided the model for a strati-graphic unit. Note how she describes such non-layers: 'in fact any *disturbance* in the soil'. Throughout the chapter on excavation techniques, such things are repeatedly described as disturbances, that is, defined in reference to the layer which they break. Indeed both in her and Wheeler's books, there is a clear sense that the two basic components of a site are layers and structures; tellingly, structures are never given numbers, only layers are (and disturbances of layers). More significantly interfaces and/or cuts do not receive numbers – but only solid deposits (see Kenyon's section in Figure 4).

In other words, even though Kenyon recognised a pit as a unit distinct from a layer, the concept of what a pit was, stratigraphically, was very much in terms of a layer – that is, what was recorded was the pit *fill*, not the pit cut. This is what got numbered, not the line defining the extent of the disturbance. Harris also quotes Kenyon in this respect, but he tends to give Wheeler and Kenyon the credit for recognising the interface as a unit of stratification, when in fact this is misleading (Harris 1989: 11). Certainly they recognised the importance of the interface as distinguishing between deposits, a fact which comes out forcefully in their espousal of strong lines in section drawing (see p. 208); yet to say that they recognised the impor-tance of the interface as a unit in its own right is incorrect. This was surely Harris's major contribution (see p. 153; Harris 1991).

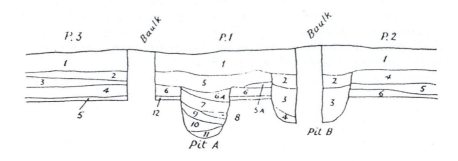

Final Periods	Working Periods		P.1	P.2	P.3	P.4 (Not shown on diagram)
		Plough	1	1	1	1
IIIb	A	Fill of Pit B	2	2		
			3	3		
			4			
IIIa	B	Pit B, cut through Period III hut floor.				
III	C	Floor of Period III hut, overlying Period II hut and Pit A	5	4	2 3	2
IIc	D	Upper fill in Pit A	6a 7			3 4 5
IIb	Di	Hearth above lower fill in Pit A	8			
IIa	Dii	Lower fill in Pit A	9 10 11			6 7
II	E	Period II hut, contemporary with	5a	5		
	Ei	Pit A, cut through occupation on Period I hut				
Ia	F	Occupation on Period I hut floor	6	6	4	8
I	G	Floor of Period I hut	12		5	9

Figure 4 Kenyon's correlation table of archaeological layers

This idea that all units of stratigraphy are essentially layers (or deposits) is still common outside archaeology in Britain and I have witnessed sheer incomprehension at the idea that one might record a cut as a stratigraphic event. This is clearly not necessarily a case of 'bad archaeology' (however much we might like to think so), but must relate to something fundamental in the way the archaeological record is perceived. I think it is important to look at the wider milieu of Wheeler and Kenyon, especially to try see in what way their perspective on excavation linked up with that of the concept of culture.

Wheeler, Bersu and the culture-group concept in European archaeology

Although Wheeler was undoubtedly extremely influential on British field techniques, he had a rival; Gerhard Bersu, who brought German 'open area' methods into Britain in the later 1930s, influenced a whole generation of famous archaeologists such as Grahame Clark, W. P. Grimes and Christopher and Jacquetta Hawkes (Evans 1989). Given Bersu's background in the 'homeland' of the culture-group concept and its concern for settlement archaeology, his focus on large, open area plans is perhaps unsurprising. Indeed, settlement archaeology extended back into the nineteenth century in much of mainland Europe with C. Schuchardt's excavations and recognition of posthole structures since the 1870s (Malina and Vašíček 1990: 49). Elsewhere on mainland Europe, people such as van Giffen in the Netherlands and Gudmund Hatt in Denmark were, like Bersu, conducting open area excavations without baulks/sections specifically to be able to discern such structures (Barker 1982: 16–20). Bersu's inaugural project was the excavation of the Iron Age settlement at Little Woodbury, conducted on behalf of the Prehistoric Society in 1938 and 1939 (Bersu 1938, 1940). However, Bersu's method has perhaps gone down as more pioneering than it really was; his excavation was not strictly 'open area', but consisted of a series of parallel strip trenches which were backfilled with the spoil from the 'seams' between them which were dug afterwards (Bersu 1938: 42; for a contemporary critique of this method by a Wheelerian, see Atkinson 1946: 43; earlier critics include Droop 1915: 22).

As Evans points out, only in the final plan does it look like an open area excavation (Evans 1989: 443); and yet exactly the same can be said about Wheeler's excavations: when completed, the baulks of a Wheelerian grid were removed to recover the whole 'plan' so that the final result might look like a section-free open area. There is little difference in the plans of Bersu and Wheeler, except perhaps stylistically as Bersu often published a naturalistic as well as schematic plan (e.g. see Bersu 1940, figures 20 and 21), although it is his naturalistic sections which are usually recalled, in opposition to Wheeler's 'compromise' sections (see Chapter 6 for further discussion of these points). Many of the differences between Bersu and Wheeler have perhaps been exaggerated – certainly they differed in their graphic representation as just mentioned, but possibly most significantly it was in their interpretation of prehistoric sites. Wheeler worked a lot on Roman as well as prehistoric sites, and much of the antagonism between him and Bersu was over the 'pit-dwelling' view of pits (Evans 1989: 444). Bersu's major influence was undoubtedly not on field techniques in general but upon the importance of recognising posthole structures in the British context and their interpretation as houses, replacing the pit-dwelling theory (ibid.: 445). Even Pitt Rivers was not very good at this and missed most structures in the areas he stripped (Barrett *et al.* 1991: 13). Yet while an open area is essential for such recognition, Bersu's method was not the most conducive to it, and certainly no more so than Wheeler's.

While it may be fair to say that Bersu gave more emphasis to the plan than Wheeler did, it is not necessarily the case that Wheeler gave greater significance to sections. This caricature was fuelled by the followers of Bersu – in their book *Prehistoric Britain*, the Hawkeses opposed horizontal and vertical approaches, associating them with modern-sociological and traditional-historical schools of archaeology respectively, albeit paying lip service to an ideal which combines both (Hawkes and Hawkes 1947: 167). And yet this is exactly what Wheeler was attempting; in the statement already quoted, although he affirmed that the 'vertical' precedes the 'horizontal', he still required both. Certainly Wheeler was almost on a mission to raise awareness of stratigraphic relations and the importance of the section, but it is also quite clear that such a method as the box system was an attempt to find the *optimum compromise* between section and plan views of the excavation.

This last is quite crucial to understanding the context of Wheeler's methods in terms of the concept of culture at the time. Wheeler's concern for stratigraphy meant that the section was raised in value, not that the plan was devalued. The force of this comes out when we consider the relationship of these methods to the contemporary culture-group concept (Barker 1982: 15; Harris 1989: 11). Petrie's concern for chronology was expressed very much as a relative phenomenon; what mattered was sequence, not absolute time (see p. 31). Contrast that with Wheeler's statement on chronology:

> To-day, when the traditional precision of history has nevertheless been extensively supplemented by broadly based cultural studies, it may seem reactionary and perverse to reaffirm, as I do, at the beginning of a book on archaeology in the field that mere dates are still of primary and ultimate and unrelenting importance. And by dates I mean not simply those nebulous phases and sequences, those date-substitutes with which

archaeologists often try to bluff us. I mean time in hard figures. I mean Bradshaw.

(Wheeler 1954: 38)

Wheeler even tells us why we need 'time in hard figures', and this is the crucial point:

First, without an absolute chronology cultures of different regions cannot be assessed: in other words, the vital causative factors of human 'progress' cannot be authoritatively reconstructed, and may be widely misunderstood. Secondly, the fluctuating tempo of human achievement – cannot be estimated: the lightning flash, for example, of Periclean Athens, or the glow of the slow-moving riverine civilizations.

(ibid.: 39)

Ignoring the specific interpretations Wheeler evokes which may sound dated, the significant aspect to absolute chronology which he highlights is its status as a *measure* – it enables cultural variability to be commensurable both in terms of change and the rate of change. The affirmation of an absolute, independent chronology made by Wheeler stands in contrast to Petrie. Petrie's evolutionary views are, for all intents and purposes, identical to Wheeler's, yet the two have quite contrary ways of articulating them: for Wheeler, assessing the progress of civilisation necessitated an independent measure of time, while for Petrie such a measure was superfluous since all that was necessary was sequence. The reasons for this difference are discussed in more detail in the next chapter, but the crux would seem to lie with the fact that for Petrie there was only one History, one Story of Progress, and the details of when this happened or at what rate were merely incidental. For Wheeler, on the other hand, history was multiple, civilisation had many faces and to understand it in all its variety meant that just those things which Petrie downplayed, rose to pivotal importance. I have argued elsewhere that the subsequent development of radiocarbon and other dating techniques can be seen in this changing conception of time to prehistory rather than as a simple narrative of progress in archaeological knowledge (Lucas 1997).

The rise of the culture group, of a pluralist conception of culture, created the necessity for an absolute framework within which to analyse that pluralism – space and time. Cultural difference was no longer *directly* relative, but had to be compared indirectly through the medium of space–time. In order to delineate cultural horizons under such a view, time and space had to be kept quite distinct, acting like a mutual check upon the other's validity. That such a model of the necessary foundation or basis upon which to understand the past should also be seen in excavation techniques is perhaps not surprising. Indeed as this distinction became more important,

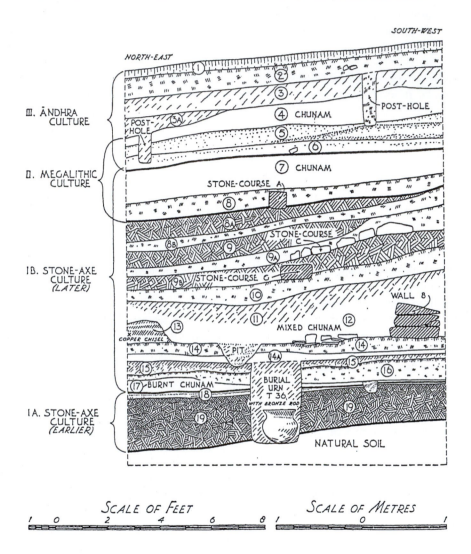

Figure 5 Wheeler's section from Brahmagiri, India

one would *expect* a debate in excavation techniques over the problems of reconciling horizontal and vertical control. This is perhaps just what the Wheelerian grid system attempted. The concern in excavation for both horizontal and vertical control is a direct expression of the wider conception of control in interpreting prehistory through the axes of space and time; locating a stratigraphic layer on a site both in plan and section is a direct correlate of the need to fix a culture group in prehistory in time and space, illustrated in the charts or tables of cultures seen in many textbooks, most famously in Childe's *Danube in Prehistory* (1929). This is *not* to say that a layer is comparable to a culture group, although it is interesting to look at one of Wheeler's sections from his Indian campaigns (Figure 5; Wheeler 1954: 48; figure 9) where major discontinuities in the section (i.e. stratigraphic sequence) are read as major changes in culture groups – a trait more common in North America. Now is a good point at which catch up with developments there and see how similar – or different – fieldwork was.

North America: stratigraphy and culture history

The early decades of the twentieth century in North America saw the rejection of cultural evolutionism and the adoption of historical particularism under the lead of Franz Boas and his students (Willey and Sabloff 1993: 91). In effect, this was comparable to the development of the culture-group concept in Europe and spurred the whole development of methods to recover cultural differentiation across time and space. At the turn of the century, spatial, that is regional/geographical, cultural complexes were beginning to be systematically articulated, particularly through the work of W. H. Holmes, who aimed to synthesise the distribution of archaeological material with known ethnographic areas (Holmes 1914). However, as Meltzer says, this work became obsolete almost as soon as it was published because the very idea of fixed, unchanging cultures was being overturned (Meltzer 1985: 258). It was not so much the spatial differences which were problematic as their association with an unchanging ethnographic present. Thus it was the chronological aspect which gained most attention and became the dominant issue for American archaeology for the first half of the twentieth century as the primary means to developing culture-historical 'area syntheses'.

This emphasis is clearly borne out in the subsequent development of field techniques, with what has been called, 'the Stratigraphic Revolution' (Willey and Sabloff 1993: 97; Browman and Givens 1996), which at first sight mirrors that in Britain under Wheeler. The methods and concerns of North American archaeologists were, however, somewhat different. Their primary purpose in employing stratigraphic excavation was to recover a sequence of material culture assemblages which, when compared or quantified, enabled a detailed chronological differentiation of an area. While stratigraphic excavation was important in understanding the site, its main aim was to prove cross-site or regionally significant sequences. Second, although it has been called 'stratigraphic excavation', this has not quite the same meaning as it did – or does – in Britain. While this practice in North America, usually meant recognition of *stratification*, excavation often proceeded by arbitrary spits rather than by the physical strata. This difference has been described as digging by 'metrical, as opposed to natural stratigraphy' (Willey and Sabloff 1993: 107; also Haag 1986: 68). In Britain, the same difference is described as arbitrary versus stratigraphic excavation (Harris 1989). Without going into which is the best terminology, the relevant point here is that the 'stratigraphic revolution' in North America was clearly quite different from that in Britain at the same time.

The key influential works on carefully controlled 'stratigraphic' excavation were by Manuel Gamio in Mexico (1913) and Nels C. Nelson (1916) and the Kidders (1917) in the Southwest. Gamio's work came about under Franz Boas' instigation and tutelage – Boas had been instrumental in setting up an International School of American Archaeology and Ethnology in Mexico in 1910 and Gamio was Boas' first doctoral student at Columbia, subsequently taking up a fellowship at the School in 1911 (Browman and Givens 1996: 90). One of the primary aims of the school was the establishment of a regional chronology after the Berlin professor Eduard Seler (who was director in the first year) had noted the great diversity of material culture in the valley of Mexico. In reporting the first years of work by the school, Boas writes:

> The question arose, how to determine the chronological sequence of these remains. A survey of the wells and brick-yards in the environment of the City of Mexico showed that this question could be studied by observations on geological sequence of strata. In the year 1911–12 a careful investigation was conducted in one single excavation in a brick-yard at San Miguel Amantla near Atzcapotzalco, which was carried out under the supervision of the Director by Mr Manuel Gamio. The result of this excavation was the definite proof that three distinct civilizations were found in the Valley of Mexico, – a primitive one, which is found in the bottom layers; a second one, identical with that of San Juan Teotihuacán; a third one, the Aztec.
>
> (Boas 1915: 385)

While Gamio's work initiated a spate of similar stratigraphic excavations by the school under Boas' supervision, a similar movement was occurring in the Southwest under the impetus of Nelson. Nelson, who had earlier excavated Californian shell mounds similar to Uhle's but with uninspired results, excavated a deep midden in the Southwest in a similar manner to that of Gamio, using arbitrary units, with even more impressive results:

> At that time it was noticed in a general way that different types of pottery fragments prevailed at different levels but no effort was made, until too late, to keep them separate. . . . A visibly stratified section of the refuse exposure showing no evidence of disturbance was selected and a block of this measuring 3 by 6 feet on the horizontal and nearly 10 feet deep was excavated. I performed this work with my own hands . . . potsherds from each separate foot of debris were kept apart. . . .
>
> (Nelson 1916)

It seems unlikely that Nelson was influenced by Uhle, especially given that his tutor, Alfred Kroeber, had been very scathing of Uhle's work (Browman and Givens 1996: 82–3). Nor, despite his association with George Pepper, did stratigraphic excavation seem to take hold with him from this source (Reyman 1989); rather, it seems that only after spending a season in Spain with famous European archaeologists did he return and adapt these stratigraphic methods to the Southwest in 1914 (ibid.: 83–4). Kidder, aware of both Gamio's and Nelson's work, was deeply complimentary, and even though his own fieldwork using stratigraphic methods came after them, it is unfair to paint him as an imitator. Kidder's approach was quite different, and his subsequent influence greater than that of Nelson or Gamio. Kidder's training was under the famous Egyptologist George Reisner at Harvard, who employed stratigraphic methods on his sites in the Near East and introduced a course on fieldwork in 1911 (ibid.: 87). By 1913, Kidder was already thinking that stratigraphic excavation would resolve problems in sequencing types, and by 1915 had started work at Pecos.

Kidder's method stands out above Gamio's and Nelson's in that instead of using arbitrary units of excavation, he followed the natural stratigraphy:

> The Pecos test pits were not divided into exactly equal cuts, as was done by Mr Nelson, but were laid out in nearly equal divisions based on sand, ash, or other strata which indicated actual levels of deposition during the formation on the mound. This was necessitated by the fact that the Pecos deposits were for the most part laid down on sloping or irregular surfaces, and cuts made on arbitrary chosen plane levels would have resulted in the splitting or cross-cutting of strata.
>
> (Kidder and Kidder 1917: 340)

Ultimately, what matters is not who was first, or who influenced whom, but that by 1920, the use of stratigraphic methods – natural or arbitrary – were widespread. The actual procedures used in such stratigraphic excavation, particularly on initial exploratory fieldwork, varied but generally two main methods seem to have been employed; one was a 'level-stripping' method whereby a trench or pit was cumulatively excavated, either by arbitrary/ metrical or stratigraphic/natural units, the other, almost the inverse of the last, was the 'block' method. This involved trenching all around a square, leaving a standing block or column which could then be excavated, again arbitrarily or stratigraphically. This method was employed by Nelson and Kidder but also subsequently by the Tennessee Valley Authority (TVA) excavation programmes which began in the 1930s (Haag 1986: 68). The advantage it had over the other, was that the vertical section could actually be used to *guide* excavation, whereas in the former, it can only serve as a *post facto* check; in terms of fixing finds to correct layers, the 'block' method had clear advantages. Superficially, the 'block' method also appears to be a negative version of Wheeler's 'box' method. It does not seem, however, as if whole areas were excavated like this but rather single pits/trenches, and it was more common to still excavate such blocks arbitrarily rather than by layer. Nevertheless, there is a clear common conception in North America and Britain of stratigraphy being understood through the section.

As if further mirroring the developments in Britain, fieldwork in North America also developed a concern for open area excavation in the 1930s, particularly in the eastern states where the traces of structures survived largely as postholes, etc., rather than as standing architecture as in the pueblos of the southwest or stone ruins of Central and South America. Previously, plans of 'features' were often only recovered from reconstructions because of the slice method, as pioneered by Putnam and others (see p. 33), but an increase in interest for such plans meant that an open area stripping or peeling method became more desirable. The major impetus for fieldwork changes came under rescue situations with the Works Progress Administration (WPA), Tennessee Valley Authority (TVA) and Civilian Conservation Corps (CCC) projects in the late 1930s and 1940s, and the individuals who supervised them such as William Webb and Fay Cooper-Cole (Dunnell 1986b: 28). While initially under the over-arching authority of the Committee for State Archaeological Surveys (CSAS) established in 1920, these projects also led to the formation of the Society of American Archaeologists (SAA) in 1934 (and its journal, *American Antiquity*) which took over the functions of the CSAS when it was disbanded in 1937, unable to cope with the quantity of work (Pinsky 1992: 166–7; Setzler and Strong 1937). The formation of the SAA has also been seen as an attempt to carve out a separate identity for archaeology in the four-field discipline of anthropology pioneered by Boas and expressed though the American Anthropological Association (and its journal, *American Anthropologist*), especially as Boas appears to have had little interest in archaeology – despite helping Gamio – because of its museum associations (Pinsky 1992: 174–5).

These rescue projects engendered a whole new generation of archaeologists and stimulated the demand for academic posts outside the restricted ambit of Columbia and Harvard. They also established consistent sets of field procedures, including the use of site grids and standardised recording forms. While Guthe published a general statement on field methods in 1930 under the National Research Council, the ultimate codification of the methods developed in the 1930s and 1940s was Heizer's *Guide to Archaeological Field Methods*, first published in 1949 and, albeit vastly modified in subsequent editions, still going strong (Hester *et al.* 1997). As elsewhere, a distinction was made between test or exploratory excavations which uncovered a part of the site using trenching and area excavation which involved stripping a larger expanse. In either case, Heizer identified two main methods: the slice or vertical face method as developed by Putnam (sometimes modified by stepping the faces, a technique known as level stripping), and the unit-level method where the site is divided into separate square units based on a grid, with each excavated independently and stratigraph-ically (Heizer 1958: 40). The latter became the main method, especially for open area sites and, as with Wheeler's box system, it deals with both the horizontal and vertical planes, exhibiting the same concerns for spatial and temporal control. The advantage over the slice method was through the better recovery of plans, and because units were excavated separately a section was always available for checking the vertical stratigraphy.

As in Britain, the new methods manifested themselves on the larger canvas of area syntheses, exemplified most famously in Kidder's work at Pecos:

> As originally planned, the work of the Pecos expedition was to be first intensive, then extensive. The intensive phase was to consist of the excavation of the pueblo, and the determination by stratigraphic methods of the sequence of the pottery types found at the site. During the second or extensive phase we were to use our knowledge of the sequence of the pottery types to arrange in their proper chronological order all other ruins which contained those types. This work was to be accomplished by a thorough archaeological reconnaissance of the Rio Grande drainage.
>
> (Kidder 1962 [1924]: 132)

Kidder's work at Pecos led to a major conference to formulate a classifica-tory scheme which in turn spawned alternatives in response, such as those by Harold Gladwin and William McKern. These are discussed in greater detail in a later chapter, but whatever the classifications employed, such area syntheses became a major goal of archaeologists in the 1930s to 1960s and were ultimately, as Willey and Sabloff note,

> an ordering of the archaeological remains of a given area in a spatio-temporal framework. The essence of this ordering was the archaeological *chronology chart*, a diagram arranged with chronological periods in vertical column and geographical subdivisions across the top, so that the various culture units . . . could be placed in their appropriate boxes.
>
> (Willey and Sabloff 1993: 128)

The ultimate synthesis and zenith of culture classifications was undoubt-edly *Indians Before Columbus*, by Martin, Quimby and Collier, published in 1947, which produced such charts for the whole of North America, appended to a long, detailed and turgid text listing the various traits of each culture group.

Cultural behaviour and context (1960–present day)

Winchester and 'techniques' of archaeological excavation in Britain

By the 1960s and the rise of rescue archaeology the 'myth' of the open area excavation as pioneered by Bersu was well established; in Graham Webster's *Practical Archaeology*, it is rated above the grid system for most sites except certain kinds (e.g., barrows, earthworks) because of its emphasis on the plan (Webster 1965: 86–7). But the open area excavation applauded by Webster, as for example that employed at Yeavering by Brian Hope-Taylor or at Cheddar by Philip Rahtz, was not the same as Bersu's open area. Much of the difference is simply related to the use of mechanical excavators allowing large areas to be opened all at once rather than successively. They were being occasionally used on sites by the 1940s, but chiefly in a rescue context and often just to cut sections or long trenches (see Atkinson 1946: 47). Atkinson suggested that their use might become more common and for stripping larger areas, especially on sites which consisted of subsoil features under an already disturbed ploughsoil layer (ibid.: 220). The growth of rescue archaeology in the 1960s undoubtedly stimulated their use to the extent that there are few sites dug today which do not employ a mechanical excavator to take off the overburden (Figure 6; see Alexander 1970: 41 and 52–3).

Certainly having a truly open area affected the perception and interpretation of sites (particularly for posthole buildings; see Barker 1969; also Bradley 1997: 64–8), but in a way this change in the 'way of seeing' had already happened; the 'true' open area came about twenty years *after* its alleged advantageous effect, as we have seen. Large-scale, mechanical stripping merely confirmed what was anticipated. Webster's *Practical Archaeology* is, for the most part, notable for the way in which it is *so similar* to its predecessors such as Atkinson's *Field Archaeology* and Wheeler's *Archaeology from the Earth*. For example, the same two kinds of entities – structures and layers – are recognised by Kenyon as 'first, man-made constructions ranging from walls to hearths, rubbish-pits and post-holes, and secondly, deposits or layers . . . of material laid down by man' (Webster 1965: 59). Significantly, though, 'disturbances' are now defined as post-depositional natural events such an root action and animal burrows, while postholes etc. are grouped under *structures* (ibid.). There are innumerable other similarities one could give, but despite all the rhetoric of the Bersu 'school' very little changed in field methods from Wheeler's pioneering work in the 1920s. The really significant shifts in field techniques did not occur through open area excavation specifically but in methods associated with it, formulated by the Winchester Research Unit in the 1960s.

Fundamental to Martin Biddle's decision to set up the Winchester Research Unit in 1961 'was a swing in emphasis away from a concept of

Figure 6 Modern open-area excavation in Cambridgeshire, England

excavation dominated by the requirements of a particular period, notably that of Roman Britain, towards the examination without period bias of a city or town as an overall archaeological entity' (Jones 1984: 17). Undoubtedly the urban context of Biddle's excavations was a causative factor, but all the same the concept of an excavation stripped of 'period bias' cannot be totally derived from the multi-period nature of most urban archaeology. There is surely more to it, especially as we consider the other concept that grew alongside this, that of 'problem-oriented' excavation (see Barker 1977: 4) and indeed this comes out when we look closely at the positive developments associated with this abandonment of period bias.

The first expression of these new developments was publicly aired at a research seminar at the Institute of Archaeology in London at the end of 1967, and published two years later (Biddle and Kjølbye-Biddle 1967, 1969). Three 'new ideas' were expounded, two of which I shall focus on here: metric, co-ordinate planning and open area excavation on deeply stratified sites. The big difference between stripping an open area on a greenfield site with little stratigraphy and a brownfield or urban site is very important to appreciate. Most if not all the work of Bersu's adherents had been done on the former, where little if anything was lost by opening large areas at the expense of retaining baulk sections. The same cannot be said in an urban context, however; one must appreciate the boldness of the Biddles' use of it in such a situation:

> One of the major problems in excavation is the need to combine the conflicting requirements of horizontal and vertical observation and record. This problem is particularly acute in the excavation of large areas. The normal solution, first devised by Sir Mortimer Wheeler at Maiden Castle, has been to excavate a grid of squares divided by baulks. In this way the excavation of a large area can be combined with a permanent record of the vertical stratification. . . . There are, however, serious disadvantages: the trench pattern is imposed on the site, often to the detriment of the pattern of structures, and once established the trench pattern is fixed. The deeper the squares go, the more difficult it becomes to view and comprehend the structures as a whole. . . . On a site with very complex stratification, correlation of layers from one side of a baulk to the other may be impossible.
>
> (Biddle and Kjølbye-Biddle 1969: 211)

In coming up with a new method to reconcile the horizontal and vertical which did *not* necessitate the retention of baulks, the Biddles developed a process of digging by 'phase'. Essentially this involved the layout of a grid of pegs across the site enabling the recording of features by a cartesian co-ordinate system (compatible with the National Grid); temporary baulks/

sections are maintained but only until a certain level is reached, defined by a 'major layer', then they are removed after proper recording (Biddle and Kjølbye-Biddle 1969: 212). The whole process is then repeated, the grid lowered as the site proceeds down and baulks either left in the same place or relocated according to the archaeology at that level. The end result is then primarily a series of 'phase' plans and 'cumulative' sections.

As the Biddles stated, such a method 'required great site discipline and well-trained workers' (ibid.: 213). In a way, this method signalled the start of the whole 'mechanisation' of excavation whereby digging becomes more a technical than interpretive process, a trend which reached its culmination in single-context recording and professional, field (i.e. contract) archaeology. Barker summed it up when he wrote in the first edition of *Techniques of Archaeological Excavation*, that the digger was a . . . 'technician producing evidence from the ground regardless of its date or function' (Barker 1977: 53). This is diagrammatically represented in Alexander's hierarchy of the excavation team which not only grades people according to their authority but includes objects such as trowels and excavators so that an impression is given of a hierarchy from human down to machine (Alexander 1970: 17, figure 1). Those people closest to the bottom are most associated with the machines, most machine-like. The so-called democratisation of field archaeology which some have seen occurring since the rise of rescue archaeology and the Winchester method is directly linked into this 'technicisation' (see Chapter 1).

While all this chimes well with the Biddles' focus on an excavation free of 'period bias', it also appears that concurrently excavation was being transformed into a process more and more removed from the interpretation of the past – and yet I do not think this is quite right. Maybe the digger is removed from that interpretation, but not the supervisor or director. Yet changes in the manner of interpretation in the field did occur, but we must rather see this in relation to changing conceptions of what prehistory and culture have meant since the 1960s. However, before I go into this, let me complete the story of the developments at Winchester, particularly the development of single-context recording.

The advantage of the Biddles' method over Wheeler's is clear in so far as sections are *always* strategically placed with respect to the archaeology, both for the clarity of the section *and* the plan. However, as the Biddles recognise, at the point at which one pauses, 'a qualitative decision is taken which may not really reflect an equally important phase in the history of the site' (Biddle and Kjølbye-Biddle 1969: 213). In other words, the particular level at which the director decides to stop and draw a plan and change the grid can only be based on his or her current understanding of the site and the stop may be too early or too late. This may only be picked up in the post-excavation analysis of the records. However, the issue goes deeper, for it makes assumptions about the way a site changes – that a site will go through major, site-wide shifts (phases) rather than a multi-linear trajectory, with different parts of the site changing at different rates or times. This problem is actually the most critical issue, and upon it hinges the change from the old combined section and plan method of digging to an effectively totally plan-driven method. The Biddles' digging 'in phase' still relied on the notion of the *layer* as the most significant stratigraphic entity and consequently the importance of the section to reading stratigraphy. In the course of post-excavation work at Winchester, Edward Harris, who worked for the Research Unit between 1967 and 1971, developed a method of relating stratigraphic units diagrammatically which had a spin-off for the whole process of recording a site allowing just for this factor of multi-linearity.

The Harris matrix and single-context planning

Harris had formulated a method of dealing with post-excavation problems in 1973 which relied on the innovations developed at Winchester. Up to the use of context sheets, the basic textual field record was the notebook which was usually ordered so that each page corresponded to a square in the grid or area within the site. The square was assigned a letter and on its corresponding page the different layers were listed and numbered (though numbering always started from zero within each square; e.g. see Kenyon 1953: 129–31). This basic two-tier method of a letter (square/area) and number (layer) goes back at least to Petrie and is chiefly linked in to a means of identifying the provenance of finds (Petrie 1904: 51–2). With the Biddles' use of co-ordinate planning, letter and number systems were dispensed with so that every find or feature could be located by specific x–y co-ordinates as in a cartesian grid (Biddle and Kjølbye-Biddle 1969: 208), and more significantly in this context, one could also then have a single running sequence of numbers of every stratigraphic unit for the whole site.

The basis of the Harris matrix is that any stratigraphic unit can only have three possible kinds of direct relationship to another: none, earlier/later than, or equivalent to (Harris 1989: 36). In practice, contexts may have *indirect* relationships with other contexts (i.e. through a common context which is earlier or later) as well as the more direct relationships. The nature of this indirect relationship cannot be determined stratigraphically but must be discovered by other means, which involve *grouping* (or phasing) the matrix into broad divisions which are approximately contemporary; ideally this would be done through major horizon breaks in the sequence and/or independent dating through finds association (e.g. pottery, coins). Essentially this is the question of permutations of the matrix which occur in all multi-linear sequences (e.g. see Harris 1984; 1989: 129–32; also Dalland 1984).

The idea behind the matrix derives from critical path analysis, a technique in quantitative geography: 'This method [i.e. the matrix] of presenting a stratigraphic sequence might be seen as a form of critical path analysis' (Harris 1975: 119). Critical path analysis was formalised in the 1960s as part of the same statistical and quantitative 'revolution' which hit most of the social sciences, including archaeology. Essentially it presents in a diagrammatic form the shortest route in time on a *one-way* path, the critical path being the longest path through a network of possible routes. Interestingly, the work Harris quotes, *Quantitative Geography*, suggests that critical path analysis

> might also provide a new approach to studying the course of history, since certain events could not happen before the completion of others. The motor car of the present could not be made before the invention of the internal combustion engine using petrol. This in turn had to await the invention of the sparking plug – and so on.
>
> (Cole and King 1968: 572)

From the Biddles' co-ordinate planning and Harris's work on the matrix, the idea of recording stratigraphic units on separate *pro forma* sheets and planning them individually, produced a whole new possibility in conceptualising fieldwork. The first instances of the use of context sheets for describing stratigraphic units occurred in the 1970s; single-context planning was first suggested to Harris by Lawrence Keen (Harris 1975: 121; 1989: 95) and developed with Patrick Ottoway on New Road site, Winchester in 1975 (Harris and Ottoway 1976; Harris 1989: 95). It was developed as a means to avoid reliance on multiple-feature or, more commonly, composite plans – that is, plans which record all or phased features respectively, on the same drawing.

The combination of the matrix and single-context recording effectively meant that all baulk sections could be dispensed with and everything excavated in plan. For the first time, stratigraphy became truly *independent* of the section. The basic conceptual difference between Harris's formulation of stratigraphy and that based on the section is that, for the former, *physical and stratigraphic relationships* are not conflated but distinct. This difference will be explained below, but it was quite a momentous occasion in the history of field archaeology in Britain. Statements such as the following, in a 1974 publication on archaeological reports, once uncontested, swiftly became untrue: 'The whole presentation of the excavator's stratigraphic analysis and hence his interpretation of the site has depended upon his sections, so they stand as the only record of that interpretation' (Grinsell et al. 1974: 41). Harris's methods were quickly adopted, most notably in London by the Department of Urban Archaeology (DUA) who first used them at the GPO site in 1975

to overcome the time constraints of on-site interpretation and the corresponding need for phase and composite plans (Spence 1991b). (Schofield
(1977: 101), however, stated that these methods were being used as early as
1974.) In the following discussion, I will deal with the DUA, or MoLAS
(as it is now known – Museum of London Archaeology Service) system, as
it undoubtedly represents the most refined development of the Harris–
Winchester method, though most other units in the country, especially urban
units, have adopted a form/degree of single-context recording and the matrix
(e.g. for York, see Pearson and Williams 1991).

The primary consideration in the excavation and recording of sites using
this method is the stratigraphic sequence. The method is particularly useful
on urban sites with deep, complex stratigraphy where some external control
is required which does not solely depend upon on-site interpretation. The
basis of the approach is to divide up the site into discrete units or contexts
which are excavated and recorded according to their stratigraphic position:
'*Any single action, whether it leaves a positive or negative record within the
sequence, is known as a "context*"' (Westman 1994: §1.2; emphasis in original). The definition of the unit is thus in terms of its physical, that is
spatial, limits which are defined either negatively (e.g. a cut) or positively
(e.g. a deposit) and interpreted as representative of a single action or event.
This spatial definition means that even if what appears to be a single feature
such as a dump layer is bisected by a cut, and if there is no physical contact
extant between the two halves, then they are treated as two separate units.
The approach has to be consistent; the identity of the two halves can
always be established subsequently in the record. Each unit then has a
stratigraphic position – that is a position relative to other units in terms
of the sequence – and this is represented in terms of the Harris matrix
(Harris 1989).

The single-context recording system and the stratigraphic matrix are both
extremely useful methods in understanding a particularly complex archaeological site; by viewing it as a palimpsest of discrete events (either of
deposition or removal), the sequence of development on site can be understood with maximum control (Figure 7). It views the site or even a part
of the site as a dynamic, creative process. In a way, it represents the apoth-
eosis of techniques developed in the late 1960s and 1970s and best illustrates
the conception of fieldwork as the investigation and retrieval of an archaeological *record*. No longer a physical site, made of dirt and sharp stones,
no longer the location of buried treasure, but an abstract, immaterial structured set of lines, numbers and text.

Field archaeology in North America since 1960

North American archaeologists started to encounter large-scale excavations
comparable to the rescue or Cultural Resource Management work as early as

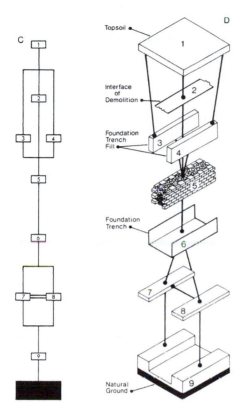

Topsoil

Interface
of
Demolition

Foundation
Trench
Fill

Foundation
Trench

Natural
Ground

Figure 7 Harris matrix

the 1930s and 1940s through the Works Progress Administration and Civilian Conservation Corps programmes (Dunnell 1986b: 23). It was in such situations that many of the innovations which were introduced in Britain in the 1960s had already been implemented, innovations such as standard recording forms and cartesian grids (ibid.: 28). Mechanical excavators were also starting to be used at the same time, especially by the Tennessee Valley Authority and other salvage excavations, and, unlike Britain, they seem to have been instrumental in opening large areas and uncovering whole settlements (Wedel 1951; Haag 1986: 70). If the USA had already established many of the developments which took place a little later in Britain, what innovations in fieldwork did occur at this time? A look through the various editions and transformations of Heizer's original guide from 1949 up to its present incarnation shows that the same basic procedures, developed in the 1930s and 1940s, continue to form the core of excavation methods, in particular the 'unit-level' method of excavation. Most other field manuals which started to appear from the 1960s onward, also cite the unit-level method as the favoured technique (e.g. Joukowsky 1980; McMillon 1991).

The only major shifts within this scheme were the standard preference by the 1960s for excavating after the natural stratigraphy wherever possible rather than using arbitrary spits, and the subsequent adoption of the Harris matrix by the 1980s. The continued use of a horizontal grid as a larger excavation unit, however, distinguishes the US from the British approach with an accompanying greater concern for sections or profiles. In this regard, the layer remains the primary element of a site; thus features such as pits are often still described as 'disturbances' of the stratigraphy rather than stratigraphic units in their own right (Joukowsky 1980: 150–7). McMillon even gives a detailed breakdown of such phenomena under the subtitle of 'excavation problems', where he divides them into 'distortions', 'interruptions' and 'disturbances' (1991: 77–84). The importance of the section for understanding the site is highlighted by Joukowsky, for it 'can only be learned by the study of exposed sections and section drawings, which are scale drawings of the stratification of the site' (Joukowsky 1980: 153).

Nevertheless, while it may appear that field techniques did not develop as dramatically in the 1960s as they had in the 1920s and 1930s in North America, this is only a partial view. While it may be fair to say that *excavation* methods were not radically different, more general aspects of fieldwork were, specifically in the area of sampling and research design. Both on the larger scale of the landscape and the micro-scale of the site, sampling strategies were undoubtedly a major innovation in fieldwork around the 1960s. Use of grids for field survey, geophysical and geochemical methods of site prospecting, and the routine adoption of on-site screening (i.e. sieving) and flotation of deposits for environmental and other remains are all major developments that took off after this time (Haag 1986: 70–3; Dunnell 1986b: 28). The same trends also occurred in Britain and are clearly linked to the new concerns and questions of archaeology after the 1960s – site distribution and regional settlement systems on the one hand, and environmental and ecological components on the other. Both these issues were of course raised in the decades before the 1960s, but it is only after this time that they became routine aspects of fieldwork because of changes in the perception of the archaeological record.

Fundamental to this change was the idea that the recovery of data was inevitably dependent on what one was looking for. Binford, in an important paper on research design, criticised most earlier fieldwork for treating sites as essentially 'mines' for the recovery of artefacts with little regard for features or the relationship between artefacts and features (Binford 1964). While this was perhaps overstating the case, his main issue was that fieldwork was usually too constrained by what was within the often arbitrary limits of trenching or survey, and that the relationship between what was in or on the ground and what was actually recovered remained unproblematised. He argued for a need to consider proper sampling strategies and a thought-out research design using two basic units of sampling – the region and the site – the one being covered by surface survey and the other by excavation. For the former, he drew on the by now common trio of random, systematic or stratified sampling procedures, while for excavation he suggested a staged investigation employing methods which were already in use: an initial test pit survey to identify the presence of remains, a secondary block area excavation to provide a representative spatial cover, and finally an open area stripping to provide the detailed contextual data (ibid.). By implementing a research design, the relevant data about sites could be properly recovered, with, more importantly, some control over their recovery (e.g. see papers in Mueller 1975).

Modern field methods and 'action archaeology'

The rise of New Archaeology around the same time as these developments in field techniques is of course no coincidence. The use of a matrix and single units is reminiscent of systems theory diagrams and we have already commented on its pedigree in geography's critical path analysis. More specifically though is the equation made between a stratigraphic unit and an event or action, for just as objects were no longer viewed as direct, normative representations of cultures nor were the contexts of those objects. Culture came to be seen as more complex, articulated through all kinds of different behavioural events/actions rather than simply a normative repository of traits. This complexity of culture is equally manifest in the SCR system of excavation which sees a site as a complex of actions/events rather than a simple sequence of cultures or cultural change as in 'phase' excavation. While this thematic link to excavation methods was perhaps stronger in Britain, in the USA these developments were accompanied by a group of related studies – ethnoarchaeology, experimental archaeology, taphonomy, formation processes and Middle Range Theory – all of which in various ways tackle the question of the relationship between the archaeological record and behaviour (see Chapter 5).

Willey and Sabloff have suggested that the development of 'feature' excavation in the 1930s ultimately stimulated the concern for context and understanding behaviour patterns in the archaeological record (Willey and Sabloff 1993: 144). It certainly may have been a necessary precondition, but such behavioural concerns do not really appear until much later and in Britain a case can be made for clearly linking them to SCR with its focus on the 'event' or 'action' nature of archaeological deposits. For Wheeler or Kenyon excavation was largely a matter of construction sequence; while we have inherited this notion, our focus on the stratigraphic unit as representative of an event seems a clear departure, in the sense of viewing a site as a site of actions and events. Of course Wheeler saw this too, especially through his imaginative reconstructions, but the difference is that for Wheeler the events are pulled out of the stratigraphic sequence and woven into a traditional historical narrative while under SCR they form the very basis of the sequence. Our concern today is understanding a structured activity or set of activities, not simply a series of unique events; the site is composed of this.

Economic and ecological dimensions of the culture group as developed by such people as O. G. S. Crawford and Grahame Clark in Britain and, slightly later, Julian Steward and Leslie White in the USA, can be seen as anticipating this behavioural turn. However, their work focused on improving the retrieval and analysis of environmental finds, rather than explicitly studying behaviour patterns through context or stratigraphic units. It is only when assemblages were studied in these terms that major changes were made in viewing the archaeological record – for example the studies on social organisation made on Pueblo sites in the American Southwest by Hill, Longacre and others and those on mortuary practices by Binford and others (Binford and Binford 1968). In Britain, similar studies ultimately developed into a contextual archaeology under the influence of Ian Hodder (e.g. Hodder 1982b). Just as the culture group concept influenced the way sites were excavated, so processual/post-processual archaeology through its concern for behaviour/action has affected the way we perceive sites today.

Looking back over the developments in field archaeology since the 1880s, several major changes in perception can be identified. For Pitt Rivers and others of his time, the archaeological site was a repository of objects which, if carefully excavated and linked to types of monuments, were instrumental in the construction of evolutionary typological sequences. For Wheeler, Kidder and their contemporaries, the site became a repository of an artefactual assemblage indicative of a culture group, and, if stratified, the locus of critical information on the chronological changes within this assemblage. For us, the site is a repository of behavioural patterns, structured activities revealed through close analysis of contextual association within or between assemblages.

One can see how each of these views is linked to the prevailing conception of the past – as the evolution of culture, as the history of culture groups, and as cultural behaviour (however this is viewed). These changes should not, however, be seen as completely disjunctive, for many of the themes from preceding periods were carried over. We still use typologies and systems of classification developed in the late nineteenth century and we still use regional culture differences inherited from the earlier twentieth century. The history of fieldwork is one of continuities and change and it is important to see the two together. Moreover, while there is no doubt that fieldwork methodologies also tend to channel the process of recovery in relation to theoretical perspectives, this is not necessarily a closed relationship as the productive re-examination of earlier excavation archives shows (e.g. Barrett, Bradley and Green 1991; Barrett *et al.* 1983; Wilcox 1981). This issue of the openness of archives is something I return to at the end of this book in terms of the concept of 'iterability' and the fact that excavation and fieldwork in general are not necessarily the unrepeatable experiments we often regard them as.

Chapter 3

Splitting objects

It is very easy to forget why a site report is structured like it is – we read it without really questioning the partition and order of information, indeed we even expect it to look a certain way. A ceramicist may turn to the back and flick through, looking for figures and descriptions of pottery, knowing that such reports usually occur near the end and as distinct sections of text within the report. The faunal remains person, the lithics specialist, and so on, may do the same. Someone interested in the site phasing may look for phase plans, or for a quick summary of the site interpretation, and will go to the final discussion. It is very predictable, very repetitive and – boring? Well, perhaps, but this is not really my point. The site report as it usually appears today presents a whole classification of archaeological knowledge, one which is not necessarily 'natural', 'scientific' or the best, but one which has developed out of specific historical and theoretical circumstances. The very partitioning and order of information presented in a site report is as implicated in the history and conceptualisation of the discipline as the fieldwork which precedes it.

In this chapter, I want to explore this classification of archaeological knowledge. I want to focus in particular on what appears to be a dual sense of such classifications: on the one hand, the separation of the site's features (its pits, postholes, ditches, walls) from its finds (its potsherds, bones, seeds); and on the other, the separation of different kinds of finds from each other. I want to examine how archaeological objects came to be split off from each other, and from their context of deposition and how these splits were accompanied by a similar classification of archaeologists – ceramicists, faunal analysts, palaeobotanists, etc. Such a classification may seem natural to us, or expedient – no one can be an expert on everything they excavate; but the issue here is not merely with a classification *per se*, but with the particular structure in use now. Why the split between features and finds, between pots and flint, or artefacts and ecofacts? Why do these *particular* axes of partition operate as opposed to any other? Why and how did they develop and, perhaps most importantly of all, what effect do they have on our interpretations of the past?

The classification of archaeological knowledge

The development of specialisms in archaeology

How did object specialisms emerge? To understand this, it is important to realise that such specialisms were prefigured in the way that objects were split up and discussed in a site report, even though the excavator was usually also the one to write about all the finds. For example, Pitt Rivers generally discussed most of the material himself. A survey of selected reports published in Britain between 1913 and 1996 shows how over the course of the century, this changed as more and more specialisms developed (Figure 8). The exceptions to this pattern are the environmental or non-artefactual remains, principally unmodified bone (both human and animal) and preserved seeds or insects. Early studies of faunal remains from archaeological sites were conducted by zoologists or palaeontologists (Reitz and Wing 1999: 16). Some of the earliest work was done on the Swiss lake dwellings in the 1860s by L. Rütimeyer who differentiated wild from domesticated species and also reported on butchery marks. However, on the whole, reports on faunal remains throughout the late nineteenth and early twentieth century were brief and usually only taxonomic, that is, identifying the range of species present. Occasionally more extended discussions can be found, but these usually dealt with comparative anatomy and produced tables of bone measurements, etc. The attention to such topics is not surprising as they formed the major concerns of the day, and in fact the same basic topics can be seen in reports on human remains, with particular emphasis given to cranial measurements and the associated issues of race. Such a style of faunal reports continued until the 1950s, when a major shift occurred in the interest in animal bones from archaeological sites when they start to be viewed in terms of information on the economy. A classic example is Grahame Clark's Star Carr published in 1954 in which both faunal remains and wider environmental data form a large part of the text (Clark 1954), while in the USA the work of Gilmore was pioneering and his association with Walter Taylor cannot be coincidental (Reitz and Wing 1999: 21).

The shift is clearly related to wider changes in the conception of the archaeological record and past societies which are discussed throughout this book. It is from this period that archaeologists trained in faunal remains start to emerge as opposed to zoologists working on archaeological material. By the 1960s, these new specialists were developing their own sets of issues and problems particular to archaeology, the two major themes being domestication and taphonomy. Among these specialists the German Joachim Boessneck was perhaps the pioneering figure in Europe (Davis 1987). These themes, especially the latter, remain central to zooarchaeology, and most faunal reports today will not only contain basic quantified species information, but also taphonomic data such as evidence for butchery practices and bone

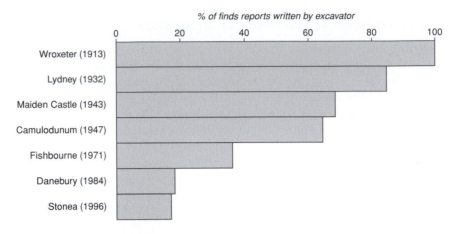

% of finds reports written by excavator

Figure 8 Graph showing rise in specialist reporting in a sample of major British site reports

size/fragmentation. Related to the latter was the concern to recover smaller bones – either from small animals (such as fish) or through greater fragmentation – and sampling deposits has become a major component in the control for fine bone retrieval (Payne 1975).

The study of plant remains from archaeological sites followed much the same pattern; early work was conducted by botanists, especially on sites with waterlogged material such as the Swiss lakes (Renfrew 1973: 1–6). As with the faunal reports, these early studies were confined to noting species present and discussing issues pertinent to taxonomic interpretation. The development of palynology and its introduction into archaeology occurred around the same time as the interest in wider economic and environmental issues in the 1950s. By the 1960s, specialist palaeoethnobotanists started to develop their own agenda, focusing on issues such as domestication and retrieval methods. One of the problems with much of the earlier work on plant remains was its reliance on chance recovery, for example the cache of carbonised seeds in a pot. There was a growing realisation that most sites could yield preserved plant material but it was not being recovered because of the excavation methods. During the late 1960s and early 1970s there emerged a range of sampling techniques which used a liquid medium to separate out material and a mesh to collect it (Streuver 1968a; Jarman et al. 1971; Williams 1973; Minnis and LeBlanc 1976). Commonly the process has come to be known as flotation, although in general it utilises a double process of sampling by density (flotation) and size (sieve). Most sampling today employs these techniques developed in the 1960s and 1970s with minor modifications (Jones 1991).

Other specialists only emerged much later; as Figure 8 shows, over the course of the twentieth century, the proportion of the finds which the exca-vator reported on diminished as others (frequently women) began to appear as specialists in various fields. For example, with ceramics, much of the early work was conducted by archaeologists also associated with excavation; thus the typological approach which dominated ceramic studies until the mid-twentieth century is linked to people such as Pitt Rivers and Petrie from Britain or Kidder and James Ford in the USA; their work on pottery was integral to their excavations. It was not until the mid-twentieth century that ceramic specialists emerged,[1] the most influential perhaps in the English-speaking world being Anna Shepard. She brought together many of the previous themes associated with pottery – chiefly chronology and distribution – with a greater emphasis on technological and analytical study of the ceramics themselves (Shepard 1956).

The technological aspects of pottery and the emergence of specialists studying ceramics helped to re-focus attention on issues about the nature of ceramics – for example that they were not proxies for people, but objects which were made and used by people. A number of important themes thus arose after the 1950s, including the life-cycles of pots and the technology of their production. Informed by ethnographic work such as David's study of Fulani pottery in Africa and that of of De Boer and Lathrap in South America, issues of the ceramic life-cycle became a major focus of interest, expressed through the term 'ceramic ecology' (David 1972; De Boer and Lathrap 1979; see Arnold 1985 for a major statement on this position). In tandem with these studies, work on pottery fabrics also developed, to eluci-date themes such as production and use, provenance and dating through a variety of techniques from thin-sectioning to thermo-luminesence (see Orton et al. 1993 for a summary).

A similar development can be traced for studies of worked stone or lithics. The very earliest studies of stone tools were linked into establishing the an-tiquity of humans and they became classic type fossils for nineteenth-century archaeologists such as W. H. Holmes in the USA or John Evans in Britain. This chronological facet remained in the early part of the twentieth century a key component of lithic studies and, again, such studies usually conducted by the excavators themselves and/or nameless assistants. The rise of lithic spe-cialists began to develop in the 1950s and 1960s, in particular through exper-imental replication studies by archaeologists such as Don Crabtree and François Bordes. These studies, while in themselves not new, were the medium through which a specialism emerged (Andrefsky 1998: 3). Another element associated with the emergence of this specialism was use–wear analy-sis, pioneered in the former Soviet Union by Semenov, whose work became more widely available in the 1960s when it was translated (Semenov 1964).

Use–wear analysis helped to shift thinking away from a static view of stone tool morphology, and lithic form was increasingly seen as a product of its life-cycle as much as of its original design, and thus issues of stone tool function became as important as any chronological index. Thus, as with ceramics, the development towards lithic specialism can be closely linked to a greater concern for processes of production, use and discard against purely typological analysis, a change which undoubtedly relates to broader shifts in archaeological thought in the 1950s and 1960s.

While this brief outline of the emergence of specialists has shown the broad links with larger conceptual issues in archaeology, I want to narrow the focus a little and trace in particular how objects became separated from the site in the first place, whether to be studied by a specialist or not. Some of the earliest archaeological reports – often in the form of narratives or letters – discuss the finds in the context of their discovery; this is typically the case with the Barrow excavations of the mid- and later nineteenth century, where grave goods are listed and described as the graves are, and figures of such objects intersperse the narrative (e.g. Greenwell 1877; also see Hodder 1989b). Yet by the end of the century the separation of finds from contextual or site description was in place and soon became the standard presentation of archaeological data and the classic form of the archaeological report as we know it today. How did this come about? Pitt Rivers was one of the first to deploy this method of presentation indeed the typical sequence of discussion in his volumes on Cranbourne Chase began with the site as a whole, followed by feature descriptions and ended with the finds. Is there a model for this sequence – which has essentially remained unchanged?

Hinsley, in a study of nineteenth-century graphic presentations of the archaeological process, showed how there was a typical three-stage narrative to such presentations, exemplified by Layard's discoveries in the Near East (Hinsley 1989: 89–90). The story begins with an image of the site as a place of lost grandeur (the moment of discovery), which is followed by an image of the site under investigation with the removal of structures or objects from it (the process of recovery through technology), and finally ends with a depiction of these structures or objects in their resting place, usually the museum (the appreciation of knowledge/beauty). Hinsley argued that such a presentation was guided by a desire to narrate Western ideals, and it is not difficult to see how this worked. However, what interests me in this study is the particular sequence, specifically its ending: the object as a source of edification. Can one say that perhaps the same narrative structure guided early archaeological reports, with the finds occupying pride of place?

Certainly, if one looks at the amount of space given to the presentation of finds against the site and its features, the early reports seem very biased towards the finds, although by the 1930s the balance has shifted so that treatment of finds against the site are more or less equivalent. The changes to this presentation can to some extent be explained by the changes in fieldwork practice described in the last chapter. My concern here is really to focus on the history of how finds are split from their context and each other; if Hinsley's nineteenth century narrative of the archaeological process helps us to understand the former, how do we understand the latter? If the end point of this narrative was the object on display – either in the museum or on the printed page – how were objects arranged and divided?

The origin and development of museums has a vast literature but the particular aspect which concerns me here is the relation between the ordering of objects and their conceptual classification. Ole Worm's seventeenth-century *Cabinet of Curiosities* employed a classification derived from earlier works but his was the first general treatise to cover specifically archaeological and ethnographic objects (Schnapp 1993: 174). Significantly, his division of artefacts is based on material criteria: clay, amber, stone, gold, silver, bronze, iron, glass, plant, wood and animal products all form the basis of his divisions, the only exceptions being coins and the unclassifiable. The material basis to classification was to become the important element in the development of the Three Age System, but it is significant that this has formed such a long-term axis of classification in Western thinking. However, Worm's classification is interesting for another reason, in that he did not use the previously common distinction between *artificiosa* and *naturalia*, but rather saw the two as inseparable (ibid.). These two innovations can be seen as related; indeed the classification of artefacts by natural categories is an explicit demonstration of the continuity between *artificiosa* and *naturalia*.

This material basis for the classification of objects, best exemplified in the Three Age System, was more generally widespread in the treatment of finds during the late nineteenth century. Pitt Rivers' Cranborne Chase volumes categorise the finds in ways no different from today – the South Lodge finds, for example, are divided into bronze, iron, bone, flint and pot (Pitt Rivers 1898). Similarly, at Glastonbury, Bulleid arranged artefacts according to clear material categories, under headings such as objects of metal, shale, wood, bone, antler, flint, baked clay (Bulleid and Gray 1911/1917). There are exceptions, such as pottery (distinct from baked clay), weaving combs or spindle whorls which, though of antler or other materials, are not categorised under those general headings but separately. The reason partly relates to their recognition as familiar objects, as the name given to them testifies – though this cannot be the whole reason. Nevertheless, the same basic categorisations of finds seen in Pitt Rivers' or Bulleid's reports have more or less remained constantly in use throughout the twentieth century, as a glance through any site report will reveal. There is the same splitting of objects, either using special categories for familiar finds (pottery, brooches, coins), or generic categories based on material for the less familiar (objects of bronze, iron, bone, stone, antler, baked clay, etc.). These divisions largely existed *before* the specialists who later emerged to study them.

The same approach is seen in the USA – an early collection by the American Bureau of Ethnology of material from New Mexico and Arizona is arranged by explicitly material classifications, the objects listed as articles of stone, bone, clay, vegetable substance, animal substance, horn and bone and wood (Stevenson 1883). However, in Fewkes' report of fieldwork in Pueblo ruins, the finds appear more idiosyncratic in their grouping, although in many ways the principal division is between recognisable types (e.g. pots, baskets, prayer-sticks) and more generic categories (e.g. bone implements, horn implements; Fewkes 1904). Similarly, in the later reports such as Webb's and de Jarnette's Pickwick Basin excavations, Cole's study of Kincaid or the more recent American Bottom FAI-270 investigations, to choose a few at random, categorisations of objects are most often based on their material (Webb and de Jarnette 1942; Cole 1951; Fortier *et al.* 1984).

Is there any significance to this twofold division of specific types based largely on perceived function or use, and generic categories based on raw material? Interestingly, in Webb's and de Jarnette's publications of finds from the Pickwick Basin, they have a section at the end on special arte-facts, where they state that their distinction comes from the fact that they are unusual but more significantly characteristic of the culture, in this case the Moundville complex (Webb and de Jarnette 1942: 287). Could there be a link between the cultural specificity of finds and their categorisation in specific rather than generic terms? Perhaps. In fact, to give it another angle, if we divide reports on the basis of the *antiquity* of the material recov-ered and examine the ratio of the two categorisations, an interesting pattern seems to emerge. The older the objects, the more likely it seems they will be categorised by their generic material. This is suggested in Table 2, in which the figures are taken from a selection of major site reports from Britain where, proportionately, finds are more likely to be categorised gener-ically on prehistoric sites than on historic (in this case Roman) ones. Now one might explain this by reference to familiarity with the object – the more recent the find, the more likelihood that it will be familiar to us anyway; but I think there is more to this than meets the eye.

Table 2 Ratio of generic to specific finds categorisations by period in major British site reports

Period	Site	Generic categories	Specific categories
Prehistoric	Durrington Walls (1971)	5	1
	Orkney (1979)	3	1
	Danebury (1984)	10	5
Roman	Camulodunum (1947)	8	10
	Fishbourne (1971)	10	12
	Stonea (1996)	11	14

Consider Pitt Rivers' image of the development of ethnographic weapons from Australasia (Figure 9). The illustration is a visual representation of his idea of evolution, from the simple to the complex, from a single original form to a diversity of forms. The effect of the arrangement encourages us to perceive the over-riding significance of the centre – that this stick is the origin, the prototype or universal form of all the other types. Significantly, Pitt Rivers also conceived of a museum on this plan – the 'rotunda' was to be so organised that the visitor began at the centre moving outwards into increasing differentiation, thus retracing the steps of evolution (Chapman 1985). This idea comes out equally forcefully when he is referring to the notion of degeneration; his examples, including Evans's study of British coins and his own of Papua New Guinean tribal masks, expresses the idea of an original artefact of which subsequent types are simply degenerate copies as the original is lost and undergoes successive reduction of accuracy in replication (Pitt Rivers 1906).

Linked very closely to this idea is that of the *natural*; that the lower the civilisation, the greater the similarity of form to a natural form. Thus, in the Australasian example, the various implements 'show evidence of being derived from natural forms such as might have been employed by man before he had learnt the art of modifying them to his uses ' (Pitt Rivers 1906: 11). Thus there is a certain affinity established between the natural and cultural form through an *originary* conception of material culture. The same association between artefacts and the concept of the *original* and the connotations of the natural which go along with it, articulated Worm's conflation of *artificiosa* and *naturalia* and continue to influence our conception of the archaeological object today. That very contemporary phrase, *material culture*, encapsulates this relationship; the archaeological object as both cultural and natural.

For Pitt Rivers, interpretation of an artefact in evolutionary (i.e. cultural) terms is guaranteed through its origin as a natural object; cultural evolution or reason stands in contrast to or outside nature yet at the same time nature lies at the origin of culture. A similar ambiguity is still perceptible in the constitution of archaeological objects; the word we usually give to an archaeological object is *artefact*, which means something artificially made, that is, non-natural – a cultural product. A pot, an axe, even a pit or a ditch is an artefact. Yet one might observe that even such objects as pots are not *totally* cultural in so far as they are composed of natural resources or materials – for example, a pot is made out of clay. This was Worm's point and underlay Pitt Rivers' evolutionary typology. And while we may no longer trace the *form* of the cultural object to a natural object (e.g. a club to a stick), its *substance* – its materiality – is fully grounded in nature.

Related to the question of this duality of the archaeological object, there is also that of the duality of archaeological objects; for archaeologists also study natural objects or ecofacts too – pollen, seeds, shells, soils – and this

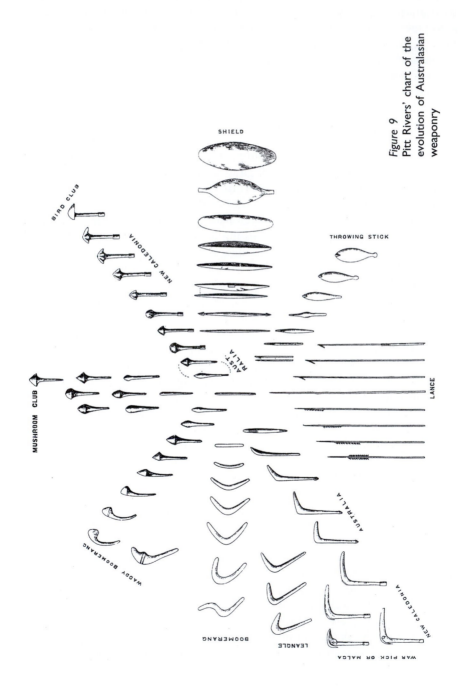

Figure 9
Pitt Rivers' chart of the evolution of Australasian weaponry

SHIELD

BIRD CLUB

NEW CALEDONIA

THROWING STICK

MUSHROOM CLUB

AUST-
RALIA

LANCE

WADDY BOOMERANG

AUSTRALIA

BOOMERANG

LEANGLE

NEW CALEDONIA

WAR PICK OR MALGA

usually forms part of an attempt to understand site formation processes or the interaction between human groups and the environment. Yet the distinction between natural and cultural objects is not that clear. Take the example of domesticated cereals: the pollen or seeds from these plants are from one point of view natural – humans did not make the plant as they made the sickle which cuts it down. On the other hand that plant is often the way it is because of human involvement – and deliberate involvement at that; selective breeding has altered the form of the plant. A domesticate is an artefact. More generally, though, the distinct splitting of faunal or botanical remains from other objects often fosters a more naturalistic interpretation of them. By looking at animal bones separately from the rest of an assemblage, the typical faunal report tends to focus solely on physical characteristics of the fauna – age, sex, butchery marks, etc. – and this is translated in the discussion into terms of purely economic or ecological, that is, *natural* considerations.

Adams, in discussing the nature of archaeological entities, has highlighted the fluidity in the distinction between artefacts and ecofacts, but then maintains the nature/culture distinction in terms of two sets of attributes of an artefact – its cultural and environmental 'enhancements' and 'reductions' (Adams 1991: 5–6). In other words, Adams is relocating the nature/culture distinction away from the object itself to processes affecting the production of the object. This does not really resolve the issue but rather defers it. One might ask what constitutes a cultural as distinct from an environmental process? The response appears to revolve around the action of a human being – that is, if a human participates in the process then it is a cultural process. But how easy is it to make a clear distinction between a process which has involved human actions and one which has not? Pot-making might be a clear example, domestication is a little more ambiguous but what of something like slopewash caused by deforestation? How far removed in the chain does something have to be, to be non-cultural – and is it possible to say of anything, that humans are not involved at some remove? The other side of this problem lies with the use of the human being as the signifier of culture; how does this work and what does it imply? That humans are not natural? What is it in the equation 'Human = Culture' that we take for granted? Is not this a circular argument, in that it implies that what is specifically non-natural in humans is culture, while what distinguishes nature from culture is the presence of the human signifier.

Taking the issue further, we can look at the way sites are seen in terms of the same duality; for example, on site – particularly on rural sites – the concept of 'the natural' is used every day in field archaeology to denote the undisturbed natural substratum, such as the underlying chalk or gravel. *Undisturbed.* It is as if the natural provides the baseline upon which the archaeological record is laid. And indeed that is just what it is – the canvas or backdrop for archaeological features. The 'natural' gives us that element of certainty when digging a feature, it gives us the *limit* of the archaeology, of the cultural, in the same way that the natural as the environment gives us the backdrop and limit of cultural behaviour. The fact that on many urban sites 'the natural' may never be reached, or that features are cut through other features and not through natural, does not counter the point being made here; all this does is tell you to *carry on digging*. It can be an unsatisfactory experience not to take a site down to natural; there is a feeling that reaching natural gives you the sense of completion, of certainty in having circumscribed the limits of the archaeology, of the *cultural*.

Thus it would be difficult to envisage an archaeology which did not have the concept of the natural, at least in principle, with which to delimit, or offset against, that of the cultural – or archaeological. In determining whether a flint object is an artefact or has been naturally fractured, or a layer is undisturbed, basal natural, we need this concept to define the limits of what is archaeology. If this provides the other measure of splitting objects, is there a way in which the two senses identified here link up? Is there some connection between the splitting of objects from their context and from each other? I think there is, but to understand this, it is necessary to go one stage further and examine how objects are further split within specialisms – that is, how typologies emerged in archaeology.

Evolutionary typology and the erasure of context

Given the early emphasis on the *collection* as the mainstay of archaeological research in the late nineteenth century, it comes as no surprise that finds were divorced from their associated features. Yet traditional narratives of archaeological historiography tend to define its emergence, particularly as distinct from antiquarianism, with a concern for context:

> In a sense, archaeology is defined by its concern for context. To be interested in artefacts without any contextual information is antiquarianism, and is perhaps found in certain types of art history or the art market. Digging objects up out of their context, as is done by some metal detector users, is the antithesis in relation to which archaeology forms its identity. To reaffirm the importance of context thus includes reaffirming the importance of archaeology as archaeology.
>
> (Hodder 1986: 120)

All this therefore raises the question that if this *is* the case, why is the separation of finds from context still such a prominent aspect of archaeological procedure? This cannot be relegated to the 'physical' issue of the portability or removal of finds from site after the excavation or destruction of the feature – for there is nothing to prevent the writing up of finds alongside the writing up of features. But this is not done – finds and features are separated in most site reports, as if they were completely unrelated, even though they may be reintegrated in subsequent interpretation or discussion. What needs to be explained is that, *in spite* of the growing concern for context, which undoubtedly contributed to define the emergence of archaeology as a scientific discipline, the study of finds is still kept separate from the study of features and only later in the process are the two brought back together.

The answer lies, partially at least, in the fact that the original researches on collections were still dominating the way archaeology and the archaeological record were perceived at the end of the nineteenth century, as I argued in Chapter 1. It was the prevailing concern to understand the differences *between* objects, which ultimately necessitated the separation of these objects from associated features. The two kinds of partition were thus inextricably intertwined from the very start and it could be said that the subsequent development of specialisms within archaeology was inevitable. To understand this, it is important to look at how finds, as collections, were studied in the latter part of the nineteenth century because it demonstrates, quite unequivocally I believe, that despite the wider concern for context, such studies seemed to promote the erasure of context.

The system under which such collections and finds were studied was, of course, typological, but within the framework of an evolutionary, and universal concept of culture, famously synthesised in Lubbock's *Prehistoric Times* (Lubbock 1869; Trigger 1978; 1989: 114–18). Typological developments therefore took on an increasingly evolutionary tone over the period. Christian Thomsen's original construction of the Three Age System was based on dividing objects according to their function (e.g. cutting implements) and then using a form of seriation, ordering variations (based on material and form) of each type of object in a chronological series (Gräslund 1987; Trigger 1989: 75–6). While evolution played little role in the details of Thomsen's sequence, the general move from stone through bronze to iron was informed by current evolutionary thinking.

Classification at the end of the nineteenth century in North America was less developed than in Europe, and early work as such as Thomas Rau's and Thomas Wilson's classification of arrowheads and spearheads was primarily descriptive with limited attempts to associate variability to chronology or regions (Dunnell 1986a: 157–9). Essentially, variability was arbitrary and of no explanatory value; with such an attitude, it is a wonder that any classification was attempted. Dunnell sees part of the problem in the choice of object, lithics generally displaying less variability and therefore less sensitivity to change (ibid.: 160); this is questionable, and it is perhaps better to see this as a result of a lack of interest in chronology. In spite of an evolutionary paradigm – or rather because of it – the prevailing attitude was that the indigenous Indian population had not progressed, and therefore had no history to speak of, unlike the Old World.

In Britain the evolutionary perspective on such sequences was much stronger. Daniel Wilson, who was the first to introduce Thomsen's ideas into British archaeology, gave a rudimentary sequence for axes and spear-heads based on an explicit view of progress. He prefaces this sequence with: 'The following is an attempt to define such a system of classification ... assuming every additional improvement, complexity, or ornamentation as evidence of progress, and therefore of work of a later date' (Wilson 1851: 252). Further classification was taken up by John Evans with his work on stone and bronze implements (Evans 1872, 1881) although this went little beyond broad categorical divisions in relation to the Three Ages. Probably the greatest exponent of evolutionary typology in Britain however was Pitt Rivers; his schemes were highly speculative and when he wrote his famous essay on classification he was clearly influenced by analogies from natural evolution (Pitt Rivers 1875). To some extent this can be traced to his reading of natural classifications and work on firearms (Thompson 1977; Chapman 1985; Bowden 1991). In his examples of prehistoric classifica-tions a simple unilinear scheme is presented, as with the development of spearheads and axes from a common 'ancestral' cordate implement (Pitt Rivers 1875; plate I).

The master synthesiser of evolutionary typology however was Oscar Montelius, a Swedish archaeologist, although others such as Hans Hildebrand also played an important role (Gräslund 1987; Trigger 1989: 155–61). Montelius' method was basically similar to Thomsen's although using more data and greater finds control; with it, he was able to refine the Bronze Age into six sub-divisions (Montelius 1885), and later applied the same tech-niques to the Neolithic and Iron Age. However, there is one aspect to Montelius' work which distinguishes him from Thomsen, and that was the way he drew out evolutionary implications in the sequence (Figure 10). In particular, he tended to give primacy to evolutionary development over context, as this extract from his major work on the Bronze Age testifies:

> The method which is used here is very simple in principle. Firstly, I have defined the most important series of weapons, tools, jewellery, belt ornaments and decorative styles in order to understand the course of development and to see, based on their own criteria, in which order the types follow each other. Then I have gone through the grave finds and all the other finds known at present from the Scandinavian area which may throw light on the date of the particular types.
>
> (Montelius 1986 [1885]: 26)

I have already mentioned the debate between Sophus Müller and Montelius at the end of the nineteenth century (see p. 28). Montelius certainly made use of a seriational approach based on context (i.e. find combination of closed assemblages), but he tended to stress the importance of developmental

Axes	Swords	Brooches	Belt boxes	
			D	VI
F	G		C	V
E	D	F / E	B	IV
C D	C	D / C	A	III
	B / A	B / A		II
A / A	A			I

Figure 10   Montelius' typology of Bronze Age artefacts

typology in dating finds while down-playing the contextual aspect. As Gräslund points out, Montelius' grand work *Dating in the Bronze Age* (1885) relies heavily on the method of find association to work out the chronology, yet in contrast, when he describes his method in this work and elsewhere, he gives priority to typology (Gräslund 1987). This question of find association and its relation to typology was the basis of a critique by Sophus Müller against Hildebrand and Montelius in his *A small contribution to the methodology of Prehistoric Archaeology* (1884), who argued that their approach could not possibly be prior to a contextual analysis; Montelius responded by saying that the two went together in practice, but ought to be separated analytically for clarity (ibid.).

However, the important question which Gräslund ignores is *why* Montelius was so keen to forget the importance of context in chronology, indeed why he and others from the 1870s onwards gave so much significance to evolutionary typology. Part of the answer lies in the growth of Darwinism and the often quoted parallels between cultural and natural evolution in typological studies such as Hildebrand's *Scientific Archaeology* (1873) and Montelius' *Typology or the Theory of Evolution Applied to Human Labour* (1899). But I think the greater reason must lie with the fact that evolutionary typology was an *explanatory* concept as well as (if not more than) a methodological one. Indeed, for archaeologists working in the late nineteenth century, it was far *more* explanatory and interpretively useful than mere find combination. Archaeologists just were not interested in why objects were associated except as a means to an end. Evolutionary typology not only ordered finds in a chronological sequence, it also carried a basic historical philosophy, a paradigm for understanding prehistory.

In 1900 Montelius gave a series of lectures at University College London on his chronological system and its application to British data (Montelius 1908). His ideas were very popular – for example, in 1909, Greenwell and Brewis published an evolutionary typology of the spearhead. They mention the lack of systematic classification in Evans's work and provide a list of types and stages of development of the bronze spearhead in Britain. The most interesting thing, however, is perhaps the reasoning behind the typology and why they see the changes happening.

> The progress in the development of the spearhead had throughout been towards simplicity and efficiency, and this was carried out so fully in the leaf shaped heads that there appears to be no further room for improvement in that direction. Henceforward any advance that was made was by means of economy in the use of metal, which at the same time reduced the weight.
>
> (Greenwell and Brewis 1909: 451–2)

In Egypt, Petrie was developing seriation techniques similar to but far more explicitly laid out than those of Montelius; we tend to think of Petrie as a pioneer of seriation as it later came to be conceived in the 1920s onwards, especially in the USA (see p. 81; Trigger 1989: 202). However, Petrie was an evolutionist and even though he advocated a mixture of methods in his seriation, evolutionary typology was one of them (Petrie 1899: 297; see his second method). More importantly, he saw the final sequence, however it was worked out, in evolutionary terms. This was his concluding statement to 'Sequences in prehistoric remains':

In all of these series of changes in slates and tools we see a regular progression, yet this dating results solely from the pottery with which they were found; and thus this regularity of the results is the strongest proof of the true and solid basis of the classing by sequence dates.

(Petrie 1899: 301)

This regularity of the results is the strongest proof . . ., sums up the whole explanatory power of evolutionary typology.

Even though within a couple of decades the whole edifice of evolutionary typology crumbled in the wake of a new concept of culture, the legacy of studying finds independent of context and using typologies has remained a central aspect of archaeological work. Both the legacy of earlier disciplinary divisions such as zoology and botany, and the initial dominance of evolutionary typology are responsible for the current specialisms and splitting of objects from their context and each other. How did this legacy affect the way archaeologists subsequently dealt with finds? This is quite a complex history and needs to be traced not only through the culture historical phase between the 1920s and 1960s, but also through the processual and post-processual movements since then. The important thing to bear in mind is that the context of the object suddenly became far more important than it had previously been, and yet this had to contend with the long tradition of regarding finds as independent objects. On the one hand, then, typological studies flourished as never before, especially in the culture historical phase, in order to relate variability with context – which in this case was largely understood as cultural affiliation (defined spatially and temporally). On the other hand, however, the broader divisions of finds – faunal remains, ceramics, lithics – remained untouched.

It can be argued that such specialisations have had a detrimental effect on the way we study objects, in particular the way they privilege some objects over others. A glance through any site report will show that while some objects such as pottery or lithics receive selective and extended attention by a designated specialist, others such as fired clay, uncommon pieces of metalwork or other occasional objects are invariably lumped together, sometimes reported on by a single person (the 'small finds person'). Such 'residual' finds also tend not to carry the same academic weight, either generally or specifically within the site report. The reason for this is clear, as Walter Taylor long ago pointed out – such finds are neither as numerous nor exhibit as much variability as the more classic finds categories such as pottery (Taylor 1948: 131). As such, they do not offer themselves easily to a traditional typological approach and consequently they are devalued.

Yet the whole valuation of frequency and variability is not given but derives from the concerns of a typologically obsessed attitude to finds – a contextual attitude would and often does transform their significance radically. And this is exactly how the two means of splitting objects link up:

it is this very same variability of the major finds categories which also guarantees
the stability of the broader divisions discussed above – ceramics, lithics, etc.
Indeed, as typological schemes developed and became more and more elaborate throughout the twentieth century, these broader divisions became
even more sedimented in practice and unquestioned. I believe that these
two divergent processes sustained – and continue to sustain – each other;
the more one engages in typological work, the more one is forced to ignore
broader categorisations. In the next section I want to trace the subsequent
history of how artefact variability has been interpreted, first through the
heyday of typologies between the 1920s and 1960s, and subsequently through
the functional and contextual approaches since the 1960s. I will argue
that the problems and debates characterising this history can be tied back
into the broader issue of specialisations because of the specific ways in
which variability is conceived.

The interpretation of artefact variability

Early classifications of the later nineteenth century were largely simple,
unilinear schemes – the progression of spearheads or axes, the succession
of ceramic forms or brooches. Rarely did they encompass more complex
configurations, particularly taxonomic – that is hierarchical – systems. Pitt
Rivers' figure (see p. 72) of the evolution of Australasian weapons is highly
unusual in so far as it illustrates a kind of genealogical system of development. Yet such systems ought perhaps to have been more common, especially
given the biological metaphors frequently employed in their discussion. Pitt
Rivers drew heavily on these metaphors:

> Human ideas, as represented by the various products of human industry,
> are capable of classification into genera, species and varieties, in the
> same manner as the products of the vegetable and animal kingdoms,
> and in their development from the homogeneous to the heterogeneous
> they obey the same laws.
>
> (Pitt Rivers 1906: 19)

Typology was the archaeological equivalent of evolution.

Montelius also made similar analogies, for example in *Typology or the*
Theory of Evolution Applied to Human Labour published in 1899, as did
Hildebrand even earlier in his *Scientific Archaeology* (1873). Indeed such
analogies were far more characteristic of nineteenth-century typologies, and
while there are some later examples in the early twentieth century, published
at the height of culture classification, these were not widely accepted. Nils
Åberg's paper 'Typology' published in 1929 explicitly cited Darwinism and
suggested that the evolution of artefacts resembled that of organic life, while
V. A. Gorodozov's approach, which was translated into English in 1933

(Gorodozov 1933), was an articulation of a scientific typology on the basis of principles of causality, evolution, borrowing and a 'struggle' for survival. In the USA such views were associated with taxonomic approaches such as Hargrave's schema which presented a taxonomic system boldly referencing biology (Table 3; Hargrave 1932).

Such attempts soon came under severe criticism, the most famous being Brew's chapter entitled, 'On use and abuse of taxonomy' in *The Archaeology of Alkali Ridge*. Here he criticised typologies along two lines: first, that they are simply tools of analysis and not an inherent structure in material culture; second (and related to the first), that analogies with biology are misconceived (Brew 1946: 46–7). Part of the problem as Brew saw it was that many of the authors of classifications were trained in biology or zoology, including Hargrave and Colton, but the real problems lay in attributing characteristics to material culture which they do not have, captured in his phrase, 'pots don't breed'.

The prominence of the taxonomic systems that developed in the USA around the same time was undoubtedly linked to the fact that the chronological dimension became significant for the first time, unlike in Europe. Many of the earlier studies of the 1920s were linked to the new concern for stratigraphy and there was intense use of seriation as a technique; excepting Uhle's work, the first major study to have an impact was by Kroeber on Zuñi pottery in the Southwest, which used surface collections and employed a frequency rather than occurrence seriation (Kroeber 1916). His work was expanded upon in the following year by Leslie Spier who gave a much more explicit definition of seriation, actually employing the term which is absent in Kroeber's work and setting the standard for the Southwest (Spier 1917). The most developed study of seriation and typology was Irving Rouse's *Prehistory in Haiti* published in 1939. Using frequency seriation of attributes (which he called modes), he explicitly condoned the assumption of a cyclical frequency curve, also asserting that such frequencies may vary independently (Rouse 1939). At the same time, James Ford was working on developing a method which was influenced by the idea of popularity curves although this only crystallised much later on in the 1950s and 1960s (Willey and Sabloff 1993: 114–16).

Table 3 Hargrave's artefact taxonomy

kingdom	artefacts
phylum	ceramics
class	vessels
order	fabric
ware	surface colour
genus	surface finish
type	ware (e.g. Flagstaff Red)

Underlying such seriational studies was of course the necessity of a synthe-sising typology and there was an increasing degree of discussion about typological schemes. A major critique of such schemes came from Krieger who argued that such taxonomies were too restrictive in trying to identify universal criteria (such as shape or material) rather than accepting that different typologies might require different criteria as their basis (Krieger 1944). Rather, he argued, it was more important to agree on universal processes or principles of classification – in other words to define a typo-logical *method*, distinct from any particular attributes which might define any particular classification (Dunnell 1986a: 164). Part of this critique can be tied in to the abandonment of a universal concept of culture and the realisation that different cultures will categorise material differently. Brew made similar points in his paper already cited (see p. 81).

Following Kreiger's critique such classifications were eventually replaced by systems which prioritised the method rather than the criteria, a method which, although it differentiated types on the basis of attributes, did not prejudge what those attributes were but rather tested them against their responsiveness to spatio-temporal location. Two main methods emerged: Rouse's analytic classification (Rouse 1960) and the type-variety method, developed in the late 1950s by Gifford and others and still in use today (Gifford 1960). Both bear superficial similarity to the older taxonomic approach in using a hierarchical approach, but while the aim of the analytic approach was simply to classify attributes in terms of their cultural signifi-cance (what Rouse called modes), the type-variety method produced a typology by the selection and grouping of attributes. The two approaches are not necessarily exclusive. Indeed Rouse said that a typological (what he called taxonomic) classification should be based on the analytic classi-fication (Rouse 1960), while others using the type-variety method have claimed that a proper classification should integrate and use both (Sabloff and Smith 1969). The differences between these two approaches, however, is of less relevance here than their similarity, particularly in how they envis-aged the social significance of classification – how was such variability captured in a classification accounted for?

Typological debates between 1940 and 1960

This problem crystallised around the issue of what the type meant or referred to. In general, types were viewed as reflective of customs or mental templates/ ideas in the minds of the makers – types as cultural norms. Childe summed it up well:

> Indeed an archaeological datum is a type just because it results from the behaviour pattern of a single society. It is a type too because it is a con-crete expression and embodiment of a concept. This concept is – or was

– objective in as much as it exists – or did exist – not in the maker's head alone, but in the heads of a society that transcended and outlasted each and all its members.

(Childe 1956: 10)

The same basic idea underlay both the analytic and typological classifications – under the type-variety system, types referred to objects patterned and conditioned by a 'majority held value orientation', while the varieties were determined by 'individual or small group motivation' (Gifford 1960). Rouse's interpretation of his modes was a little more advanced, identifying two types: conceptual, referring to ideas and standards of the artisan, and, more interestingly, procedural, relating to the process of manufacture and subsequent use (Rouse 1960). Rouse's distinction is interesting for the way it anticipates a basic theme in contemporary studies of production, particularly operational and behavioural chain analyses; I discuss these further below so I will not dwell on them here. My main concern presently is with the typological debate which developed about the significance of archaeological classifications and how this debate implicated finds specialisms.

The emergence of a typological debate can be traced to the fact that views as to what a type meant and the process of constructing and using types, were unrelated theoretically (although assumed to overlap), and so when archaeologists in the 1950s began asking explicitly what was the relationship, the culture-history approach was found greatly wanting (Dunnell 1986a). The problem was first aired in Taylor's A Study of Archaeology, published in 1948. In a chapter on classification, he argued that types must be related to the cultural context in which they operated, that is they must refer to actual categorisations of the culture being studied (Taylor 1948). He made a distinction between empirical and cultural classifications, such that for example the divisions of bone, stone, clay, etc. fall under the former, while food, dress, hunting fall under the latter, and to be meaningful the two should correspond as much as possible (Taylor 1948: 114–15). The same point had been made by Steward and Setzler also, some years earlier, in a paper entitled 'Function and configuration in archaeology' which prefigured many of the themes in Taylor's study (Steward and Setzler 1938). They criticised most archaeological reports for treating artefacts as simply material objects rather than cultural ones, a fact which was

implied in the use of such descriptive headings as objects of 'bone', 'horn', 'stone', and others based upon materials, instead of such functional headings as 'horticulture', 'food preparation', 'hunting', 'fishing', 'dress', 'adornments', 'household', and others appropriate to the culture.

(Steward and Setzler 1938: 6)

What is interesting is that it clearly raises issues about finds specialists and how objects are studied, not just how they are presented; in the 1930s and 1940s such an approach was perhaps still conceivable, as the excavator and primary author may still have been also the one discussing most of the (artefactual) finds. However, Steward and Setzler's point was never really taken up, for although they reference examples – and no doubt more could be found – most reports continued to use material or typological divisions. The reason relates to Taylor's important distinction between empirical and cultural classifications; by creating this difference, a compromise was ostensibly made which enabled current typological divisions to be sustained so long as a correspondence could be identified between them and cultural classifications. And yet, despite Taylor's stipulation, it is hard to envisage how this ever could have been the case – at least with the examples he and Steward and Setzler gave. Indeed, this is precisely where the issue in some ways shifted ground; while it seems difficult to see how a classification of pottery, stone or bone can *directly* correspond with one based on activities such as eating, hunting or weaving, there might be a way in which such divisions could correspond to ethnic classifications of objects. And this is exactly the direction the subsequent debate took; instead of being about different ways to split and group objects by reference to activities, the issue was reduced to whether archaeologists' object typologies reflected cultural classifications of objects.

It was James Ford who first criticised the idea of a cultural classification, claiming that archaeology must go beyond the specific details of a culture to a more objective, scientific understanding of general principles of culture change – something only an empirical typology allowed (Ford 1952). With Albert Spaulding's response to Ford's paper, a heated debate started. In 'Statistical techniques for the discovery of artifact types' (1953), Spaulding tackled two deficiencies in the culture-history typological approach: the *ad hoc*, trial-and-error method of selecting and testing viable attributes as criteria in defining types; and the uncritical attribution of social or cultural meaning to such types. For the former problem, Spaulding introduced a statistical technique (chi-squared) to test the attribute combinations which defined types – in other words, he provided a means of defining *and* assessing the validity of a conventional type identification by demonstrating non-randomness. The implication was that this was a real pattern, inherent in the data and not imposed, and therefore reflective of cultural phenomena. Spaulding's types are not units of measurement but empirical entities referencing behaviour and therefore having the significance which culture historians claimed for their types, but which was never demonstrated. The emphasis on the behavioural correlation with typology can clearly be seen as part of the major 'behavioural turn' which came in with the New Archaeology a decade later; indeed the typological debate represents one of the earliest anticipations of two major themes which emerged in the 1960s, quantitative techniques and behavioural explanation.

At the heart of the difference between Ford and Spaulding lies the distinction between emic and etic types – the former being types recognised as meaningful by the people whose material culture the archaeologist studies, the latter being constructs of the archaeologist. Essentially, it is the same distinction Taylor made between empirical and cultural. Ford suggested that the statistical types which Spaulding identified are accidents of sampling and that types do not correspond with the cultural categorisations of the makers, but with the archaeologist's abstractions (Ford 1954). He argues that although societies do categorise the world, this is a fluid affair both on the level of formal abstraction and in terms of time and space. The typologies archaeologists construct are simply heuristic, and help to order the data at a particular level but in no way refer to emic categorisations. Spaulding thought, like Taylor, that the etic and emic should correspond.

What makes Spaulding's approach most distinct from the culture-history method is that he restricts his analysis to the level of the assemblage in the first instance, because this is the level at which behaviour operates (Spaulding 1953: 305). In other words, unlike in the culture-history typologies, it does not operate across assemblages but within them and any typology thus generated may therefore be of limited application. The emic–etic debate is thus entwined with the issue of the *level* at which emic units refer and this has often caused confusion in the subsequent debate (Dunnell 1986a). For example, we may construct a simple typology around the temper and surface treatment of pots and show that grit-tempered pots usually have stamped surfaces, while shell-tempered pots have smooth surfaces. On this basis we have a typology – but it is not *necessarily* useful beyond its specific context because it may be that, chronologically or regionally, such associations or attributes are meaningless – but this has to be demonstrated by its recurrence on each assemblage. The critical point is, as Dunnell remarks, that the types defined by Spaulding and which serve as the basis for all current theoretical discussion of typology, work *only* in the particular cases in which they have been identified (Dunnell 1986a: 192). More significantly, this exclusivity opens up the possibility of multiple typologies, all equally valid but referencing different behavioural patterns within the same community.

Time has sided with Spaulding in this debate, and most discussions on typology since the 1960s have viewed archaeological types as culturally meaningful constructs. However, because of the acceptance that such types are behaviourally specific and that more than one classification can be valid for the same set of objects, the interpretation of what *kind* of behaviour different types refer to subsequently became a major issue. Suddenly, the notion that a type can be explained away by cognitive templates or some form of 'normative' ethno-categorisations was inadequate, and instead variability in objects needed to be quite specifically linked to behavioural patterns. Fortunately, an established source of explanation had been around for some time in the distinction between function and style although it was not always called by those terms. The New Archaeology did not invent function or functionalist approaches to interpretation, but what they did do was to link such explanations into typological difference. Unfortunately, in doing so, they also reinforced a typological approach to material culture, further reducing the significance of Steward's and Setzler's initial point.

The function/style debate and after

Gordon Childe made the distinction between functional and chronological attributes in the 1920s; his differentiation of culture groups was founded on a small number of diagnostic artefacts that possessed features which were deemed to be more or less non-utilitarian. In *The Danube in Prehistory*, he distinguished between local styles exemplified by pottery, ornaments and burial rites and others which were more widespread because of their usefulness such as weaponry and tools, causing them to spread through trade or imitation (Childe 1929: viii, 248). Utility was clearly the defining criterion. This distinction he later formalised in *Piecing Together the Past*, where he identifies three dimensions of variability in objects – functional, chronological and chorological (i.e. cultural; Childe 1956: 14–15). For Childe the functional was the primary dimension, that which separates adzes from daggers, razors, earrings, etc. By default, if not intentionally, typology or classification then became solely associated with chronology and chorology, that is the temporal and spatial variability between culture groups, which were articulated through the terms *systadial* and *homotaxial* to distinguish between similar types which share the same developmental sequence and those which do not (Childe 1956: 74). Moreover, while function was understood in evolutionary terms, the chronological and more specifically the chorological were understood in terms of those shared ideals or norms.

These earlier and more often tacit distinctions were swiftly crystallised around the dichotomy between function and style which became the subject of debate in the 1960s (Dunnell 1978). Because of the *systemic* view of a culture group espoused by the New Archaeology, material culture was increasingly being seen in terms of its function within the cultural system, and earlier discussions tended to overplay a strong dichotomy between function and style, partly in an attempt to distance the 'new' processual archaeology from the old culture-history approach (Dunnell 1978; Shanks and Tilley 1987a: 86–95). Function was clearly the most important aspect to material culture since it related to the adaptation and evolution of social systems, while style referred to those evolutionary neutral traits wherein variability was generally random and therefore an index of simple chronological or geographical differences (ibid.). As such, style became equated with the old-fashioned typology which was dry and unexplanatory; not to be discarded, but clearly supplemental to the main business of artefact study – function.

As processual archaeology matured, this dichotomy between function and style became increasingly problematic, and the impetus for an explanation of style rather than an appeal to randomness became stronger. It might be claimed that the radiocarbon revolution made the old typology as chronology superfluous (e.g. Dunnell 1986a), and this raised the question of the value of types as styles – what does 'style' actually refer to? Amongst processual archaeologists the resolution was commonly to expand the notion of function so that it incorporated style within it – in other words, the old meaning of style with culture history as defining a group was revamped as a function of that group. Most commonly this took the form of group identity or ethnicity – in other words style functioned to create or maintain group boundaries through its communicative nature (e.g. Wobst 1977; Weissner 1983). However, Sackett criticised such 'iconological' approaches for equating style with non-utilitarian aspects of an artefact, whereas he makes the distinction between function and style on the one hand, and, on the other, the instrumental and adjunct form of an object, both of which can have style (Sackett 1982; 1990). His 'isochrestic' concept of style equates it with cultural norms which determine the particular way in which function is manifested. As Sackett says, style is merely 'function writ small' (Sackett 1990).

In response, Weissner argued that Sackett's notion of isochrestism as passive is unnecessary in that these passive symbols of ethnicity can be manipulated actively (Weissner 1983, 1990). Either way, the Sackett–Weissner debate is ultimately founded on a notion of style as cultural norms or ethnicity, and whether one stresses that they give specific form to a general function or are active as opposed to passive, the question of why these norms or traditions exist in this particular way is still ignored (Conkey 1990). The question of style is still tied to the old culture-history concept in processual archaeology, and as a result no issue is ever raised about *why* it takes the form it does. The problem of style is reduced to function – either as iconic communication or isochrestic variation, and the issue of ethnicity or cultural norms is side-stepped.

The problem with such studies of style lies in their conception of culture; as long as they worked on the assumption of a social system *primarily* responsive to the environment (i.e. adaptive), function would always set the terms within which style would be discussed: style is what is left over, the surplus, residual after function (Shanks and Tilley 1987a: 92). Part of the innovation of post-processual archaeology was to redefine the concept of culture as meaningfully constituted, and the issue of variability came to be seen primarily in terms of social meanings rather than adaptive functions. The question of the function–style dichotomy in post-processual archaeology has been re-phrased as one of a dialectic rather than dichotomy (Hodder 1985); whereas the processual responses to the dichotomy tended to reduce style to function, the alternative approach emphasises the context of variability and sees function and style as dimensions of the context or meaning (Hodder 1987a). In this respect, the importance of context as that through which meaning is created, maintained or transformed becomes of paramount importance; context is what provides the means to assess relevant dimensions of variability (Hodder 1986). An important consequence of this debate is that the original opposition between function and style has largely been broken down and replaced perhaps by a more general concern with the interpretation of design through use or consumption. This has developed in two quite different directions, largely mirroring the theoretical divides laid out in the function–style debate.

Many classic examples of post-processual or contextual approaches to design variability appeared in the 1982 volume *Symbolic and Structural Archaeology*. Daniel Miller's study of contemporary ceramics in India showed how vessel variability expresses notions of pollution and broader caste divisions, and that the development of such variability may in part be a product of the need to maintain such divisions which are transgressed through repeated practice (Miller 1982; also see Miller 1985). Thus one cooking pot type to emerge recently in the community he studied was a copy of a metal type in use in only the wealthier households and only for certain non-meat foodstuffs. This pot not only signalled emulation by lower castes of upper castes, but also acted to re-assert the categorisations of certain foods with certain vessels and maintain boundaries against pollution. It was clearly bound up in a rich social context, as were the pots and other items of material culture in the Dutch Neolithic examined by Ian Hodder (Hodder 1982d). He argued that pottery shape and decoration became increasingly more differentiated through the Neolithic as settlement fission and expansion developed, creating instability and contradiction in the face of traditional social ties and practices (especially burial). Similarly, when such elaboration on the pottery decreases in the later Neolithic, it can be associated with a resolution of these contradictions and an attempt to deny ⸲arlier social divisions.

In contrast to these approaches, other studies, particularly from the USA, have continued to look at design in very functional terms, although there has been a great deal of development in how function is conceived since the 1960s. While in general, function remains defined naturalistically, there is a broad and sometimes subtle difference between those who employ ecological (i.e. systemic) criteria and those who adopt more evolutionary (i.e. selectionist) ones. An ecological or systemic method would see design as being adapted to intended use or function – thus the use of a certain kind of temper in a cooking pot might experimentally be shown to be more efficient than another kind, while, more generally, the use of certain clays and tempers will be constrained by availability and costs in acquisition. Dean Arnold's studies of ceramics is a good example of such an approach (e.g. Arnold 1985).

Evolutionary or selectionist approaches criticise such explanations for their presumption of intent – just because a design is adapted to a certain function, does not mean it is an *adaptation*. Dunnell was the first to address selectionism seriously and he initially linked function with adaptive traits and style with neutral traits (Dunnell 1980); more recently, however, a distinction has been made between traits which increase adaptiveness and are under selective control and those that are not, thus moving beyond the style–function dichotomy (O'Brien and Holland 1992: 46). Thus a trait might be functionally adaptive but is not necessarily selected – this has to be demonstrated over time by *directional* movement. Braun's study of the increasing thinness of vessel walls of pottery of the Woodland period has been hailed as an example of such selectionism, as has O'Brien and Holland's study of the shift from grit to shell temper in the Midwest (Braun 1983; O'Brien and Holland 1992). Both show directional trends in the adoption of such traits and can be contrasted with others which exhibit more of a random drift.

I will discuss selectionism further in the next chapter, but enough has been said here to show how it differs from more ecological approaches. Common to all of these approaches, the post-processual studies included, is that they have tended to interpret artefact variability or design primarily in terms of *use* – however this is defined, functionally or symbolically. The focus on use and more generally the contextual field of objects might seem to have finally moved in the direction first espoused by Steward and Setzler and by Taylor, with archaeologists looking at how objects are actually used by the people or culture – no more the obsessive concern with typologies as if objects had a life of their own. And yet there is a sense in which all these studies still leave everything as it was; such studies invariably rely on prior classifications, divisions and typologies – it is not that objects have been re-arranged and classified using different groupings, but rather that the variability in pre-existing classifications is associated with contextual variability, whether this is interpreted functionally or symbolically. The same divisions of pottery, stone and bone, and the same specialists studying them, remain embedded in archaeological work, and the recent studies described above never contest these basic divisions but work over or alongside them. This twofold approach, first manifest through the emic and etic distinction proposed by Taylor, remains with us in the distinction between typological and contextual studies. I discuss this relation in more detail in Chapter 5, but in taking this chapter to its conclusion I want to explore another dimension to this duality, that between production and consumption. For if such studies have tended to focus on use, how do they view production?

Partly because of this duality, production falls within the realm of the specialist and, until recently (see p. 90), has largely been a technological side issue. This has been fuelled by the fact that while functionalist interpretations have tended to put the relation between production and use as harmonic or homogeneous – a pot for example is intended to be used for cooking and so its design can be partially explained by this intended function – the symbolic interpretations on the other hand have placed this same relation as heterogeneous, the actual use of an object potentially having nothing to do with its intended use. The pot may have been built for cooking, but it can also be incorporated in practices for which it was not intended, such as its display in a museum case. While functionalism stresses a univocal use, a symbolic approach emphasises the polysemous nature of objects. This is not to say that functionalists do not recognise that an object can be used for many purposes, or that in a symbolic interpretation an object might have had an intended use – rather, it is how the *design* of the object is primarily interpreted.

The two approaches, then, are perhaps not necessarily incompatible but in both cases production becomes secondary to consumption, either because the production of an object is narrowly defined by its intended use (functionalism) or is under-determined by its potential use (symbolism). Production itself, beyond technological issues, has not until recently been problematised as a field of social activity, but is subsumed under and deferred to issues of use/consumption. This lack of problematisation of the production process, and more generally the relation between production and consumption, is critical in understanding how the current specialisms are maintained. Thus, to end this chapter, I want to look first at recent studies of the production process and more generally at the life cycle of objects – how they both challenge and yet still reinforce specialist divisions – and, second, to examine the broader relation between these life cycles and the issues of classification and, ultimately, specialisations.

The temporality of objects

The natural history of the object

Rouse in his method of analytic classification drew attention to the procedural element of the production process and artefact design; indeed his classification can be used to reconstruct the process of production, or those relevant elements of it (Rouse 1960, figure 1). However, studies on the *process* of production have, until relatively recently, been largely ignored. The most common production processes studied, perhaps unsurprisingly, have been those of lithics and ceramics – indeed the basic methods used in the production of stone tools have been understood for a long time (e.g. Semenov 1964). Common to both approaches, though has been a rather restricted conception of technology in terms of how the material behaves when subject to certain actions – how flint fractures, how clay fires for example – and thus reconstructing the sequence of actions which produce the final result primarily in terms of material properties.

The major exceptions to this conception have been the work of Schiffer, with his behavioural chains, and others in the USA, and in France, the work of Leroi-Gourhan and more recently of Lemonnier, with operational chains (*chaînes opérataires*). Schiffer's behavioural chains form part of a wider theory on material culture but are specifically an attempt to reconstruct the sequence of actions or events within the life history of an object (Schiffer and Skibo 1997: 29; also see Schiffer 1998). As such his approach has a strong bearing on the production process, especially through the notion that the technical choices which structure the production process affect the subsequent performance characteristics of an object through its formal properties. For example, the performance of a pottery vessel in cooking is greatly affected by a quality known as thermal shock resistance (that is, the ability to withstand the repeated stress of heating and cooling), which can be manipulated through a variety of formal properties of the vessel such as temper, shape or surface treatment. The significant question, though, is how the technical choices are made. Schiffer recognises that many alternatives are possible and that a sequence of events is not necessarily linear – a point which also underlies operational research approaches to production (e.g. Bleed 1991). While recognising the influence of the knowledge and experience of the artisan, greatest emphasis is placed on situational factors in constraining technical choice, by which is meant the wider context within which the activity takes place (Schiffer and Skibo 1997: 34–9). Thus everything from access to and quality of raw materials to the time and place at which the pottery is produced can affect the technical choices made.

While outlining a broad spectrum of factors, there is a sense in which the approach Schiffer proposes is almost too general, and by emphasising the situational component the complexity can appear overwhelming. In contrast the French operational chain focuses much more on the knowledge and skills of the artisans, in particular the cultural milieu in which they work. By focusing on the detailed structure of the process of production, particularly identifying points at which choices are made, we can describe a logic which shows how an artefact acquired its particular form (e.g. Lemonnier 1986, 1990, 1993). The method recognises that even though certain physical or natural constraints may act upon the design of an object (strategic components), there are still a number of alternative pathways possible, and by identifying points where decisions are made, one identifies the influence of the social. A good example is van der Leeuw's study of pottery production in which he demonstrates that even though the technical requirements of potting may limit the choices, the range of available options remains very large (van der Leeuw 1993). Thus he presents several different examples of forming a pot, from throwing on the wheel to coil-building, all of which ultimately achieve the same goal and cannot be explained by reference to the material properties of the clay, since this itself can be modified anyway. The differences must therefore relate to the social context of production, and he identifies two dimensions: the broader conceptualisation involved (in this case, of shape) and the tools used during the forming process (e.g. moulds, rotary supports or wheels). This distinction is also underlined by another – that between largely unconscious cognitive structures (a 'tradition') and more conscious choices.

In many respects, the operational chain appears to share similar features with a normative concept of culture, as exemplified in Sackett's isochrestism, not least in the fact that it offers no rationale for the particular choices made – it merely identifies them, as exemplified in Lemonnier's use of the term 'arbitrary' to designate the non-technical dimension of choices (Edmonds 1990). The underlying attribution, ultimately, is the distinction between the natural/physical (as constraint) and the social (as choice); the assumption is that we can identify the former and any remaining variability is to be accounted for by the latter. It is this opposition set up between natural constraints (function/technology) and social choices (style/symbolism) that is the heart of the problem, which Lemonnier himself recognises as something he cannot do without (Lemonnier 1993: 10; also see Boast 1997 for a similar critique). Nature dictates the problem, culture provides the solution. Indeed, Lemonnier argues that function cannot be totally reduced to social strategies – that objects do have certain properties because they are adapted to a use, what Leroi-Gourhan called *tendence* (Lemonnier 1993: 23–4). Morever, while Schiffer's emphasis on situational components appears more sophisticated, it downplays the history of production. Yet, even when this is considered, such history is described in terms of feedback and selectionism which while addressing change, do not really articulate this in relation to continuity (Schiffer and Skibo 1997: 34).

Van der Leeuw is a little more sceptical of the opposition between natural problems and social choice. He seems to argue that while the operational chain employs the distinction between the invariant component or essence of a technique and its variable components, its choices, this does not have to map on to the older distinction between material and cultural, but should rather focus on the artisan's conception of this difference (van der Leeuw 1993: 242–3). His distinction between tradition and choice does go some way in breaking down this normative conception and is something I have also developed in a study of clocks (Lucas 1995a); moreover, his observation that the conceptualisations embedded in a tradition might be identified in other cultural spheres is highly significant (van der Leeuw 1993). For example, his description of the conceptualisation of pot shape is all about how a group perceives the spatio-temporal dimensions of form – how is the transformation of the clay to the pot conceived. Is the pot made from the rim down or the base up? Is it made from discrete elements (e.g. rims, bodies, bases) or as a continuous whole? Is it made both horizontally and vertically (e.g. coil-building) or primarily vertically (e.g. wheel throwing)? The important point about understanding these conceptualisations is that the same structures may recur in other contexts, that the spatial concepts which pervade the production of pottery may also recur in other social situations.

For example, in a study I made of the deposition of Neolithic pottery in northern England, I argued that there was an intentional selection for specific parts of broken vessels (the rim) and that this selection was reinforced by the extent of elaboration in the design (decoration and moulding). Thus the same partitive division in the production process which separated the rim from the rest of the pot, also recurred in the depositional process, which might even be seen as an inversion of the former (Lucas 1995b). Such an example shows how the same conception of space or topology is used in different contexts or activities. Clearly there is a sense in which conceptualisation, as a way of thinking – whether continuous as a tradition or as manifest in ostensibly different contemporary activities – is a useful component in understanding design, a component which essentially transcends the immediate situational context of production.

Perhaps one might argue that we need both, that Schiffer's situational context needs to be bonded with the notion of tradition. However, while such themes provide a much more sophisticated understanding of the social context of production, it should be pointed out that the production process itself is still enfolded within a certain teleology – that is, that the activity, of say, potting is nothing other than the process of making a pot. This might sound strange at first, for what else would potting be about? But consider Childe's reconstruction of a flint knapper:

> To make a D scraper, collect a flint nodule (1) at full moon, (2) after fasting all day, (3) address him politely with 'words of power', (4) . . . strike him thus with a hammerstone, (5) smeared with the blood of a sacrificed mouse. . . . Technical and scientific progress has of course just been discovering that (1), (2), (3) and (5) are quite irrelevant to the success of the operation prescribed in (4). These acts were futile accessories, expressive of ideological delusions. It is just these errors that have been erased from the archaeological record.
>
> (Childe 1956: 171)

Childe's example is clearly over the top, but it was to prove a point about the technological element of material culture – a point which is still implicit in contemporary studies on the process of production, as a technological activity. More importantly, though, it also defines activities in terms of their material production – the object provides the teleology of the process and the whole activity is defined in terms of this teleology. Of course it is reasonable to say that potting is about making pots, but it can also be about other things, specifically the affirmation and maintenance of social relationships, for example between women if potters are all female, or between master and apprentice in this kind of labour structure. The whole production process – like any activity – reproduces social (and conceptual) structures and relationships between individuals as well as objects.

A good example of an approach which considers just such themes is Shanks study of a Greek perfume jar. Shanks's argues against the dominant view in classical archaeology which sees pots in art historical terms, in particular as chronological and 'stylistic' exemplars (Shanks 1992b). Rather, he argues, attention should be paid to the social context of production, and this not only includes tradition, but also the social context of its consumption. Thus he views the design of a late eighth/seventh-century BC Greek perfume jar, both as drawing on long traditions of vessel forming and firing, yet as a radical break in terms of its decoration, expressing risk and transgression which would have appealed to the aristocratic consumers.

While Shanks's study opens up the field of production towards its wider social context of use, it is important to recognise why such approaches are not widely taken up, a resistance which relates to the fact that the teleology of most studies of production is enfolded within a wider conception of objects. One only needs to look and see where most studies of objects start: with the properties of the raw material. As much as an end, studies of production need a starting point, an origin, and it is precisely the material which provides this. Rouse placed the material at the top of his procedural pyramid, while even Childe in his example above starts with 'collect a flint nodule'. The movement between the raw material and the finished artefact presents the whole process as a movement from the natural to the cultural. Indeed it is Pitt Rivers' phylogenetic process writ small as ontogeny. It is at this point that I would draw a connection between the broad specialist divisions and the detailed study of finds: both clearly draw on the material or natural basis of their object as a point of origin. I want to explore in more detail this 'ontogeny' of the object, and see if there is another way of articulating life cycles without relapsing into an originary interpretation which fixes an object through its material nature.

In conceptions of the taphonomy of objects, there is a typical life cycle of production, use and discard, rather like a metaphor for the biological cycle of birth, life and death. An underlying motif is the transformation from natural object to cultural object, a transformation which takes place in the production process (e.g. Schiffer 1987, ch. 2). It is perhaps no accident that most studies in the past on production have tended to be very physically oriented, looking at the material properties of objects, while approaches to consumption or use have been more socially geared. Indeed, the transformation from raw material to artefact could almost be taken as a metaphor of the western epistemological process and classification of science, with interpretation and understanding correspondingly harder as one moves along the life history of the object from its natural to social status.

While the operational and behavioural chains go some way in breaking down this association, the critique needs to be pursued further, in particular to consider not just production but the whole life cycle of an object as a social phenomenon – to consider the social life of objects (Appadurai 1986). To shift away from the dichotomy of nature/culture towards a more complex and dynamic image, it may be useful to consider an artefact's life history in biographical terms (Kopytoff 1986). A biography requires recognition of a persisting object, that which is the subject of the biography – as such the artefact denies time by enduring. A megalith or a stone axe endures, indeed in many cases for vast stretches of time. This very property is what constitutes the archaeological record and excavation is simply a part of its ongoing life story. However, what makes the biography into a story is the fact that the artefact also changes – for example, the axe moves from a multiplicity of contexts during the 2,000 years of its life and during this time may suffer modification, such as wear, polish, perforation, breakage, patination and painted numbers. This paradox of the object is implicit in the notion of an individual as persisting yet changing – the same but different. How do we reconcile this paradox?

We are never explicit about this but the tendency is to associate the permanence or durability of the object with its essential characteristic, namely its physical or material being, and its mutability or transitoriness with accidental qualities such as meaning. In practice the two can be confused so that the very materiality of material culture lends its meaning a certain durability – that durability of meaning *derives* from material durability (Eighmy 1981; Fletcher 1989). But this takes us back to the dichotomy I want to avoid. Alternatively, I would consider what is really the issue here – time. Any object which moves from one context to another carries with it part of its life history – an heirloom passing through the generations may go into different houses or rooms and takes on new associations but also retains older ones. When something is buried and recovered 4,000 years later it still carries something of its past – both of its last context, the burial, and potentially scars of its former ones including its context of production. When one picks up a stone axe 4,000 years old, it is *not* its physicality which has endured while its meaning is lost, mute; rather, it is one part of its biography which has endured, its context in the hands of a knapper and before that in volcanic eruptions. Its materiality or substance is no more essential than its axe shape – it is just the product of an earlier history. The axe shape is as much dependent on this earlier history as in any biography and here we come to the crux of the issue: the knappers who made the axes were aware of this – they may not have articulated it in the same way as we do, but the stone presented certain properties which constrained what could be done to it, as the operational chains and other studies of production affirm. However, it is important to recognise that these constraints are biographical too. The real dialectic is not between matter and form, natural and cultural, but between past and present: the paradox of the object, of biography, is a temporal paradox, not a material one. This insight is of tremendous help in understanding the process of differentiation we make in splitting objects, for in recognising the temporal conditionality of objects we are in a position to rethink the way we split objects from their context and each other.

Typology and the reproduction of objects

What matters perhaps more than most things in archaeological work is knowing what *kind* of object one has, because it is only by identifying the objects that one can begin to understand better the relation between them. As Childe said in *Piecing Together the Past*, the type constitutes the archaeological datum:

> an archaeological datum as such must remain an abstraction, an instance of a type. It can never attain the full concreteness of individuality and remain an object for archaeological study. A really unique creation, the result of an act never repeated nor imitated, would slip through the archaeologist's classificatory net and thus elude his interpretation unless it were helped out by some extraneous circumstance – a contemporary written description or an explanatory inscription. It might become an *objet d'art*. . . .
>
> (Childe 1956: 6)

Childe's quote raises an interesting point about the type – it is an abstraction and stands in contrast to the individual object. And yet, at the same time, I am uneasy when I read Childe's reference to a unique object, the *objet d'art*, as escaping the classificatory net; there is a paradox in here, one which links up with the paradox of the object in time discussed above.

The process of working with typologies has been usefully described as a dialectic, in particular between the process of sorting or ascribing individuals to a class and the act of defining those classes (Adams and Adams 1991). These processes can also be expressed by saying that typology or indeed any general process of classification works on a double aspect to an object – that it is both an individual artefact and a type. *This* axe is also *an* axe. One cannot have the general class or type without specific examples, but conversely – and here is what in Childe's statement makes me uneasy – one cannot really have a unique individual. Take the most obvious example – me. There is no other Gavin Lucas – yet if I am unique, I presuppose that with respect to which I am unique; specifically other people. It presupposes I am a person and in that respect at least I share something in common with others. It is impossible to conceive of uniqueness apart from the idea of collectivity. And yet my name encapsulates this duality –

or indeed paradox; my first name 'Gavin' identifies me as an individual while my surname 'Lucas' affiliates me with a group – my immediate family and wider patrilineal kin. Of course kinship can be and has been regarded as a kind of classification.

How does typology deal with this duality? A major difference exists between those typologies which are constructed on the basis of attribute association and those on object clustering (Whallon and Brown 1982). To some extent this is a European/North American divide too, but the critical difference is that attribute association techniques define types by recurrent associations of diagnostic *attributes* for a group of objects, while object clustering techniques define types by grouping *objects* on the basis of overall similarity. In brief, attribute association uses chi-square (or other similar) tests on contingency tables of attributes (initially on a simple pairwise basis, but later on a hierarchical model; Spaulding 1982). As an example, consider a group of fifty pottery vessels which for simplicity we analyse as a pairwise table of two attributes/variables, form and colour, each with two values, plate/bowl and black/red respectively (Table 4). By looking at the frequency of values for each variable against the other variables, a pattern might be exhibited which suggests some association of variables. In this case, it appears as if red is closely associated with bowls and black with plates.

A test for non-randomness would then demonstrate whether this is statistically valid, and if it shows that it is, we could argue that there is good evidence for two distinct types, red bowls and black plates. A hierarchical approach, bringing in more variables, might help to account for the residuals, so for example we might demonstrate that the three red plates are of a different fabric from the forty-seven bowls, and that once fabric as a third variable is taken into account, all residuals are accounted for and the type is more closely defined. This is of course a very simple and too-perfect example, but one which nevertheless highlights the basic conception of a type under this approach as a monothetic set of attributes or variables.

The criticism of this approach is that it is *too* monothetic in its conception of a type. While in practice it may well tolerate residuals which even under a hierarchical approach cannot be smoothed out, in theory the type is a distinct entity characterised by a certain exclusive combination of attributes. The object clustering approach, by contrast, explores the relation between objects. Developed from David Clarke's use of numerical taxonomy

Table 4 Pairwise table of hypothetical pottery assemblage

Form	Colour	
	red	black
plate	3	45
bowl	47	5

in the 1960s, and championed by Hodson, this approach compares every object in a group to every other object in terms of similarity across as many variables as one chooses to employ, using a similarity co-efficient (Clarke 1968; Doran and Hodson 1975: 173–84; Hodson 1982). The result is a hierarchic structure, typically rendered as a dendrogram, where objects are linked together at different levels, from the unique to a unity (Figure 11). The dendrogram appears to express in a very clear form, the *relationship* between the objects as individuals by showing the *degree* to which each is unique or more similar to other objects. The proponents of this view argue that it matches reality more closely, taking objects as the starting point and not attributes.

It might seem from this that the object cluster approach is therefore a far more sophisticated technique for expressing classification, embracing as it does the polythetic nature of classes – that is, not every instance of a type has to share a fixed set of attributes, and thus is an inherently fuzzy entity. None the less to be useful, a *key* has to be created which identifies the values of variables which distinguish one cluster/type from another, for without it there is no way of knowing what exactly a particular type is or of being able to sort new objects into the classification. Methods of achieving this have included the K-means which simply finds the most significant level(s) of clustering (Doran and Hodson 1975: 180–4). Ultimately, to be successful, object clustering requires the variability to dissect into two very distinct kinds – minimal (within a cluster) and maximal (between clusters), expressed in the phrase 'internal cohesion and external isolation' (Hodson 1982: 23). The problem is, however, that different algorithms used to enhance identification of clusters can produce different results; in other words, using similarity as a technique of classification masks the multiple ways in which objects may cluster. In short, they are faced with the reverse problem of the attribute association approach – in theory, they aim for discrete clusters defined by specific values but in practice they cannot escape the consequences of the polythetic nature of their approach.

Thus, if the same group of pottery vessels used as an example above was analysed using the same variables and values by numerical taxonomy, there would emerge *four* types not two – red plates, red bowls, black plates and black bowls. The reason is that the measure used is purely one of similarity which is *insensitive* to the composition of the assemblage. In effect what this means is that while it can produce clusters of objects and call them types, there can be no definition of what any *specific* type is without a key, and finding a key is not that easy. Its very strength, as a polythetic classification, is also its weakness, because if there is no specific definition/key, there can be no way of ascribing objects to a type without going through the whole procedure again – which is highly impractical. Moreover, even if a key is created, the cluster simply becomes transformed into an attribute association reached by another route. Many actually see these two approaches in this way and therefore as complementary (Read 1982: 68).

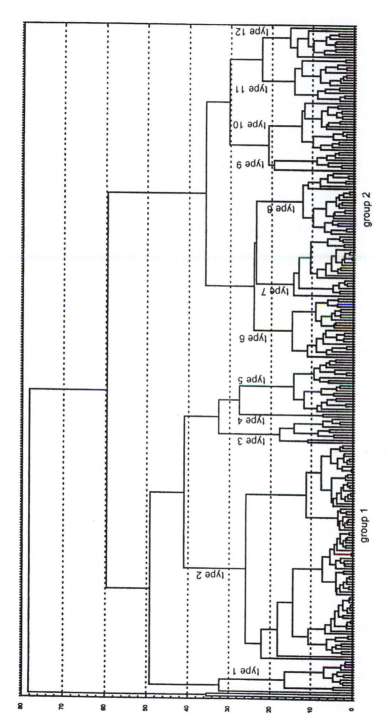

Figure II Cluster analysis dendrogram of obsidian points

Attribute association always faces the problem of residuals by defining the type in strict monothetic terms while object clustering frequently cannot decide on where clustering is significant because of its polythetic definition. Both of these problems occur because of what can be described as an essentialist tendency, one which ultimately tries to collapse the distinction between an individual and the type of which it is an instance. With attribute association, the individual object is bypassed in order to define the type in terms of attributes; the individual object is thus *either* an instance of a type *or* a repository of attributes – in itself it is not recognised. With object clustering, the type is bypassed in order to define an individual object in relation to other objects in terms of attributes – clusters of objects may be identified but these do not constitute types in themselves for the type itself is not theorised.

Despite their more pragmatic approach, Adams and Adams, in facing the same problem, also resolve it in favour of reducing the individual to a type, rather than sustaining an open, oscillating relationship. While admitting the typology may be open and fluid, *at any one time* the relation between an individual and the typology is not: at the end of the day, they want to assign an object into a prescribed type. Maybe I can be accused of pushing this point too far in that what I am talking about is no longer typology or classification. Childe summed it up well: 'Archaeologists consider phenomena almost exclusively as members of a class or, as they say, instances of a type. They ignore that it is the particular peculiarities, accidental or intentional, that in fact distinguish each specimen' (Childe 1956: 6). A typology which does not reduce the individual to a class, is not really a typology.

And yet, for me, it is precisely this relationship between the individual object and its more generic description which is interesting – more interesting than typologies or classifications which ultimately collapse the relationship in favour of the generic description, i.e. reduce individuals to types. But how does one sustain this tension in a meaningful way? In a study I made a few years ago on English domestic clock dials from the seventeenth to the nineteenth century, I noticed that, regardless of the specific changes, different design elements had different *rates* of change (Lucas 1995a). A chart of these elements was useful in showing these different rates, which could be taken to mark continuities and discontinuities at multiple scales without resorting to any reduction into successive types as in classification (Figure 12). More generally, though, it highlighted the fact that there is no single trait which one can point to and say, this is essentially what defines a clock. We could argue that the simple presence of hands for example remain constant – I just have not included them in the chart. However, many modern (i.e. post-1860) domestic clocks do not have hands (e.g. digital clocks); furthermore, other instruments such as barometers, chronometers or watches have hands and thus hands are not exclusive to clocks.

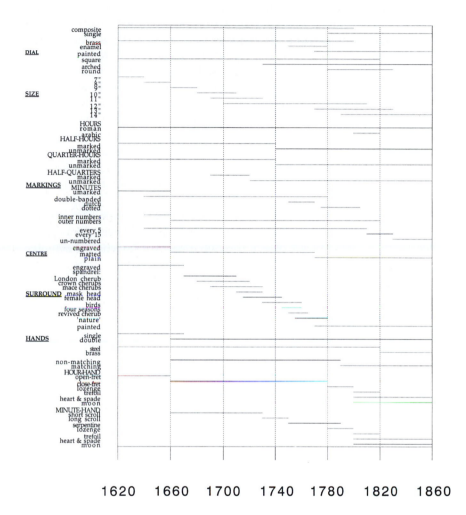

Figure 12   Chart of principal design changes on English domestic clock dials
(1620–1860)

The normal way to view this phenomenon is to say that the absence of
some attributes signals a different type – for example, a digital clock is a
different type of clock to an analogue one, one of the critical attributes
being the presence/absence of hands. But this emphasises difference at the
expense of similarity; this is not to say I want to reverse this equation, but
rather sustain the two together. I could for example have increased the
sample of objects to include barometers, chronometers and watches, or
restricted it to longcase clocks; in either case the *character* of the chart

would in all respects be no different. There would still be no essential defining feature of identity but rather a stratified identity which involves degrees of generality/particularity. One must not read the essential from the general. This is exactly the same point we made about the biographies of objects, that just as objects have no stable or originary basis through materiality, neither do typologies through the categorisations we use. In this way although we can draw boundaries around our analysis, we cannot absolutely define them – the chart can be seen as simply a selective perspective dependent on the context of analysis. Moreover, a mobility of resolution is directly related to the stratified nature of the chart, and in archaeological terms this is highly significant for it suggests that we might adjust the degree of dimensionality (i.e. inclusiveness of objects) to the degree of chronological resolution at our disposal.

The point of this method is precisely to show the discontinuities within a single analysis without resorting to a classification. Classification tends to divide the analysis of an object through two contrastive and complementary terms, the variable (or attribute) and the value (or state) which the variable possesses – for example, red being a value of the variable colour. An essentialist definition of a type has to be given – even if any particular definition can change, the condition of possessing an essential definition cannot. Under classification, attributes/variables/dimensions are the immutable element of an object while the value is the mutable aspect. A distinction between essential and accidental properties is presumed and as a result fixes the limits of an object. For example, all pottery has a fabric (fixed) which varies according to a number of factors such as temper, hardness etc. (variable). What the stratification of the clock chart demonstrates on the other hand is that variables and values are not fixed but relative – any attribute or trait can be both a variable *and* a value depending on its degree of generality or particularity relative to other attributes. Even the most general attribute could become a value if the horizons were altered, horizons which will also affect what constitutes the object in question. Thus, just as the chart can be used to show the fluidity not only between different types of clocks but also between clocks and other dialled instruments, so pottery merges with bricks, tiles, figurines, etc., in sharing fabric, but equally with other containers such as metal or wooden vessels which share not fabric but form.

Questioning the parameters in such an analysis, thus challenges some common ascriptions; in other words, in what sense do we ascribe a common identity to the category of clock or, more generally, pottery, for example? In the case of pottery, how can we say that Neolithic pottery in Britain bears any significant relationship to Romano-British pottery? Perhaps we cannot and do not, although we might argue that the two share certain analogies by virtue of their material properties. But then we are back with an originary basis to classification and specialisms. Consider the material

artefacts we call cutlery – spoons, knives and forks have all existed as
distinct objects of Western material culture for a long time, especially knives
and spoons. But is it reasonable to draw any association between Roman
spoons and knives, or between these and our present cutlery set? The latter
developed only in the eighteenth century with changes in dining patterns,
and this shift is marked through the design of the object in terms of matching
motifs such as the rat-tail pattern etc.

This example shows that what we commonly describe as the same object
can actually have very different existences, despite the analogies. A similar
but reversed situation occurs with objects of similar form in different
materials, for example ceramic, wooden and metal bowls. Is there a justification for a specialist in ceramics, woodwork and metalwork, or, to put
it another way, is it reasonable that the categories of clay, wood and metal
are used to define such specialisms? Certainly the different histories of these
materials before human modification are significant. But what do we do
when faced with bone and wooden awls which look the same, or vessels
of the same shape but in ceramic, metal and wood? Is it still legitimate to
separate woodwork from bone, ceramics from metalwork? Such things are
not necessarily very common, and this has to do with the different properties of their raw materials – but at the same time, we may often be *missing*
similarities because of this preconception.

More commonly, take the case of funerary pottery – it might equally be
wrong to study it alongside domestic pottery simply because it shares certain
formal similarities. This is not to argue against such comparative study, but
rather to highlight the relevance of prior categorisations to their study. The
study of funerary pottery alongside other funerary objects might be a more
appropriate course but, equally, it might be appropriate to study such vessels
alongside domestic pottery – but not because of their formal or material
similarity, but because the social context of their production might need
to be seen against the production of domestic vessels – are they made by
the same potters?

It is through the concept of production – or rather, perhaps, reproduction, that the relation between classification and the biography or life cycle
of an object is best articulated. Consider the problem of the European
Beaker, a class of late Neolithic/early Bronze Age pottery. Throughout the
twentieth century, there have been attempts to classify this form in Britain,
the most detailed being David Clarke's which used complex statistical
analysis (Clarke 1970). However, neither Clarke's attempt nor those of the
others have been entirely successful, and in terms of the chronological
implications of their typologies none of them worked when recently tested
in a radiocarbon dating programme (Kinnes *et al.* 1991). In contrast, since
the 1980s, a number of contextual approaches to vessel variability have
revealed far more interesting patterns (Hodder 1982d; Shanks and Tilley
1987b; Boast 1995). Why is it that the British Beaker (and indeed other

prehistoric pottery) has proven intractable to typological analysis, unlike pottery of later periods? The answer lies in the concept of standardisation: Beakers are simply *too* variable. Typologies depend on the right amount of variability – too little, and one hardly has a basis for any classification at all as Taylor remarked many years ago (see p. 79), but, on the other hand, with too much one cannot know where one type might begin and another end. The degree of variability or standardisation is a key issue and it is this which links typologies into the social contexts of production and reproduction.

To take an opposite case, Bronze Age metalwork in Scandinavia is highly standardised. It is this very aspect which made it so amenable to Montelius' typology which still more or less stands today. It worked, not necessarily because it was the right method but because it was the right material. Sørensen has taken this point further and suggested that this very fact is important in terms of understanding contexts in the *reproduction* of material culture (Sørensen 1989, 1997). Indeed, perhaps our very concern for typologies derives from the fact that we live in a society where such contexts foster standardisation and relative trans-contextual stability – mass-production or specialised guilds which sustain closed traditions of manufacture. The fact is, a great deal of archaeological material is going to be unclassifiable except in a broad sense of using generic identities which must change according to context. Beaker typologies have never worked and they never will, because the conditions under which Beakers were made are too context-specific; in contrast, much of Bronze Age metalwork is trans-contextual and, in these cases, a typology of the traditional sort is possible.

By heeding the social context of production, archaeology may be in a position to reconsider categorisations which have been in place for too long and the bias such systems carry towards the more numerous and typologically variable objects. I am not arguing for the abandonment of specialisms, nor that all the specialist divisions need to be re-structured. There are very good reasons why a lithics analyst or ceramicist are useful specialists and, concomitantly, why lithics and pottery are useful categories of analysis. A pot specialist does not just look at how the pot was formed, or consider the properties of the clay, but also examines evidence of use, residues, even how a pot was broken. Similarly, a zooarchaeologist will not just identify the species and sex of an animal but will look at pathologies, age of death, butchery marks and other clues of *post-mortem use*. Objects do not just offer information about the context of deposition but carry the scars of other contexts, so many of which we, as archaeologists, rarely get a chance to see. Similarly, the strategies of reproduction, either of animals or pots, are mediated by processes of continuity and change which often favour high degrees of standardisation and at least exhibit continuity of form at some level, permitting recognition of them as types. The common thread is the need to be aware of the temporality of objects.

The issue comes to down to recognising this duality: that while all objects are context-specific in that they take their meaning or significance from their context, at the same time most objects are capable of transcending contexts either as individuals (biographies) or as types (design traditions). Because so many of the studies on objects since the 1960s focused on the issue of use, the context of objects became a primary articulation of variability. And yet archaeologists never encounter objects in a dynamic context, that is they never witness their life cycles or biographies, but usually only see one context, that of deposition. Of course production sites are excavated, and various 'pompeii' situations are occasionally encountered, but the majority of contexts in which objects are recovered refer to the final point in the life cycle. This fact may have contributed to the dominant blindness of archaeologists in regarding the ability of objects to move through contexts, despite the growth of taphonomic studies. Indeed, such taphonomic studies are invariably not about the life cycle but about the 'death cycle', the post-depositional processes affecting objects.

Maybe now we can re-appraise Steward's and Seltzer's (1938) critique of the way objects are split; while they were right to argue that material culture ought to be seen in its cultural context, this cultural context cannot be taken to be homogeneous. One could say this was a product of the current normative view of culture, even despite their call for a more functional interpretation, but this is beside the point. Objects clearly move and work through multiple cultural contexts and while the call for multiple classifications might have been a response to this recognition, it really misses the point. In moving through contexts, objects bring with them traces of the effects earlier contexts have had on them, the most durable and impressive of which is their context of production. The significance of typology today must be seen in terms of this context – that typological variability is but a shorthand way of referring to the continuity and change in design traditions in the context of production. Of course this needs to be linked into contexts of consumption through the notion of reproduction, but, more importantly, the very issue of variability and differentiation between objects has to be temporalised.

It is precisely this temporality, therefore, which must be foregrounded so that what specialists study is related to what other specialists are doing, as well as being integrated with the site in general. Such integration may or may not have been a component of projects in the past, but it is clear that, in being studied and written up, the finds tend to become far removed from their association with each other and their context, and the more this process goes in one direction the harder it seems to pull it all back together. It is rare to find a final synthesis in a site report which does justice to the various specialist studies preceding it. More integration at the point of recovery is clearly a necessary direction to move in, and one which projects such as that at Çatalhöyük are moving towards (Hodder 1997). It may be salutary to remind ourselves that just as there are no universal classifications, there are no universal specialisms – most ceramicists are also specialists in the ceramics of a particular region and period, and if we can accept this level of contextualisation, there is no reason not to tolerate even tighter levels.

Chapter 4

The measure of culture

Gordon Childe was famous for his breadth of knowledge of prehistoric Europe – indeed, he was probably one of the last archaeologists who could claim to know in some detail the material culture of prehistoric Europe based on first-hand knowledge through visits to sites, museums and libraries around the continent. As McNairn observes in her study of Childe's theoretical perspectives:

> At a time when the trend was towards detailed, particularistic, research, Childe's texts such as *The Dawn of European Civilisation* (1925), *The Danube in Prehistory* (1929), or *Prehistoric Communities of the British Isles* (1940) stand out as great works of synthesis patterning the whole of European prehistory.
>
> (McNairn 1980: 1)

Such syntheses as exist today, are often multi-authored and based on secondary or tertiary published material (e.g. Champion *et al.* 1984). How could it be otherwise? Just as in the early days of archaeology when finds specialists emerged, so did period or area specialists, both groups increasing after the 1930s alongside the increasing amount of material recovered and the number of archaeologists in universities.

At the end of the nineteenth century and into the first decades of the twentieth century, archaeologists could quite seriously consider themselves students of human or world prehistory. One of the first important texts was Lubbock's *Prehistoric Times* (1865) which happily crossed millennia and continents. Of course there were studies which focused on specific areas – Daniel Wilson's first major work, and a landmark in British archaeology, was concerned with the prehistory of Scotland (Wilson 1851), but even he turned to more general works such as *Prehistoric Man* (1862). The point is, that even though archaeologists might focus on a specific area, the general concern was with 'man', and specifically the evidence which archaeology revealed of cultural or social evolution. By the 1930s, such grand schemes had been replaced in Europe and America by a more historically and regionally specific understanding of local culture groups as evolutionism lost favour.

This is not to say that more cross-cultural concerns about human society and prehistory were – and are – no longer addressed by archaeologists. The functional and ecological–economic approaches from the 1930s to the 1950s and the symbolic archaeology from the 1980s to the present all attest to a continual interest in these broader issues. But these are also always historically and locally situated and usually researched by people who have developed an area and/or period specialism in which they articulate these ideas. Indeed, it is *expected* of most academic archaeologists today that they do have such a specialism over and above the material specialism they may have (e.g. zooarchaeology). Area/period 'floaters' are frowned upon, decried as fickle and said to never know any material properly. These professional divisions are no accident and are directly related to the historical development of the discipline, in particular the emergence in the 1920s of the culture-history or culture-group approach, which, though it no longer holds sway, still affects the way we work. Yet ironically, although archaeology has developed these regional or area specialisms, there has remained a strong tendency for generalisation in archaeology to be of such a nature that it directly contradicts such a specialism – that generalisation is, *de facto* cross-cultural. This is a complex issue which I will reserve for the end of this chapter, but the theme of generalisation and its relation to both area/period specialisms on the one hand and the interpretation of spatio-temporal variability on the other will be a critical undercurrent throughout.

In the last chapter I discussed the influence of finds categorisations and concomitant specialisms in archaeological work, categorisations which stretch back a long way and in many cases may be deleterious to study. In this chapter I want to begin by exploring the development of culture history and examine its legacy in current practice, for it reaches into issues concerned with the professional period/area specialisms and how we circumscribe the limits to these specialisms. For example we may choose to specialise in the Bronze Age of Britain – but why the Bronze Age and why Britain? Clearly this is a historical question of how the particular divisions became inscribed and is partly a product of both nationalism/modern political boundaries in the case of space, and older evolutionary period divisions in the case of time. But there is an even broader question buried here, about how such specialisations relate to the role of space and time in archaeological explanation or interpretation and, even further, how this relates to the nature of generalisation in archaeology and broader disciplinary divisions.

The classification of culture

The partition of culture in Europe and North America

In the late nineteenth century, differences in archaeological assemblages were linked into a temporal difference on the assumption that culture was universal and therefore developed in a similar way everywhere; any difference would then *have to be* a temporal difference. As Daniel eloquently puts it: 'That was the keynote of the old epochal idea – that man's cultural development could be represented as a single sequence, and read in a cave section, just as the geological sequence could be read in a deep cutting through the sedimentary rocks' (Daniel 1975: 244). The later nineteenth century saw an increase in sub-dividing Thomsen's Three Ages into smaller temporal divisions which culminated with the work of such people as Mortillet and Montelius. Mortillet's elegant chart of French prehistory of 1897 sub-divides the Three Ages into periods and these are further subdivided into epochs (see Figure 13), while Montelius' typological studies of the Bronze Age produced a detailed sub-division of six periods. The epoch or period thus became the lowest-level time horizon and concomitantly the lowest level of cultural difference.

Periodisation was thus integral to the evolutionary paradigm for it provided the specific methodology for turning the idea into archaeological reality; without it, neither ordering nor – more importantly – comparison was possible. Although the grand evolutionary narrative is no longer a part of archaeology, its methodological expression through periodisation remains, even to the extent of the names we give periods although they may be often inaccurate and inappropriate. Regardless of these semantic issues, however, periodisation is still a fundamental part of our conception of archaeological reality; how was this transformed with the emergence of the culture-historical approach?

It is interesting to see how the concept of the culture group emerged out of the idea of periodisation and the affinities they share. Part of the impetus came from archaeological fieldwork which began turning up anomalies – Daniel lists several examples where a previous epochal difference was being shown as in fact contemporary. Similarly the same cultural sequence in Europe was difficult to apply elsewhere in the world – the lack of a Bronze Age in sub-Saharan Africa, for example (Daniel 1975: 239–42). Concomitantly, greater emphasis was being placed on regional variation, specifically to link it into an ethnic group (e.g. Celts), which was part of a wider historicising trend associated with classical archaeology on the one hand and a nationalistic archaeology on the other (Daniel 1975: 242–3; Trigger 1978: 80–2; Trigger 1989: 155, 161–3; Díaz-Andreu and Champion 1996; Graves-Brown, Jones and Gamble 1996). The culmination of all this, as is often stated, was Childe's *The Dawn of European Civilisation* (1925)

TEMPS		AGES	PÉRIODES	ÉPOQUES
Quaternaires actuels.	Historiques.	du Fer.	Mérovingienne.	Wabenienne. (*Waben, Pas-de-Calais.*)
			Romaine.	Champdolienne. (*Champdolent, Seine-et-Oise.*)
				Lugdunienne. (*Lyon , Rhône.*)
	Protohistoriques.		Galatienne.	Beuvraysienne. (*Mont-Beuvray, Nièvre.*)
				Marnienne. (*Département de la Marne.*)
				Hallstattienne. (*Hallstatt, haute Autriche.*)
		du Bronze.	Tsiganienne.	Larnaudienne. (*Larnaud, Jura.*)
				Morgienne. (*Morges, canton de Vaud, Suisse.*)
			Néolithique.	Robenhausienne. (*Robenhausen, Zurich.*)
				Campignyenne. (*Campigny, Seine-Inférieure.*)
				Tardenoisienne (*Fère-en-Tardenois, Aisne.*)
Quaternaires anciens.	Préhistoriques.	de la Pierre.	Paléolithique.	Tourassienne. (*La Tourasse, Haute-Garonne.*) Ancien Hiatus.
				Magdalénienne. (*La Madeleine, Dordogne.*)
				Solutréenne. (*Solutré, Saône-et-Loire.*)
				Moustérienne. (*Le Moustier, Dordogne.*)
				Acheuléenne. (*Saint-Acheul, Somme.*)
				Chelléenne. (*Chelles, Seine-et-Marne.*)
Tertiaires.			Éolithique.	Puycournienne. (*Puy-Courny, Cantal.*)
				Thenaysienne. (*Thenay, Loir-et-Cher.*)

Figure 13 Mortillet's chart of French periodisation

where the explication of cultural difference is drawn as a spatio-temporal mosaic, best exemplified in a table from the slightly later book, *The Danube in Prehistory* (1929) (see Figure 14). As Childe himself said of the charts in *The Dawn*, they 'present the distribution in time and space of cultures, assemblages of archaeological phenomena that should reflect the distinctive behaviour patterns of human societies' (Childe 1925: 341).

Comparing an earlier epochal chart by Mortillet with Childe's culture-group version (Figures 13 and 14), the contrasting conceptions of cultural difference are quite clear; and yet maybe there is also a deeper similarity which we too easily ignore. For to some extent the groundwork for a culture-group concept was already laid by the concept of the period or epoch, a point which Daniel makes when he says 'the French system of "epochs" like the Acheulian, the Azilian, or the Cébénnian was, in a way, a step towards the recognition of cultural groups . . .' (Daniel 1975: 147). This is wonderfully illustrated in a story Daniel relates about an altercation between Mortillet and a museum curator:

> De Mortillet had arranged the collections in the Saint-Germain Museum according to his carefully graded subdivisions. He was infuriated because the curator of the Museum, Alexander Bertrand, changed the word Epoch on the labels in every case to Type. Adrien de Mortillet characterised this action as a craven compromise with the opponents of prehistory.
>
> (ibid.: 125–6)

By labelling epochs as types, the curator was in effect re-interpreting them; moreover there is even the suggestion that Bertrand may have regarded such changes in terms of ethnic migrations as he saw the transition from the Stone Age to the Bronze Age in terms of an Aryan invasion (Childe 1956: 27–8). Ironically, as Childe says:

> de Mortillet himself helped to show that one assemblage of type-fossils could be used to define, not only a period of archaeological time in France, but also a nation known to written history; the types, charac-terising his 'Marnian' in France and Switzerland, proved in Italy to be distinctive of the Gauls, known to have descended from that direction.
>
> (Childe 1956: 28)

We can see even further affinities between the epochal and culture-group conception of prehistory when we look at the way such schemes were for-malised in particular in terms of different scales or hierarchies. A hierarchi-cal approach to the culture group was developed by Childe in *Piecing Together the Past*; there he defines three levels – the culture-cycle, the culture and the variant, which had clear spatial connotations (1956: 142–3). If we juxtapose Childe's spatial and Mortillet's temporal hierarchy of divisions, the two are

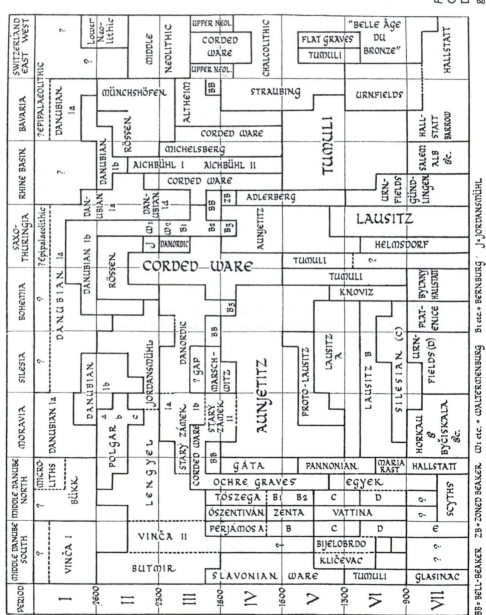

Figure 14
Childe's chart of
Danubian culture
groups

remarkably similar (see Table 5). No direct correlation is implied in this table, that is, the Bronze Age is not equatable with Childe's culture cycle, but that is not the point; it is that the way in which the archaeological concept of culture is articulated is similar, and that given the way the epochal definition of culture was scaled, such a scheme as Childe's might have been inevitable. More significantly, at the time when the culture-group concept was still relatively new, there was a great deal of overlap which is well illustrated by the confusion Childe discusses surrounding the ways in which a period was conceptualised (Childe 1956: 94–9). He gives three – as a subdivision of one of the Three Ages, as an epoch, or as a culture-period – of which the latter for Childe was the clearest, for it is defined not in terms of technology (as in the Three Ages) or cultural evolution (as with epochs) but by the culture group and its temporal limits.

However, despite the affinities between periodisation and the construction of the culture concept, there was also a point of tension. The development of prehistory was defined though periodisation, specifically the Three Age System and material culture was primarily organised along these divisions. However, when more specific culture-historical concerns developed, there was an inevitable clash between these traditional periodisations and the need for independent chronology. Childe summed it up well:

> Thomsen's three ages did enable him to arrange his collection of Danish relics in the right chronological order. It would have broken down had it been extended to collections from Greece and Greenland. To determine what Danish products should be displayed as contemporary with Bronze Age relics from Greece or Esquimaux Stone Age artifacts a time scale quite independent of the material must be invoked.
>
> (Childe 1935: 2)

The problem was synchronicity – how to determine, for example, if the Bronze Age in Britain occurred earlier, at the same time, or later than in, say, southeast Europe. This was not so important in the nineteenth century because it was the general evolutionary progress of European prehistory through these periods that mattered, not the absolute dates of when it occurred (see Chapter two). However, with the emergence of interest in

Table 5 Mortillet's (left) and Childe's (right) schema of the partition of culture

Times (*Temps*)	–
Ages (*Ages*)	Culture cycle
Periods (*Périodes*)	Culture
Epochs (*Époques*)	Variant
Site / Assemblage	

specific culture histories, one of the major issues was that of diffusion, in particular of distinguishing similarities between culture groups caused by diffusion from those which resulted from historical or independent development. Periodisation merely conflated this problem because it was relative to that which one was measuring, not absolute; it was necessary to have an independent chronology.

Thus Childe's innovative space-time charts of archaeological cultures explicitly eschewed the use of periodisations along the time axis in favour of dates, even if the exact position of the culture group or focus along the chronological axis might be imprecise and subject to change. Thus control of time was a critical factor in Europe (and North America) during this period of archaeology; whether it was to offset the Three Age System or break down the culture-area concept (see p. 47), absolute dates were decisive in the articulation of the culture-historical approach. Indeed, the necessity for an independent chronology can be seen as the driving force behind the development of absolute dating techniques, which initially depended on cross-dating from historical/written sources but were eventually dropped in the wake of the radiocarbon revolution (Renfrew 1976). This 'revolution', however, must not be painted as some kind of progression of archaeological science but was a development driven by the particular historical conditions of the 1930s and 1940s which demanded such a technique. One might go so far as to say the development of radiocarbon dating was an inevitable consequence of these conditions (Lucas 1997).

Childe's definition of culture remained a key notion in archaeology; thus the British archaeologist Stuart Piggott wrote on the eve of New Archaeology:

> An archaeological culture has to be defined in terms of its material content, but these have to be related to the dimensions of time and space. By the various means of dating . . . the significant assemblage of material traits taken to define the culture has to be given its chronological limits so far as possible. Its spatial bounds can be approximately determined by plotting on a map all finds of the relevant archaeological types which constitute the culture.
>
> (Piggott 1959: 97–8)

Almost as soon as it was written, this notion of culture should have become redundant; and yet it lingered. Indeed, as late as the 1960s, David Clarke developed a hierarchy similar to Childe's of technocomplex, culture group, culture, subculture and site/assemblage which is much more detailed in its articulation (Clarke 1978: 366, figure 75). He himself said of this model, however, that

> archaeological entities do not really exist in simple hierarchical levels and that many of the most tantalising problems are false problems

arising from a model which is not entirely adequate. . . . The evidence rather more closely approximates with a continuous multidimensional system of elaborately networked multistate elements.

(Clarke 1978: 413)

In other words, the partition of material culture at different spatial – or for that matter temporal – scales is highly fluid and need not fall into discrete levels. The fact is, in the context of the New Archaeology, Clarke's system was incredibly anachronistic and out of place. While Binford and others were arguing for more behavioural and socially complex understandings of the variability of material culture, any scheme which proposed a fixed, over-arching classification is reminiscent of the older culture classifications of the 1930s and 1940s.

While such culture classifications played a role in British and more gener-ally European archaeology, their development in the USA was far more progressive and explicit – indeed, they are perhaps the defining feature of the period (Willey and Sabloff 1993: 121–5). Part of the reason for their importance is clearly linked into the concern for chronology, and most of the systems had explicit or implicit chronological implications. Indeed, it was precisely the fact that the earlier culture-area divisions such as those of Holmes were viewed as too ahistorical (being ethnological) that more complex classifications were required. Because of the nineteenth-century assumption that the indigenous peoples did not really have a history, there was and has always been a close link between ethnography and archae-ology in the USA and the cultural boundaries and divisions which were recorded for the present were largely projected into the past as stable enti-ties. However, with the rise of culture history and the greater awareness that changes in material culture had occurred, the stability – indeed utility – of such culture areas was thrown into question. The earlier culture clas-sifications were partly explicit attempts to avoid the culture-area concept because of the way that genetic relations could be inferred from cultural similarities – it meant that the historical connections were highlighted. Unlike in Europe, North American archaeology was not seeking local chronologies to avoid problems with periodisation but to break down the culture-area concept. Indeed, it is ironic that while in Europe the culture-group concept developed out of the emergence of ethnological concerns for ethnic/tribal divisions as exemplified in the *Kulturkreislehre*, in the USA it was precisely a retreat away from this kind of association that drove culture classification.

This concern can be seen in a debate that briefly arose between Steward and McKern, over the need for cultural taxonomies (McKern 1939, 1942; Steward 1942). Steward argued that using a Direct Historical Approach (i.e. an analogical interpretation of prehistoric societies using historic data) could furnish the information which cultural classifications aimed at.

McKern argued that the Direct Historical Approach was not comparable to taxonomy since it used ethnological criteria not archaeological ones. He did not preclude the two working together, indeed he even encouraged it, but the archaeological classification concerned itself with similarities in material culture and not with ethnological divisions, because such divisions were fluid across both space and time (McKern 1939: 303).

The first attempt at a cultural classification came from the Southwest, particularly through the work of Kidder. Following his synthesis in his *Introduction to the Study of Southwestern Archaeology*, published in 1924, a conference was convened at Pecos where Kidder had conducted his excavations (see Chapter 2), in order to work out a general classificatory scheme for the region (Kidder 1927). The basis of the approach was chronological and a series of periods was agreed upon which defined the various phases of Southwestern culture. While the periodisation is still used with some modifications, it had one major drawback: even within the area of research, it was soon found that the periodisation was not as applicable in all regions of the Southwest. This manifested itself primarily through asynchronicity between regions (i.e. time lag), and furthermore the whole scheme was better adapted to the northern region (where Kidder worked) than the south. Essentially, it was the same problem that European archaeologists faced with their general periodisation which generated the concern for absolute chronologies independent of periodisation.

The critique of the Pecos classification came from Winifred and Harold Gladwin in their paper *A Method for the Designation of Cultures and their Variations* published in 1934. They argued that because of this asynchronicity the Southwestern periods were better termed stages, and they developed a more generalised, dendritic or tree-like scheme which, while it had genealogical implications, was independent of chronology (Gladwin and Gladwin 1934). Thus at the base of the tree was the root which referred to the broadest cultural divisions in the Southwest. The root was subdivided into stems, then branches and finally phases which was the smallest cultural unit. It was presumed that the increasing cultural differentiation through the tree system had chronological implications so that, in other words, genetic relationships could be inferred through the branching system and, more dubiously, all the cultures in the Southwest ultimately derived from a common ancestor exemplified in the root traits shared by all.

The system was modified by Colton in the light of the Midwestern system (see below) but while the smaller subdivisions remain in use, the genetic model as a whole has been dropped. Contemporary with the Gladwins' system for the Southwest was the Midwestern classification developed by a conference group in 1932 and revised by McKern a few years later (McKern 1939). Unlike the Gladwins' system, this had no genetic implications and was more a purely formal taxonomy based on cultural similarity, a fact which may partly have related to the lack of deeply stratified sites and the wealth of unintegrated museum collections which existed in the Midwest (Willey and Sabloff 1993: 123–4). However, more importantly, the problem with genetic interpretations of the tree is that they do not allow for any cross-cultural contact between phases – that is, all cultural similarities are subsumed under a genetic model which cannot show diffusionary processes across the splits (McKern 1939: 312). Nevertheless, it did not preclude genetic interpretations and formally, it looks very similar to the Gladwin's system (see Figure 15).

The Midwestern taxonomic method was perhaps the most successful; it was copied for other areas and also used to modify the Gladwin system. At the bottom of such systems were the sites, or more specifically (given multi-period sites), the component (i.e. the assemblage). It is this which provided the basic material on which cultural similarities were compared, much as they did in Europe (cf. Table 5, p. 113). As the theoretical ground shifted in the 1950s, however, such taxonomies began to decline and the only terms to remain in use were the smallest and largest (as well as the component), with foci simply arranged chronologically and geographically, enfolded within a larger pattern (Rouse 1972: 76; also see Rouse 1955). However, it was the smallest, the focus (and its relation to the component) which remained the primary unit. Culture historical syntheses reached their zenith with *Indians before Columbus* (1947) by Martin, Quimby and Collier, which was essentially a descriptive list of traits defining culture areas and regions for the whole of North America, with accompanying chronology charts at the back. Although not explicitly adopting the terminology, the text and charts exhibit a clear minimalist classification based on the focus which they termed the 'culture', which was located in a spatio-temporal framework (Martin, Quimby and Collier 1947, figure 122).

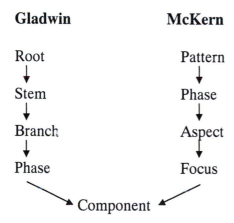

Figure 15 North American culture classification schemes

The shift towards a more minimalist culture classification (as used in Europe) was theoretically marked in a paper by Gordon Willey and Philip Phillips (published in two parts in 1953 and 1955), and later expanded into a book, *Method and Theory in American Archaeology* (Willey and Phillips 1958). The problem with the taxonomic classifications remained the inherent pull of a genetic interpretation to cultural similarity because of its root structure, and so cultural similarities tended to be predominantly viewed – and explained – in genealogical or genetic terms. As the 1950s witnessed an increasing concern for functional interpretations, the need to actually examine the relationships between cultures (i.e. phases or foci) rather than simply classify that relationship became more important. Thus Willey and Phillips constructed a scheme which employed only the most basic elements of the taxonomic systems, the component and the focus (what they called the phase), which were cross-cut by two axes, the tradition and the horizon (Willey and Phillips 1958: 41). Adopting Kroeber's concept of the horizon style as a dissemination or diffusion of traits over a large area for a delimited period, they offset this with Willey's concept of tradition which designated the long-term persistence of traits within the same area. The two concepts of horizon and tradition provided what they saw as an integrative approach to providing area syntheses, yielding a balanced model between genetic and diffusionary relationships between cultures.

In a response to the first part of Willey and Phillips' original paper, Rouse re-affirmed the central importance of the component and focus/phase and elegantly argued for the importance of a staged approach using solely these units and their correlation across time and space (Rouse 1955). He found the concepts of tradition and horizon inadequate and argued for the need to correlate foci/phases in a more systematic way, promoting a three-step process: descriptive (i.e. formal or typological), distributional (i.e. through physical contiguity, either spatially or temporally) and finally genetic (i.e. through diffusion or temporal continuity). The critical point was that no classificatory scheme could encompass these possibilities within a single model since both distributional and genetic correlations could be highly variable (Rouse 1955: 720). None the less, while there were many innovations in Rouse's and Willey and Phillips' scheme, both reinforced the basic principle of culture classification, if not taxonomically, then minimally through the preservation of the focus and its determination in space and time. Essentially, this is what was occurring in Europe, where the culture group was the equivalent term to the focus/phase (Rouse 1955: 713). Indeed, despite the rise and fall of taxonomic systems in the USA, in their aftermath the same basic approach to cultural division as seen in Europe remained intact, with the culture group forming the basis of understanding variability in the archaeological record.

How influential are these cultural classifications today? While few would openly adopt the taxonomic or hierarchical method, the basic idea of a cultural area or region defined by similarities in constituent assemblages remains a dominant, if not always explicit concept in archaeology. We still draw general temporal and spatial limits around our data, which are often based on the same culture divisions created earlier in the twentieth century, whether it is broad periods such as the Three Age System or more particular ones such as Beaker or the Hopewell. The word 'culture' frequently still stands as a shorthand or generic term for the circumscription of assemblages of material culture in space and time. To this extent, the culture classifications of the 1920s-1950s still influence the way we do archaeology today, including the fact that as archaeologists we usually specialise in a particular area and period which was defined by these classifications. At this level, the historical reasons for contemporary practice are perhaps quite clear and to some degree unsurprising. Most archaeologists base their interpretive research within the framework of culture historical divisions; much of archaeology is taught at an undergraduate level on a region and period basis; and if an archaeologist were to work in a new or unknown area, there is little doubt that one of the first tasks of fieldwork would be to construct a local chronology or type series. There remains a strong sense in which time-space parameters of material culture form the basis to any interpretive study. What validity though, if any, do such classifications have today?

Ethnicity and the critique of the culture concept

To help understand this question, it is important to consider further how the concept of culture has been articulated in archaeology over the past century or so (e.g. Kroeber and Kluckhohn 1952; Trigger 1978; Watson 1995). It was only by the eighteenth century that the term 'culture', which derived from Latin and was associated with agriculture (i.e. cultivation), took on its meaning of human enlightenment of progress (Trigger 1978: 75; Díaz-Andreu 1996: 51–2). Very soon afterwards, both in Spain and Germany, it also came to be used more specifically for the customs or beliefs of a particular nation or people, by writers such as Herder or de Masdeu (Díaz-Andreu 1996). Its use continued into the nineteenth century where, in Germany in particular, it became associated with a growing field of culture historical studies (*Kulturgeschichte*) associated with Gustav Klemm. In contrast, in Britain and France the word 'civilisation' was used instead – typically by E. B. Tylor – although towards the end of the nineteenth century the word 'culture' was slowly adopted and eventually replaced 'civilisation' by the middle of the next century. Thus Tylor's classic definition: 'Culture or Civilisation, taken in its widest ethnographic sense, is that complex whole which includes knowledge, belief, arts, morals, law, custom and other capabilities and habits acquired by man as a member of society' (Tylor 1871: 1).

Throughout the nineteenth century, cultural differences also had racial associations, although this classification usually had an influence on a wider sphere between the West and the Rest. Nevertheless, archaeological studies of the later nineteenth century and early twentieth often linked racial types (based on skulls) with particular cultural periods. In terms of material culture and artefacts, the association of particular types with this partitive concept of culture was prefigured in earlier post-Renaissance attempts to link historically attested people such as the Saxons and Celts with material remains although under quite different epistemological conditions (Hides 1996). This only developed more systematically in the later nineteenth century where ethnic groups were linked to material culture by researchers such as Montelius or Rudolf Virchow. The classic expression of this approach was however by Gustav Kossinna in *Die Herkunft der Germanen* (The Origin of the Germans) published in 1911. In this work he promoted the notion of culture as definable archaeologically through spatial and temporal continuity of a number of traits and made identifications of major ethnic groups such as Germans, Slavs and Celts, as well as more particular tribes (Jones 1997: 16). Both Kossinna and later Oswald Menghin were key influences on Gordon Childe, who is regarded as the pivotal figure in the establishment of the culture-historical approach in archaeology although, as Sian Jones remarks, many of his contemporaries such as Crawford were using the term in similar ways (Crawford 1921; Jones 1997: 16–17). While Childe first used the term 'archaeological culture' in *The Danube in Prehistory* (1929), it was in his classic paper 'Changing methods and aims in prehistory' (1935) that he defined culture more explicitly:

> The culture is not an a priori category elaborated in the studies of philosophers and then imposed from outside upon working archaeologists. Cultures are observed facts. The field-worker does find specific types of tools, weapons, and ornaments repeatedly associated together in graves and habitations of one kind and contrasted with the artifacts found in graves and settlements of another kind. The interpretation of the observed phenomenon is supplied by ethnography. The traits of a culture are thus presented together to the archaeologists because they are the creations of a single people, adjustments to its environment approved by its collective experience; they thus express the individuality of a human group united by common social traditions.
>
> (Childe 1935: 3)

Childe's understanding of culture underwent various changes in his lifetime. In particular he grew more and more cautious over identifying the archaeological culture with any linguistic, ethnographic or political unit (e.g. Childe 1956: 132–3; see McNairn 1980: 46–73). However, the interpretation of the archaeological culture as a bounded unit of material traits and equivalent in some way to a bounded social unit remained, and it is a basic understanding which persisted until its critique in the 1960s and 1970s (Jones 1997: 24).

In the USA, the association between the archaeological culture and an ethnographic conception of culture was even stronger due to the close links between ethnography and archaeology and the predominance of the culture-area approach (see p. 47). In a classic review paper by Dixon entitled 'Some aspects of North American archaeology' published in 1913, he describes archaeology as 'prehistoric ethnology and ethnography – the incomplete and wasted records of cultures which, often in vain, we try to reconstruct and affiliate with their historic descendants' (Dixon 1913: 558). For Dixon, such an approach characterised a scientific and systematic archaeology, distinct from mere antiquarianism (ibid.: 565–6). Dixon's call was later to crystallise into what became known as the direct historical approach, first coined by W. R. Wedel (1938); it was a method which involved working backwards from the ethnographic to the archaeological record to establish continuities. On its own, it had severe limitations, not least its presumption of the ahistorical nature of ethnographic groupings and lack of concern for chronology. However, despite some differences, it was retained as a useful tool in the reconstruction of culture history in conjunction with the taxonomic methods (McKern 1942). With the development of culture classification and taxonomies in the late 1920s and 1930s, the ethnographic link with archaeological cultures was increasingly downplayed although a broad association with 'a people' was tacitly assumed (e.g. Colton 1942). As late as 1972, Rouse was still arguing that his cultural complexes were effectively the assemblages associated with a cultural group (Rouse 1972: 87).

The implicit understanding of culture in archaeology until the 1960s was thus one of a bounded, homogeneous entity which 'more or less' corresponded with a comparable social unit – a people, an ethnic group and, in some cases, a race. It was this normative concept which came under fire in the New Archaeology. However, an important distinction needs to be made between two uses of the word 'culture', a distinction made by Taylor in 1948 between a holistic and partitive conception (Taylor 1948: ch. 4). The holistic sense applied to culture as an attribute of humans and human society – it was a generic term which distinguished humans from other animals. The partitive sense was the one I have been discussing above – it is a particular manifestation of the generic sense among a group of people. The distinction, though made by Taylor, existed tacitly before – archaeologists such as Childe sometimes talked about culture in a more holistic sense, particularly in distinguishing the biological and racial aspects of humans (McNairn 1980: 52–3). More generally, it is a distinction simply between the diversity of humans and their common humanity.

Most critiques of the culture concept since the 1960s – both the processual reaction to traditional culture-historical archaeology and the post-processual reaction to the New Archaeology – have focused on the former, holistic sense of the term. Processual archaeologists discuss culture as an adaptive or functional system, while post-processualists view it as symbolic or meaningfully constituted for example, and so on. The focus of this debate has largely been at this generic level of the culture concept since the 1960s (e.g. see Watson 1995). In contrast – and as a consequence – discussion of the partitive sense of the term was largely backgrounded. The kinds of critiques that did emerge about the partitive meaning of culture were mostly about the polythetic nature of cultures and their 'fuzziness ', a point which however went back to Childe (Childe 1956: 33–4; cf. Clarke 1968: 35–7, 263–6). Colin Renfrew took this argument to an extreme in 1977 when he argued that the notion of a culture group was a fiction. His paper 'Space, time and polity' accentuated the problem of the fluidity of the culture group:

> For it is easy to show how spatial distributions, equivalent to the tradi-
> tional cultural entities, can be generated by the archaeologist out of a
> continuum of change. If uniformities and similarities in artefact assem-
> blages are viewed as the result of interactions between individuals, and
> if such interactions decrease in intensity uniformly with distance, each
> point will be most like its close neighbours. Consider the point P lying
> in a uniform plain, with its neighbours fairly regularly spaced around
> it. Similarity in terms of trait C decreases with distance from point P.
> At the same time the variables A and B vary uniformly across the plain
> with distance along the axes x and y. If the excavator first digs at P
> and recovers its assemblage, he will subsequently learn that adjacent
> points have a broadly similar assemblage, which he will call 'the P
> culture'. Gradually its boundaries will be set up by further research,
> with the criterion that only those assemblages which attain a given
> threshold level of similarity with the finds from P qualify for inclusion.
> So a 'culture' is born, centring on P, the type site, whose bounds are
> entirely arbitrary, depending solely on the threshold level of similarity
> and the initial, fortuitous choice of P as the point of reference.
>
> (Renfrew 1977: 94–5)

Renfrew's argument is in many ways the same as that given by Ford years earlier regarding the question of whether types are real (Ford 1954; also see Chapter 3). Yet as Hodder pointed out and Renfrew admitted, the notion that 'culture' is a homogeneous continuum *may* be the case, but not necessarily. Such a situation is only true if the association between the groups is random; analysis can distinguish if the discontinuity is random or not and at what scale it operates (Hodder and Orton 1978; Hodder 1982: 6–7). Indeed, in his paper Renfrew does not really overturn the notion of bounded entities in the past but rather reformulates them in terms of neo-evolutionary social organisation and the archaeological correlates of such entities. More importantly, though, just as processualists never really addressed the concept of style in artefacts, so they never really grappled with the problem of identity or ethnicity in culture.

Thus, despite the shift from a normative to a functional (and later symbolic) conception of culture, the issue of cultural identity was largely pushed to one side in the wake of the New Archaeology (Jones 1997: 27). While there were severe critiques of the normativism implicit in this concept of culture, there were few attempts to address the nature of specific cultural identity or ethnicity (but see p. 138). In fact, in many ways the use of culture classifications, as I have already mentioned, continued – and continues in practice with little thought for what this might mean (ibid.). Part of this relates to the fact that such classifications are often considered an empirical rather than interpretive question – yet, as this chapter is attempting to show, such a distinction is highly flawed. However, another part is related to the fact that ethnicity remained implicitly regarded as a normative concept and, given the processual turn, attention naturally turned to more dynamic and functional interpretations of spatial and temporal variability. In the next section, I want to examine these other dimensions and look at how variability has been interpreted across space and time since the 1960s. At the end of the chapter, I will return to the theme of iden-tity and, in particular, raise issues about the consequences for an archaeology which abandons a partitive concept of culture – at least as a privileged axis of differentiation.

The interpretation of spatio-temporal variability

Settlement and spatial archaeologies

The demise of the normative view of culture was already presaged in the late 1940s with the call for more functionalistic interpretations of culture such as those of Steward and Setzler (1938), a trend in the USA summarised in a paper by Bennett (1943). However, Taylor's 'A study of archaeology' and its promotion of a conjunctive approach was the first in-depth critique of culture classification – or the 'comparative approach' as he termed it. He called for the study of the relations *within* cultures as well as between them: 'This attitude, the conjunctive approach, considers a site to be a discrete entity with career and cultural expressions of its own. It is no longer just one more unit in a spatial and temporal range of comparative units' (Taylor 1948: 96).

Taylor's conjunctive approach was important in highlighting the impor-tance of a site as a locus of activity, rather than just a manifestation of a culture group, and it was this critical recognition which was pivotal in changing the way spatio-temporal differences in assemblages were viewed. Two kinds of approaches to a more site-oriented archaeology developed in the second half of the twentieth century, both in Britain and the USA, one coming from a more ecological or economic context, the other being more social or political in orientation (Trigger 1968). Such approaches in the USA took their direct influence from Steward, whose work was ecolog-ically oriented, rather than from Taylor who, despite addressing a wide range of fundamental issues, for a number of reasons never had the impact he deserved (Watson 1995: 685–6). Julian Steward's *Theory of Culture Change* was, with Willey and Phillips' *Method and Theory*, a major theo-retical text of the 1950s. Published in 1955, it explicitly distinguished between a scientific, generalising approach and a historical, particularising approach, boldly favouring the former (Steward 1955: 3). Outlining his famous concepts of multi-linear evolution and cultural ecology, of partic-ular relevance here that he uses of different levels of socio-cultural integration (e.g. the family, the community, the nation); moreover, he crit-icised the 'culture-area' concept of cultural classifications, arguing that it had serious limitations when trying to analyse process or function.

While Steward's work was perhaps the most important of its kind in the 1950s, subsequent ecological and environmental approaches were perhaps more influenced by Leslie White, especially through his student Betty Meggers. Meggers adopted a quite explicit environmental determinism along with White's more rigid unilinear evolutionism, both of which she outlined as the basis for a new synthesis in archaeology in the volume *New Interpretations of Aboriginal American Culture History*, published in the same year as Steward's book (Meggers 1955; also see Meggers 1954). This volume is interesting in that many of the papers read like traditional culture history with merely a nod in the direction of environmental and evolutionary factors, and Meggers' claim for 'new interpretations' seems rather hollow, her own work excepted. It was in Britain and Europe that many of the more explicit models in an ecological approach were developed. Topographical approaches to archaeology had a long pedigree in Britain (see Chapter one) and between the 1920s and 1950s the work of Cyril Fox, O. G. S. Crawford and especially Grahame Clark all helped to estab-lish the importance of seeing an archaeological site in its environmental context.

Grahame Clark's first general book *Archaeology and Society* published in 1939, argued from a functionalist standpoint but in direct opposition to Childe's Marxism. Clark asserted that the primary function of any society was survival and that therefore ecological constraints acted on all societies. The importance of understanding the environment and its effect on societies was therefore basic to archaeology. Indeed he claimed, as did others of the period, that the economic aspects to a society were easier to understand in archaeological contexts than those of social organisation or belief because of the material nature of archaeological data. Clark's ideas received their applied expression through his work on the mesolithic site of Star Carr and his general synthesis *Prehistoric Europe: The Economic Basis*, both published in the 1950s (Clark 1952, 1954). The latter explicitly related broad economic systems to ecological zones, drawing on the concept of ecosystem.

The direct descendant of Clark's approach came in the 1970s with the work of the Cambridge-based palaeoeconomic school. Using geographical models, Eric Higgs and C. Vita-Finzi developed the concept of site-catchment analysis which made far more explicit the ideas of the previous generation on the importance of environmental context (Vita-Finzi and Higgs 1970). By circumscribing an area around a site, the available resources and access to those resources could be mapped out and associated with the subsistence of the site. Through two books edited by Higgs, the palaeoeconomic approach was developed further and focused on the relationship between population and resources, although it is the model of site-catchment that has remained the enduring contribution (Higgs 1972, 1975).

The other strand of settlement archaeology, while not excluding environmental factors, focused much more on the social organisation of settlements, examining settlements in relation to each other rather than just to their environment. In the USA, Willey and Phillips, although heavily influenced by Steward, went beyond his ecological approach to consider this broader relationship. In their *Method and Theory in American Archaeology* published in 1958 they similarly describe different levels of integration, although clearly from a more archaeological perspective, defining three types of archaeological data – the first being the formal or material type (i.e. the component and focus), the second two being spatial and temporal. These latter two are manifest at different scales, primarily defined by the spatial: thus the site lies at the lowest level, then locality, region and area, with temporal sequences based on these spatial ones (i.e. local sequence and regional sequence; Willey and Phillips 1958: 17–27). The idea that differences between assemblages might relate to functional relations between sites rather than simply demarcate cultural entities gained practical application in Willey's project in the Virú valley, Peru, published a few years earlier. Encouraged by Steward but going beyond his cultural ecology, Willey looked at the different kinds of sites in the Virú valley (such as cemeteries, settlements, temples) in terms of changing patterns of social and political organisation (Willey 1953). Willey's study stimulated a spate of similar surveys such as Robert Adams' research in the Near East. In 1968 a volume called *Settlement Archaeology* was published in which Willey looked back and interestingly appraised such studies as indicative of new *approaches* but not a new *archaeology* (Willey 1968: 208; Chang 1968).

Nevertheless, the volume contained some interesting debates, particularly between Chang and Rouse over the primacy of settlement as a unit of analysis, which did not impress Willey. While Rouse argued for the primacy of the component-focus on the basis of a traditional epistemology which moved from description to interpretation, Chang saw the archaeological process as one of continual interpretation focused on typological variation within and between settlements (Rouse 1968; Chang 1968). The difference was more than procedural as Willey seemed to think, but rather went to the heart of the distinction between cultural, classificatory and processual approaches to settlement: for Rouse, the culture group remained more basic, while for Chang what was important was the settlement, or the site where people lived. This point Chang had made in a paper published ten years earlier, drawing on ethnographic information for the relation between social organisation and settlement patterns. It was perhaps ten years too early (Chang 1958).

The settlement approach only really became significant under the New Archaeology where it was more fully developed in papers by Binford and Streuver (Binford 1964; Streuver 1968b). Both authors discussed the issue in terms of research design and the rise of sampling procedures, highlighting the significance of site location and distribution. A similar focus on such issues also developed in Britain (e.g. Cherry and Shennan 1978). However, perhaps the best practical example of the time was the volume edited by Kent Flannery, *The Early Mesoamerican Village*, published in 1976, which employed the same idea of different levels of socio-cultural integration as espoused by Willey and Phillips. Flannery uses a very detailed spatial hierarchy starting with the smallest unit, the feature, through activity area, household, village, and so on up to regional and inter-regional network units. While he cites Streuver as an influence, he was also drawing on human geography, particularly Peter Haggett's locational analysis (Flannery 1976: 8). It was Gregory Johnson, however, who most explicitly used geographical approaches in the USA, partly influenced by the developments in Britain (Johnson 1977).

In Britain, a similar change was occurring which was much more heavily influenced by human geography – indeed the theoretical developments in archaeology and geography often mirrored each other (Earle and Preucel 1987; Wagstaff 1987; Tilley 1994: 7). Moreover, in Britain there was a previous history of using geographical and topographical frameworks to analyse the archaeological record, especially through the work of O. G. S. Crawford who moved from geography into archaeology. His major book *Man and his Past*, published in 1921, is pervaded by his geographical background, as was his early study of the relation of Bronze Age settlement to topography and geology (Crawford 1912; 1921: 80–2). Crawford even went so far as to say that 'it is probable that most of the advances in archaeological knowledge will be made by means of geographical studies' (Crawford 1921: 132). However, while Crawford was using geographical approaches, this remained within a culture-group approach and the most his and other comparable studies ever achieved was to correlate cultural divisions with geographical ones. It was not until the 1970s under the influence of David Clarke that more dynamic approaches were taken, characterised by the sub-field of spatial archaeology.

David Clarke drew heavily on contemporary ideas in geography, particularly the work of Haggett on locational analysis to which Flannery was also drawn; Clarke even named his book *Models in Archaeology* after one of Haggett's. It was this work by Clarke, published in 1972, which created the focus for spatial archaeologies from which a number of other works followed, such as Clarke's *Spatial Archaeology* (1977), Ian Hodder and Clive Orton's *Spatial Analysis in Archaeology* (1976) and Hodder's *The Spatial Organization of Culture* (1978). It was Hodder's co-authored book which provided the heavy-duty methodological grounding for such studies, drawing on current quantitative techniques in geography such as point pattern analysis, regression analysis and spatial association. There Hodder and Orton emphasised the importance of quantitative approaches (as opposed to the usual 'dots on maps' which most archaeologists employed), as well as the related need to understand the processes which lead to the spatial patterning observed in the archaeological record (Hodder and Orton 1976: 8). It clearly represented a need to go beyond many of the more simplistic invasionist/diffusionist interpretations of distribution patterns which characterised the earlier culture-group model of prehistory (e.g. Renfrew 1969), while also being part of the scientific discourse which marked so much of the New Archaeology. Such approaches continued into the 1980s and after, as models such as central-place theory and rank-size distributions were used to analyse the spatial organisation of settlement structures, especially of more complex societies.

Spatial analysis *within* sites was comparatively under-developed until the 1980s. One of the earliest attempts was Grahame Clark's excavation of the mesolithic site at Star Carr where he looked at artefact patterning to interpret the nature of the site (Clark 1954). However, it was only in the 1960s/1970s that such studies became more common and were informed by a more explicit methodological approach. Two broad kinds of analysis can be identified; one which studies a point pattern *distribution* of an artefact (or the co-occurrence of more than one artefact), and the other which uses broader deposit or feature association with an artefact or artefacts. The former was pioneered in particular by Leroi-Gourhan and his colleagues at the Upper Palaeolithic site of Pincevent, France, inaugurating a new era in intra-site spatial analysis (Leroi-Gourhan and Brézillon 1966). This has subsequently been developed through the use of quantitative techniques and ethnoarchaeological studies, particularly by Robert Whallon and others, initially as part of the attempt to resolve the function–style debate of Lewis Binford and François Bordes (Whallon 1973; Kroll and Price 1991b: 2). The 1980s saw a proliferation of such intra-site spatial analyses which has continued and developed many of the major themes of the 1970s (e.g. see the papers in Hietala 1984, Kent 1987 and Kroll and Price 1991a).

One of the problems faced by mainly the broader, regional approaches was the heterogeneity of space – that is, the real space of mountains, rivers, coast-lines – of topography. All the more analytical studies developed in the 1970s on proximity or distance either between sites and a centre (such as regression analysis and trend surface analysis) or between all sites in a given area (such as nearest neighbour analysis and the construction of Thiessen polygons), faced this problem. Hodder and Orton's study of Oxfordshire Roman pottery, for example, showed how an apparently random distribution of sites made sense when two fall-off curves were separated according to whether sites could be reached by water or not (Hodder and Orton 1976). Such awareness of the heterogeneity of space has perhaps increased since those early days, leading to a more landscape-oriented perspective which sees a site's location less as grid co-ordinates and more in terms of local topography.

The shift from spatial archaeology to what might best be termed landscape archaeology is both a continuation and critique of the spatial archaeology of the 1970s. Landscape archaeology covers a diversity of approaches not necessarily tied to any particular theoretical orientation, and at a general level it is simply the concern to understand the archaeological record not through sites but through landscapes. In some ways the logic of such an approach is to invert the whole relationship between site and landscape, and indeed begs the question – what is a site? (this is discussed more in the next chapter). In terms of continuity of the processual and modelling approaches, the recognition of multiple scales of analysis – especially as this links into taphonomic and actualistic studies – is a major concern (e.g. Rossignol and Wandsnider 1992). Another facet of processual landscape approaches is expressed through historical ecology which focuses on the landscape as a natural and cultural formation in a historical perspective (e.g. Crumley and Marquardt 1990; Crumley 1994). These theoretical approaches, however, are frequently expressed through Geographical Information Systems (GIS) which are among the most significant innovations in recent years, developing out of the spatial archaeology and related fields such as predictive modelling (Kvamme 1999). The publication of *Interpreting Space: GIS and Archaeology* (Allen *et al.* 1989) marked a turning point, and has been followed by a number of papers dealing with its application (e.g. see papers in Andresen *et al.* 1993; Lock and Moffett 1992; Lock and Stančič 1995; for overview, see Kvamme 1999).

Most GIS studies have shown a continuation of processual, functional-environmental concerns such as mapping ease of access through a terrain in terms of natural constraints (cost-surface analysis), but this use of GIS has been criticised (e.g. Wheatley 1993; Gaffney and van Leusen 1995). Wheatley has argued that GIS should not be seen as a theoretically neutral tool and that post-functionalist frameworks might be adopted which introduce social perceptions of landscape. Use of intervisibility and viewsheds has become a common example, but Wheatley, more subtly, brings the presence of long barrows into a cost-surface analysis of the Neolithic enclosure Windmill Hill in Britain as potential access-blocks (Wheatley 1993). Another major issue lies in the question of temporality – GIS has the potential to work with a much more fluid temporality, yet so far it has not taken this up and generally uses phase or period changes (Castleford 1992).

The post-functional critique of GIS is linked directly to the more recent theoretical developments, particularly post-processualism which began to consider space as a social category and completely alters the way the landscape is studied (Wagstaff 1987; Bender 1992, 1993; Tilley 1994; Ashmore and Knapp 1999). Christopher Tilley's small book A *Phenomenology of Landscape* (1994) is perhaps the most theoretical treatment, outlining the major themes of a socialised view of space from the perspective of lived experience. A fundamental concept is that of *place*, which is the primary way in which humans experience space. We do not think to ourselves we are at such and such a grid co-ordinate (except in the context perhaps of using maps), but rather 'at home', 'at the park', 'on the bus', or even 'abroad' (Tilley 1994: 14–17). Space is always defined and experienced in such ways. On a social level, the common experience of space is defined as a *locale*, locales being parts of the *landscape* which are connected through *paths*. These concepts of locale, landscape and path are all socialised spaces, for example places of memory, landscapes of power or journeys/stories along paths; Tilley's book is mostly given over to case studies exemplifying such themes. A recent collection of papers illustrates this socialisation of landscape in other concrete ways, such as how landscape is caught up in sustaining social memory, creating identities, as a macrocosm of the social order and through long-term history (Ashmore and Knapp 1999).

Comparable approaches have been applied to intra-site analysis, although perhaps the very distinction becomes suspect (Parker-Pearson and Richards 1994); the key articulation here is through concepts of lived or occupied space, most notably (but not exclusively) exemplified through architecture. The layout of settlements or buildings and the way these associate with social or ideological categories such as gender divisions or cosmological principles is a prominent theme. The example of Later British Prehistoric houses provides a good example – at a very general level, the recurrent positioning of entrances facing east yields an east–west structuring axis which can be argued to link with a range of social classifications affecting gender and domestic tasks (Parker-Pearson 1996). Moreover, the entrance is usually marked out in special ways (deposits, porch) which emphasise its status as a threshold, mediating between the inside and the outside. Such simple architectural structures are of course overlain by more complex patterns which change through time, but they illustrate how the structure of space is socially organised through architecture.

Explanations of culture change: from evolutionism to Annales

If the spatial archaeology of the 1970s was prefigured by the shift to settlement archaeology in the 1950s, similarly one can see the development of processual archaeology and the concern for culture change in the emergence of neo-evolutionism during the post-war period. Culture history is frequently painted in sharp contrast to cultural evolution, the one a particularising interpretation the other generalising. North American archaeology, for example, in its early culture-historical period is often portrayed as violently particularistic and anti-evolutionary. Yet in the decades before New Archaeology, culture history and cultural evolution were actually regarded as complementary. Taylor's procedural approach to archaeology distinguished between archaeology as historiography and as anthropology, the one being concerned with specific cultural contexts, the other with culture itself (Taylor 1948: 44). Although it might be fairer to say that Taylor saw this distinction in terms of a temporal and atemporal approach, the same is not true of Willey and Phillips whose work perhaps had much greater impact. Adopting a similar procedural approach to Taylor, they distinguished between culture-historical integration (description) and processual interpretation (explanation), both of which had clear temporal connotations (Willey and Phillips 1958: 4). Their notion of culture-historical integration was clearly reliant on independent chronologies and essentially involved the construction of culture sequences as displayed on chronology charts. Their notion of processual interpretation, however, articulated through an interim concept called the historical-developmental approach, was basically evolutionary, despite their assertions to the contrary, and was inspired by the evolutionary schemes of Steward and Krieger (Willey and Phillips 1958). They quite explicitly argued, as did Childe (see p. 113), for the need to distinguish general cultural *stages* from historical cultural *periods* and, like Childe, they identified their stages in terms of socio-economic developments such as the transition from hunting and gathering to farming. The application of this approach was summarised toward the end of their theoretical work, and in more detail in Willey's two-volume *An Introduction to American Archaeology* published in 1966–71.

In Europe evolutionism was meshed on to culture classification through the traditional Three Age periodisation. Childe, in his classic paper 'Changing methods and aims in prehistory' (1935), attempted to retain the significance of the Three Age System by giving it a functional-economic or evolutionary interpretation. Each period was marked by a major development or revolution in social evolution – the Palaeolithic through the control of fire and other natural objects, the Neolithic through control of other living organisms (i.e. domestication) and in the Bronze Age and Iron Age through the control of other people (through weaponry). Childe is not as explicit here as I have made it, but there is a sense in which the revolutions are about power over successive elements of the world, this succession based on a hierarchy from inanimate, through animate to human. His narratives were inspired by a Marxist view of historical development, as his many general books testify, e.g. *Man Makes Himself* (1936), *Social Evolution* (1951) or *What Happened in History* (1964). The important point, though, is that this evolutionary interpretation did not stand in opposition to a more historically specific one, reliant on an independent chronology; rather the two worked together, especially in resolving the issue of diffusion versus evolution (Childe 1935: 13).

Childe and Willey and Phillips argued that the two approaches were basically complementary. Even the arch-evolutionist Leslie White saw this, although he distinguished three approaches: the historical, the functional and the evolutionary. His distinction between history and evolution in particular is interesting: 'the historic process deals with events determined by specific time and space co-ordinates, in short with unique events, whereas the evolutionary process is concerned with classes of events independent of specific time and place' (White 1945: 230). The same duality was partially translated later into Elman Service's and Marshall Sahlins' distinction between general and specific evolution, the former referring to the ideal stages of cultural development from band to state, the latter to the actual course of cultures through chronological time (Sahlins and Service 1960). One of the more recent extensive treatments of cultural evolution has been *The Evolution of Human Societies* (1987) by Allen Johnson and Timothy Earle, which explicitly takes over from Childe, White, Steward and Service, and re-asserts this distinction (Johnson and Earle 1987: 22–3).

More than being complementary, however, in many other respects the two approaches are remarkably similar, for it can be argued that cultural evolution is, essentially, a classification (e.g. Dunnell 1980: 47). The evolutionism of the nineteenth-century synthesisers, Lewis Henry Morgan, Edward Tyler and John Lubbock, was essentially a typological view of the past, where history progressed (or regressed) according to stages of cultural development such as savagery, barbarism and civilisation. The same model was used by those early in the twentieth century such as Childe in Britain or Leslie White in the USA between the 1930s and 1950s and subsequently by the neo-evolutionists such as Sahlins and Service and, more recently, Johnson and Earle. There is an underlying suspension of space and time in the fixity of these cultural forms, whether they be savagery, barbarism and civilisation, or bands, tribes, chiefdoms and states. Indeed, if the critique of normativism can be levelled at culture history, it equally applies to cultural evolution – and once again the early processualists seem to have been blind to the implications of their own critique. Cultural evolutionism, or neo-evolutionism as it has often been called since the 1960s, employed just as normative a concept of culture in its social forms of band, tribe, chiefdom and state.

Concomitantly, the notion of change is never really problematised which may partly relate to the fact that most of these cultural forms or stages are derived from observation of contemporary societies. Although neo-evolutionists would no longer talk of 'survivals', the underlying assumption that the 'ethnographic present' offers the full array of cultural forms or stages remains the same (Dunnell 1980: 46–7; McGuire 1992: 155). Ultimately, it is ahistorical since its 'history' is based on cultural forms extant in the present day or recent past. This is not to argue that neo-evolutionists do not discuss or describe change, but in many ways the processes invoked do not bear any inherent or necessary relationship to the stages employed (McGuire 1992: 151–3). The work of Johnson and Earle is a case in point – while they criticise the earlier evolutionists for giving typology precedence over causal explanations of social change, they still employ such a typology and explain the archaeological record in terms of the transformation from one stage to another with clear progressivist implications (Johnson and Earle 1987: 3–4). Moreover, their explanations, though paying lip service to the complexity and multilinearity of evolution, are explicitly founded on the primacy of the relationship between population growth and technology.

While neo-evolutionism is still a prominent theory of 'change', since the 1980s it has come under increasing attack as being something of a misnomer in so far as it claims association with natural evolution. Dunnell was one of the first to point out that cultural evolutionism is quite different from Darwinian evolution, for it was Spencer who provided the model for evolutionary theory in archaeology, not Darwin (Dunnell 1980: 40–3). Writing in 1980, Dunnell said archaeologists had yet to apply Darwinism to archaeology (ibid.: 50); twenty years on, the situation has changed and there is a growing literature of evolutionary archaeology (often called selectionism) which is quite distinct from the neo-evolutionism of the New Archaeology (Dunnell 1980; O'Brien and Holland 1992; Teltser 1995; Maschner 1996; Barton and Clark 1997). The major difference lies in the articulation of the concept of adaptation (Dunnell 1980: 49–50; Kirch 1980; O'Brien and Holland 1992; O'Brien 1996); adaptation is a functional concept and as such clearly appealed to New Archaeologists – used in an active sense, a culture which adapts simply means one which adjusts itself to its environment as in a self-regulating system. However, in biology adaptation is primarily employed in a passive sense, as in a species which is adapted to its environment – adaptation occurring not through self-regulation but by random variation and selection. The difference can also be expressed through the fact that just because something is adaptive does not mean it is an adaptation – something may be functional but that does not explain why it is present. Selectionism embraces the duality of continuity and change – continuity through the notion of cultural transmission, and change through the concepts of variation and selection. Cultural evolution was simply about change from one form to another, and because it did not properly problematise change, it did not relate this to continuity. It is this relationship which needs to be foregrounded, and although it takes a long-term perspective, the dynamics of change operate on the small scale – the reproduction of material culture, as the example given in Chapter three demonstrates. It is the long-term, cumulative consequences of the dynamics of the everyday. Selectionism, like Darwinism, does not posit a general theory of history, but of change – there is no teleology, no progressivism, no stages.

One of the key criticisms of selectionism, however, is that because of its very stress on the passive sense of adaptation, it ignores the role of agency in change – while people provide the material and variability upon which selection acts, the selection process itself is beyond the control of individuals or a society (Schiffer 1996; Spencer 1997; Boone and Smith 1998; Lyman and O'Brien 1998). While behavioural approaches would argue that selection can also come under cultural control, selectionists would argue that it is very hard to prove this. More critically, they would argue that to explain selection in terms of human intent is ultimately tautologous – it is explaining adaptation by perceived adaptiveness (Lyman and O'Brien 1998: 617–19). This may be true if explanations of human agency are constructed in purely functional terms, such as optimisation or rational decision making; but if the cultural or social nature of agency is considered, then such an argument loses its force.

Since the 1970s and the emergence of social archaeologies, the role of social and cultural factors in explaining change has become increasingly important, and is exemplified in volumes such as *The Explanation of Culture Change* edited by Renfrew (1973), or *The Evolution of Social Systems* edited by Friedman and Rowlands (1977). Although many of the papers in these volumes retained evolutionary schemes explicitly or implicitly, they also raised the importance of social factors (e.g. political tensions) over natural or environmental (e.g. ecological or demographic) ones, often drawing on Marxist models. Marxism, in particular through its manifestation as critical theory, draws on social explanations of historical change through the concept of the dialectic and structural contradiction. Early uses of Marxism in archaeology involved a quasi-evolutionary approach through the use of modes of production as stages in development, exemplified in Engels' evolution of pre-class to class societies in *The Origin of the Family* (1884). A plethora of alternative and supplemental classifications of modes of production has since been constructed – tributary modes, kin-ordered modes, lineage modes, etc., but their usefulness has been short-lived (Spriggs 1984b: 4–5).

Since the 1980s in Western Europe, through the influence of structuralist Marxism and critical theory, research has shifted the emphasis away from economic/materialist explanations towards those drawing on the significance of ideology and power. Susan Kus in particular criticised the usefulness of any classification of modes of production (Kus 1984). The work of Kus, along with Mike Rowlands, Jonathan Friedman, Barbara Bender and Kristian Kristiansen in Europe has helped to turn attention towards more socially and historically contextual interpretations through analysis of processes such as legitimation ideologies and the circulation of prestige goods (see papers in Spriggs 1984a; also Friedman and Rowlands 1977). Similarly, the work

of Mark Leone and Randy McGuire in North America on historical archaeology and capitalism has drawn on issues of social inequality in areas such
as race, gender or class (e.g. see papers in Miller and Tilley 1984; McGuire
and Paynter 1991).

Beneath this shift, however, a constant theme remains that of *conflict* as the
driving force behind social change; whereas, typically, contradictions within
the economic infrastructure between the forces of production (e.g. technology) and relations of production (organisation of labour) are seen to fuel
change (e.g. Gilman 1984), such sources of conflict have increasingly shifted
into the social and ideological realm. The emergence of social inequalities
through unequal access to resources was developed most famously in the prestige goods model. But at a broad level, Marxist-influenced approaches to social
change in archaeology today focus on a variety of power relations between and
within groups; indeed the very formation of such groups is often historically
derived through unstable power relations within prior groups, which subsequently stabilise through ideology. McGuire sums it up well when he defines
his vision of a Marxist archaeology as one which 'would look at a process of
cultural change that springs from the tension between tradition and transformation' (McGuire 1992: 169). His own study of the nature of Prehispanic
Pueblo social organisation with Dean Saitta is a good example; there they
argue that an internal contradiction between egalitarian and hierarchical
social organisations in Pueblo social life fuelled both aggregation and fission
(McGuire and Saitta 1996). Initially, a communal ideology favoured aggregation of communities, but as thresholds were reached more hierarchical
structures took over; if population declined or productivity increased, egali-
tarianism could return or group fission might occur.

A more recent example of how culture change is interpreted is through
the adoption of *Annales* approaches; over the past decade, several archaeologists have been drawing on the work of this French historical school,
Fernand Braudel perhaps being its most famous exponent (Hodder 1987b;
Bintliff 1991a; Knapp 1992). Basically, a three-tiered or scaled approach to
time is taken – the long, medium and short term – each of which is associated with different historical processes and thus requires different types
of interpretation and to some extent data (see overview in Bintliff 1991b).
Thus the long term, or *longue dureé* as it is known, is associated with long-
term structures affecting society, including environment, technologies but
also ideologies (*mentalités*); the medium term or *conjunctures* encompasses
economic cycles or social structures and ideologies again; finally, the short
term or *événements* is linked to political history or narrative history (in the
traditional sense). The problem with the approach has always been its
inability to integrate the different scales successfully, although two major
themes have been singled out which aid this: the importance of ideology
(*mentalités*) and problem history (*l'histoire problème*) (ibid.). How have these
approaches been applied to archaeology?

Bintliff's own study with Snodgrass of ancient Greece is a good example; he identifies changing demographic patterns from archaeological survey work with *Annaliste* medium-term economic and agrarian cycles (every 400–500 years). The effects of these cycles are noted in inscriptions, especially the downswing which corresponded with a rise in inscriptions indicative of crises, and also by a contemporary chronicler, Polybius (Bintliff 1991b). As a study, it shows how the medium and short term relate – although perhaps it might be said that the one is really controlling the other. Moreover, while archaeologists working in periods with written material might be able to perform this kind of analysis, what of those working in prehistory? A major problem of applying *Annaliste* theory to archaeology is that while archaeology might be able to deal with the long and medium term, the short term is often viewed as inaccessible without written documents (Snodgrass 1991: 57). In defence, it might be said that this is no great loss since these are the least decisive elements in history – indeed, Bintliff's and Snodgrass' analysis seems to suggest just this, for the events recorded in inscriptions and texts are reflective of the larger-scale economic cycles. But this is contradicted by the prominence of event history in much of *Annaliste* work, almost like the anthropological 'thick' description. If short-term events are important, how will this affect archaeology?

Part of the answer lies in what is considered an 'event'; Phil Duke's study, *Points in Time* (1991), looks at the intensification of bison hunting in the last 2,000 years in relation to ideology, in particular as this is manifest in the gender distinction between procurement and processing activities associated with the hunt. He places this ideology alongside the environmental conditions as part of the long-term structures associated with the practice, as distinct from events which mark radical breaks in these structures. Examples of 'events' include environmental change as well as European colonisation, the latter having had a deep effect on the gender divisions implicit in the difference between procurement and processing. The different *dureés* can be seen not as historical but social structures operating at different temporal scales.

Moreover, while archaeology does not have written narratives of events, it does have material narratives. Indeed the larger part of the archaeological record is made up precisely of these short-term events – digging a pit, building a house, burying a corpse. It is ironic that so much of archaeological interpretation dwells in medium- and long-term structures while its data is made up of the everyday. As Stephen Shennan has written: 'one of the problems with much existing social archaeology is that it has tried to write a history of very generalised social institutions, made up of vague roles, when it has evidence in general not of roles but of practices' (Shennan 1993: 55). Part of this relates to the problem of contemporaneity – we may have snapshots of events, which are the everyday, but we can rarely put them together except on a much larger scale because of dating resolution among other things. An intermediate level is missing (which is really perhaps the true analogue of the *Annaliste* short term). This is perhaps the character of archaeological data, as Shennan points out – that it has access both to the very long term and also to the everyday; as such its temporalities are slightly different from those of the three-tier *Annaliste* history, with more of an opposition between structure and event, an opposition which perhaps underlies *Annaliste* theory too (Braudel 1980).

Such archaeological events are thus interpreted through longer-term structures in terms of repetitive practices as in for example the structuration theory of Anthony Giddens and Pierre Bourdieu as it is applied in archaeology (Shennan 1993: 55). To some, the shift towards social explanations of culture change, especially from post-processual perspectives, has gone too far in ignoring the influence of natural/environmental factors. Indeed, while for Braudel the *longue durée* encompassed just such factors, this has tended to be downplayed, especially in favour of long-term *mentalités*. Alongside the post-processual approaches, more mainstream processual oriented approaches have emerged which attempt to incorporate many of the points about the influence of cultural factors while still maintaining the importance of the environment. Perhaps the most sophisticated and recent articulation of this approach is historical ecology (e.g. Crumley 1994).

In part emerging out of the contemporary recognition of the effects our own actions, such as deforestation and use of CFC's, have on the environment, historical ecology is a multi-disciplinary perspective which focuses in particular on local scales of human–environment interaction and can thus be seen as a kind of landscape archaeology (see p. 128). Avowedly anti-deterministic, rather than view social change as determined by environmental change, historical ecology sees the two as interactive and mutually determining. A good example comes from the Norse extinction in Greenland (McGovern 1994); Vikings colonised Greenland in the tenth century as part of a wider westward expansion, but unlike the other colonies such as Iceland, by the end of the fifteenth century, their society had become extinct. McGovern argues that this happened through a combination of environmental change and cultural response. In the thirteenth century what is known as a little Ice Age occurred in which the climate deteriorated radically; usually this is cited as the cause of extinction but, as McGovern argues, this paints the Norse as too passive; after all, the Inuit survived. Clearly the difference must lie in cultural factors, and McGovern argues that it was through clinging to cognitive structures and models of subsistence brought with them from mainland Europe that their demise came about.

What unites all the interpretive approaches discussed so far is their focus on medium- or long-term processes. Recently, a number of studies of change have focused on smaller-scale temporal processes than those just described, in particular the role of social memory in the reproduction and transformation of society. Mizoguchi's study of Beaker burial in Britain argues that the time lapse between primary and secondary interments in barrows was used as an 'authoritative resource'; in so far as the knowledge or memory of the primary interment carried greater value, the longer the time lapse. Memory of the location and position of the interment, and of who it was, was critical to a successful secondary burial and to maintaining a repetitive cycle which placed adult males as primary and females and juveniles as secondary (Mizoguchi 1993). Another example is Jo Kovacik's study of the sustained deposition of specific animal species in particular locations of Pueblo buildings in Chaco Canyon, New Mexico (Kovacik 1998). He interprets this practice as a way of maintaining a historical relationship with the site and the past and, equally, of reinforcing a communal ethos, especially given the fact that the acquisition of the species involved would have required collective effort. Thus the simple fact of a repetitive act which continued unchanged over generations requires interpretation which relies on the function of social memory.

Another area of socially constructed temporality, only recently covered, concerns the developmental cycles of social groups. Melissa Goodman, studying Andean settlement, argues that attention to household variability within settlements might yield information on the different stages of a household cycle. For example, a newly married couple in a household might organise space quite differently from an old couple or one with a large family (Goodman 1999). A focus on generational time, if integrated with other issues affecting intra-site household variability (e.g. status), will not only enrich our perspective of the past, she argues, but also aid understanding of how households and larger-scale social organisations interact and change through time. Another example, from the other perspective so to speak, is Paul Lane's ethnoarchaeological work on the Dogon of Mali. He shows how a model of the domestic cycle is maintained despite changes such as the recategorisation of space, residence mobility and ageing (Lane 1987). In particular, he highlights material practices surrounding a woman's arrival into her husband's house as being stable over time because of its association with the importance of affinal kin to the maintenance of the lineage. Both of these studies raise the importance of smaller-scale temporalities focused on the household which can be juxtaposed with other work on abandonment (e.g. Cameron and Tomkin 1993) or, more interestingly, Ruth Tringham's work on the death of the house (Tringham 1991).

Studies of this kind and those which look at social memory are extremely promising directions, for they point out the importance – and accessibility – of temporality in the relatively short term in contrast to the longer-term approaches with which archaeology is usually associated (e.g. Hodder 1987b). Moreover, they also provide archaeological examples of the more general critiques of the concept of time by Shanks and Tilley who argue that time, as with space, is a socially constructed category and needs to be engaged as such in the archaeological record (Shanks and Tilley 1987a, b and c). Indeed, if we recognise that spatial or temporal variability can be interpreted in terms of social perceptions/constructions of space and time, how might this tie in with the question of cultural identity or ethnicity? If the spatial and temporal variability of the archaeological record can be seen in terms of people's perceptions of space and time in the past, then to what extent can we see our cultural classifications and periodisations *also* as social constructs in the past – and what are the implications for archaeology and area/period specialisms if we can?

Crossing cultures

Ethnicity, periodisation and the culture concept

Both cultural classifications (in the broadest sense) and periodisations are very deeply sedimented, generic divisions of space and time in archaeology; indeed, it is often presumed that such divisions are so basic that they are almost empirical questions. Recall the point about research in a new area and how one of its first tasks would be to establish a local chronology and any cultural sub-divisions. These kinds of divisions and organisation of data are all too often treated as somehow basic and more fundamental than any 'interpretive' perspective we might have. Certainly they appear universal in archaeology and, more often than not, uncontested, standing solid as a silent foundation beneath the vicissitudes of changing theoretical orientations. But what I have been slowly moving towards in this chapter is that such a view is misguided; our periodisations and classifications are not only historically contingent, but the very idea of a periodisation and culture classification is too. It is only the historicity of archaeology which makes them seem so secure. To begin this section and illustrate this point, I will discuss some recent critiques of ethnicity and periodisation.

Sian Jones provides an excellent review of the subject of ethnicity (Jones 1997). Although the topic has only really opened out in the past few years, there were some earlier critiques in the 1980s, the most cogent of which appeared in Hodder's seminal book *Symbols in Action* which was partly an attempt to widen our understanding of this problem and marks the shift from his earlier involvement in processual archaeology to the development of post-processualism (Hodder 1982a; also see his earlier co-authored publications on the same issue). Against the tide of processual archaeology which never really answered the question, 'what do cultures refer to?', Hodder wanted at least to ask 'under what conditions do marked cultural discontinuities relate to the boundaries of ethnic groups?' (Hodder 1982a: 7). His answer was to show how the question was wrong:

> In fact it seems likely that markedly discontinuous cultural areas often do relate to peoples in some non-material sense, but interpretation in terms

of political or language units or of self-conscious tribes is not necessarily relevant to the examination of the role and meaning of the cultural boundaries themselves. To break prehistoric Europe up into blocks of material culture which are discussed in isolation and in terms of origins, assimilation and movements of peoples is to miss the central issue: what form of social and economic strategies led to boundary maintenance?

(Hodder 1982a: 188)

Another critic was Stephen Shennan who argued for the need to consider the behavioural patterns which create material culture patterning before any ascription of larger entities such as 'cultures'; in a study of the Beaker phenomenon in Europe, Shennan argued that there is a great deal more complexity than is usually admitted (Shennan 1978). A decade later, he re-affirmed this point in more general terms, arguing that a diverse range of processes can affect spatial variation, although style clearly needed more study (Shennan 1989). In the USA, McGuire addressed the issue of ethnicity in terms of historical archaeology and tied it into anthropological debates (McGuire 1982).

The 1990s have seen an increase in such studies, which are marked by a concern to show ethnicity or cultural identity as a socially constructed phenomenon and that different groups may emphasise it to different degrees and, more importantly, in different contexts (Jones 1997). Culture is not equivalent to ethnicity, but rather ethnicity may be a dimension of culture, a way of expressing *difference* like gender, and will be expressed in different ways and through different material contexts: it is not simply a reflection of a monolithic, bounded entity, as Sian Jones argues in her recent book length treatment of the subject (Jones 1997). Her example of Romanisation is a case in point; she argues that views on the adoption of Roman-style material culture in Britain after the conquest have tended to see this in block terms such as Roman vs. Native or regional tribes. This covers over the fact that, within the same group, different elements of material culture (such as pottery) may be more 'Roman' than others (such as architecture), or that different groups might adopt different elements (Jones 1997: 129–35). Another example is Elizabeth Brumfiel's discussion of the Aztec state where a supra-regional identity was explicitly fostered through the suppression and denigration of more local identities in order to reinforce the authority of a centralised state (Brumfiel 1994).

Such critiques and new directions are extremely stimulating for archaeology and they suggest that there is no primary or fundamental cultural division of the archaeological record in space. Since ethnicity or cultural identity is not given or stable, but fluid and contextually dependent, it therefore becomes one of many social or cultural (in the holistic sense) dimensions of the archaeological record – it has no primacy over others. Before looking at the consequences of this, I want to turn to periodisation.

Very little has been written on this in archaeology – perhaps one of the first to do so was the philosopher historian/archaeologist R. G. Collingwood; in the very first issue of *Antiquity* published in 1927, he raises the question of the significance of periods, as part of a critique of Spengler's theory of historical cycles:

> for though a 'period' of history is an arbitrary fabrication, a mere part torn from its context, given a fictitious unity, and set in a fictitious isolation, yet by being so treated, it acquires a beginning, and a middle, and an end. And we fabricate periods of history by fastening upon some, to us, peculiarly luminous point and trying to study it as it came into being.
>
> (Collingwood 1927: 324)

The Three Age System is just one periodisation, based on the material of which 'important' artefacts were made, arising out of the technological and evolutionary perspective held by nineteenth-century archaeologists. But other things might be considered more important today – indeed different archaeologists might see different things as important. More widely, the use of periodisations that developed in Europe and were applied elsewhere, such as in Africa through 'colonial' archaeologies, has been criticised as harmful (e.g. Andah 1995: 152). A good example is in the study of European colonialism, where periodisations in Third World countries are often radically marked by pre- and post-contact divisions. It promotes a very static and closed image of the past, where colonisers and colonised do not mix; Badillo has remarked, in the context of the Caribbean, how this marginalises indigenous populations in post-contact histories and downplays the critical process of creolisation which occurred across the globe (Sued Badillo 1995).

A more concrete example can be found in North America, where it has been shown that surface scatters which incorporate both Indian and European material are often assumed to belong to two different phases, the Indian material marking a campsite, the European material the product of later ploughed-in middening. Rarely is it considered that the Indians may be using European objects – indeed, by denying the contemporaneity of the finds, the co-existence and subsequent displacement of native populations by colonists can be downplayed (Ruberstone 1989; Handsman and Richmond 1995). The critical thing is that the use of a periodisation does have interpretive implications – it is not just a neutral way of dividing up the past. Indeed, Childe saw this point with his culture periods and the need to distinguish time from periodisation. It is surprising, however, how little attention has been devoted to this issue.

One recent study has added a new twist in suggesting that periodisation might even be viewed as a social construct in the past, not just the present (Hodder 1993a). In a paper which draws on the work of the historian

Hayden White, Hodder argues that one can see sequences of material culture (e.g. pottery) as narrative-like, exhibiting a certain coherence through narrative content, for example his own use of *domus* and *agrios* as dual stories of the European Neolithic (Hodder 1990). This narrative link has been raised before by Joan Gero (Gero 1991; also see Pluciennik 1999). Hodder, however, goes further to suggest that such narratives, as in literature, exhibit rhetorical form which, after White, follow four basic types, after their dominant tropes: Romance/metaphor, Tragedy/metonymy, Comedy/synecdoche and Satire/irony. He then illustrates this through a sequence at the Greek tell of Sitagroi. Despite the problems with this approach – notably its overly deterministic and typological structure – I think the important consequence is not so much the use of White's tropology but the connection between periodisation and narrative. Periodisation is not just a descriptive or heuristic tool for slicing up the past into segments, a product of the archaeologist, but may be actually inherent in the material culture sequences and therefore indicative of past cultural expressions of temporality or historical consciousness. Just as one uses material culture to define one's spatial boundaries against other communities, so one might do the same to define one's sense of history. Our own connotation of a new year, a new century or even millennium is clearly tied in to a purely arbitrary division of time, yet it has resounding social significance, exhibited for example in the construction of the Millennium Dome in London.

It is difficult to foresee how this approach will be taken up – if at all. The potential is certainly there, for at a very basic level it implies that multiple periodisations might be conceivable which are tied in to quite specific narratives of the past. But can archaeology be done without a single periodisation? By this, I do not mean a universal periodisation – all periodisations are limited in scope, including the biggest of them all, the Three Ages. But within a region or area, what would happen if there was no periodisation – no standard one, but many different ones? The same question of course applies to periodisation and culture classifications – indeed the two are largely related given that it is cultural classification which largely determines the extent of a periodisation's applicability. To take this point even further, I want to question some broader issues which are closely linked – those of nationalism and globalism.

Nationalism and globalism: beyond area/period specialisms and towards a multi-sited archaeology

The issue of multiple, fluid periodisations and culture classifications goes beyond the academic, for it relates directly to the question of nationalism and how archaeology is practised today, especially in terms of area/period specialisms. The culture concept and culture historical archaeology – both in its heyday and its continued, tacit use today – have strong links with nationalism (e.g. Díaz-Andreu and Champion 1996: 3; Jones 1997). The subject of nationalism has been become quite topical recently and despite some earlier publications (Trigger 1984; Fowler 1987), the number of books and papers has seen a major increase in the last few years (Díaz-Andreu and Champion 1996; Graves-Brown *et al.* 1996; Kohl and Fawcett 1995; Meskell 1998). One of the central points is how the culture concept in particular, and archaeology in general, were largely constituted by the development of nationalism in Europe (e.g. Díaz-Andreu and Champion 1996: 3). Not only was archaeology often instrumental in sustaining national ideology, but archaeology as a discipline is closely connected to the construction of the state.

The strong development of the culture concept and its links with nationalism in Germany is a widely recognised example. Gustav Kossinna was an ardent nationalist who wished to demonstrate the primacy of Germany among the Indo-European peoples through archaeological research. His particular agenda stemmed from the wider social context of the time when Germany was not only a new nation (unified in 1871) but saw itself as politically and intellectually a central figure in Europe (Díaz-Andreu 1996: 54). The links between nationalism and archaeology are perhaps best known in Germany because of the associations with Kossinna, *Kulturkreise* and the development of Nazism (Härke 1991). However, similar relations can be seen in other European countries (see papers in Díaz-Andreu and Champion 1996): in Denmark, the early professionalization of archaeology can be attributed to the loss of territory at the start of the nineteenth century, where the use of ancient remains reaffirmed a Danish 'personality'. Worsaae's *Primeval Antiquities of Denmark* was a clear manifesto of nationalism, from its opening lines to its conclusion (Worsaae 1849: 1, 149–50). In contrast, in Spain, certain aspects of the past were completely alienated in promoting the nation state – Islamic archaeology was either suppressed or 'Europeanized'.

If the concept of culture had such strong links with nationalism, is it still the case? The relationship between archaeology and nationalism was largely articulated through the concept of the 'nation' which came to stand as the model of a human group – an entity which has political and historical continuity, a bounded, homogeneous unit. To this extent, our notion of culture in the partitive sense, as 'a culture', remains bound to nationalism. As Díaz-Andreu remarks:

> Most archaeologists do not assert such an explicit equivalence of the political unit and the cultural unit. However, it would seem important to emphasise that it is nonetheless a political decision to assemble what are potentially different groups under a single name on the basis of a common material culture.
>
> (Díaz-Andreu 1996: 56)

If this is the case, then should we continue to use the concept of culture in archaeology? She argues against it (ibid.: 58), but if we do drop it, this has serious consequences. What will become of area/period specialisms? What relevance and significance will they have, since they are – and there is no way around this – predicated on the culture concept as we currently employ it?

I put this not as a rebuttal of Díaz-Andreu's point but rather as an appendix. For it really challenges us to re-think how we might do archaeology, not just from the point of view of research but its teaching, both in institutions and by public dissemination. Because we live in a nation, work in a nation, the institutional framework of archaeology might seem against this from the start. Nevertheless, we also live in a global world (if you will forgive the tautology) and the potential for transcending nationalisms is there. Indeed one way of characterising this challenge is in terms of the global and local. Marilyn Strathern's discussion of these terms reveals new ways of articulating cultural difference without recourse to a totalising articulation as in culture classification or cultural evolution (Strathern 1995). Different cultural phenomena operate at different spatial scales and the articulation of global/local is primarily about this multiplicity of scales rather than a dichotomous opposition between global and local contexts. Instead of the past being fossilised and constrained by fixed spatial and temporal divisions, archaeology can also create a much more plural and dynamic past.

This prospect has recently emerged in a volume which discusses nationalism and globalism in the Middle East and, in particular, raises issues around post-colonialism and previously silent voices and histories (Meskell 1998). Post-colonial theory in fact deals with just this problem and with how to write histories which escape the constraints of a nationalist (even Western) discourse, which includes the notion of culture as partitive. One of the major problems, in particular in post-colonial archaeologies, is how to critique old histories or write alternative histories without falling back on colonial concepts, or 'the colonial library' – using the master's tools to deconstruct the master (e.g. see papers in Schmidt and Patterson 1995). Indeed, many of the post-colonial histories to emerge from Third World academics have simply created new national histories in opposition to an old colonial one. This problem has been likened to similar issues in feminism, but Wylie argues that this problem need not be seen negatively; rather than being caught in a vicious cycle, the relation between concepts and histories is dialectical and productive (Wylie 1995: 269).

A post-colonial, or even perhaps 'post-cultural' archaeology is one which is multi-sited, which situates the global within the local; indeed, Marcus's concept of a multi-sited ethnography might be usefully applied to archaeology (Marcus 1995; also see Hodder 1999). What is a multi-sited archaeology? It is not just a question of comparing sites or drawing many sites into an analysis – archaeology does this routinely. Rather it is one where the *relation* between the sites is foregrounded and is as specific as the sites themselves. Usually such relationality is generalised, either implicitly in terms of cultural homogenisation, or explicitly through cross-cultural regularities. A multi-sited archaeology is 'cross-cultural' but in quite a different sense from either of the above senses. It is cross-cultural in both crossing cultures and crossing out 'culture' (c̶u̶l̶t̶u̶r̶e̶), rather than generalising it through homogenisation or universalisation.

Such studies remain spatially and temporally situated, yet they are mobile – the location of culture is never fixed but is fluid. A good example would be a study of exchange networks – although such studies are usually reduced to generalised principles. More concrete examples include Richard Bradley's study of ritual deposition in prehistoric Britain (Bradley 1990) or Phil Duke's study of the bison hunt in the Northern Plains (Duke 1991). Their subject is not Culture A or Period B, or cross-cultural regularities regarding hunting or ritual deposition but a specific practice in the past. Their narratives are like genealogies rather than grand histories – they follow a plot between sites and see how it is articulated and changed – they show the potential for a multi-sited archaeology and how it might move beyond traditional culture locations by area or period. Indeed, since the 1990s, such studies have become increasingly more common and though perhaps still partially constrained within conventional area/period specialisms, they do challenge it at its most basic level.

However, to some extent such studies are still not properly multi-sited. While they contest the grand totalising or generalising narratives which sought to envelop sites within homogeneous cultural entities such as cultures or periods, they still envelop sites in the name of another generalisation, namely a practice such as ritual deposition or bison hunting. Now it may be argued that archaeology, as a science, needs to generalise, otherwise it becomes mere chronicle. But this is precisely the point – who decides what constitutes valid representation of the past, a valid archaeology? This theme is usually raised in the context of global archaeology, and the dominance of Western perspectives; for example, non-Western archaeologies might often be portrayed as traditional, stuck in the old culture-history phase, with issues and problems of little interest to Western archaeologists, especially to those from allegedly more theoretically oriented nations such as Britain or the United States. Thus a scientific colonialism pervades Western and non-Western countries, where innovation in techniques and ideas is seen to come from Western Europe and North America (Olsen 1991).

The issue is not, however, just confined to a global archaeological politics, but also lies in our own backyard; while local historical and archaeological societies and individuals are frequently involved in academic or even contract archaeological projects, their views are often considered parochial and unreflective against the more serious concerns of professionals. Moreover, such a difference is not something which should be quickly dismissed as the product of alternative perspectives for it affects the practice of archaeology very deeply in terms of heritage conservation and presentation. What right does a local community have over an archaeological site in its area? Can the community be excluded from consultation, from the site's excavation and presentation? The issue is often very acute in non-Western contexts (e.g. North American Indian burial sites, Australian Aboriginal sacred sites) – but what of Western contexts?

In rescue archaeology, for example, sites are ranked by perceived archaeological significance – significance here being defined by generalising academic research agendas, rarely if ever local interests. What is one more Roman field system, or eighteenth-century orchard? What will it tell us? And even when a site is excavated, what role should the local community have? The recent case of a prehistoric timber circle on the east coast of England is a good example; there, despite opposition from a section of the local population and a number of New Age druids, the timbers were excavated and removed to another location. The situation was difficult; the local community was in fact consulted and the site was carefully and properly excavated, the prime reason being to preserve it from attrition by the elements. Yet for many, the act was still a violation and a case of establishment archaeology overpowering the wishes of a sector of the local populace.

Such an example is meant to highlight not just the problems of heritage and the public face of archaeology, but also its theoretical perspectives which are governed by a generalising ethos. Justifications such as preservation for the nation, history for all, etc., might seem democratic, but they can mask internal divisions and differences of opinion. The line between democracy and totalitarianism, as Bataille once remarked, is often very thin when considered from a certain point of view, and the role of generalisation cannot be seen as simply an intellectual or apolitical process.[1] Academic and state archaeology, in its role as guardian of the past, perpetuates the very same homogenisation of cultural values on an intellectual level which it often criticises within its own sphere. If archaeology is to take seriously the multi-sited and multi-cultural nature of its discipline, it needs to question not only the area/period specialisms within which it works, but also the national and global structures within which it operates.

Chapter 5

Eventful contexts

Pompeii, in common with many places on the Grand Tour of the nineteenth century, attracted the attention of many literary figures, including Madame de Staël; in her novel *Corinne*, published in 1807, she conjures an image of Pompeii that has become almost archetypal:

> In Rome you simply find relics of antiquity, and in these you just trace the political history of past ages; but at Pompeii the private life of the ancients offers itself to your reflection. The volcano which covered this city with cinders has preserved it from the ravages of time. If the buildings had been exposed to air, they would have decayed, but this buried remembrance is perfectly preserved. Pictures and bronzes have all their first beauty, and vessels of domestic use are in entire preservation. The amphoras stand ready for the coming feast, and the corn which was being ground is there. The remains of a lady, still ornamented with the decorations she wore on the day the volcano interrupted the feast, are seen, with her dried arms filling no longer the bracelets of precious stones which encircle them – you realise how this figure was struck down in the midst of life.
>
> (From *Corinne, ou l'Italie* by Madame de Staël, quoted in Leppmann 1966: 106)

This 'buried remembrance' is, in a way, a description of the archaeological record; and even though the circumstances of preservation at Pompeii are rare, Madame de Staël's description is interesting because of the contrast she draws with isolated relics, a contrast one might say between archaeology and art history. In the same passage, she further reflects on this distinction and in particular the imagination needed to 'penetrate the past; to interrogate the human heart across the ages'. And yet, of course, this concept of the archaeological record as being a fossilised moment in time came under great criticism in the New Archaeology, being dubbed the 'Pompeii Premise' (see p. 148). At the same time there is clearly a recognition that the remains are somehow indicative of events and not simply a repository of facts, events in which human beings are caught up.

One of the major consequences of conceptualising the archaeological record explicitly in terms of actions and/or events has been the development of a whole series of studies which attempt to understand the relationship between what is found archaeologically and the events which produced that record. But this conceptualisation has changed since Madame de Staël's day, even since the early archaeologists of the late nineteenth century. Wheeler's description of the sacking of Maiden Castle in the site report is not something commonly encountered today, or indeed among most of his contemporaries – it is an interpretation of the archaeological record through unique, narrative events, closer to Madame de Staël than to Gordon Childe:

> What happened there is plain to read, the regiment of artillery, which normally accompanied a legion on campaign, was ordered into action, and put down a barrage of iron-shod ballista-arrows over the eastern part of the site. Following this barrage the infantry advanced up the slope, cutting its way from rampart to rampart, tower to tower. In the innermost bay of the entrance, close outside the actual gates, a number of huts had recently been built; these were now set alight, and under the rising clouds of smoke the gates were stormed and the position carried. But resistance had been obstinate and the fury of the attackers was roused. For a space, confusion and massacre dominated the scene. Men and women, young and old, were savagely cut down, before the legionaries were called to heel and the work of systematic destruction begun.
>
> (Wheeler 1943: xx)

This kind of 'fictionalised' re-creation is not how we would generally understand events in the past in archaeology today; the difference is not so much in the rejection of unique or specific events (see discussion in Chapter 4), but rather with its fictional rhetoric (but see Spector 1991). When we approach the archaeological record today, we generally think of events in terms of structured activity or behaviour. This change marks a kind of 'behavioural turn' in archaeology linked to the developments in the 1950s and 1960s and can be illustrated by two examples. In Britain, the site of Glastonbury discussed in Chapter 2 and excavated by Bulleid and Gray at the beginning of the twentieth century was presented in terms of its finds – site plans invariably marked finds locations and little more. David Clarke's re-interpretation of it in the 1970s shows quite clearly how conceptions had changed – he looked at the site in terms of social units and the organisation of space (Clarke 1972). Regardless of how valid his interpretation is (for it has been subject to later critique – e.g. Barrett 1987), the very nature of it marks a radical change of perspective. Similarly, in the USA the site of Snaketown was excavated in the early part of the twentieth century, and was presented in the manner of the day in terms of artefact sequence and chronology. In 1981 it was re-examined by Wilcox who pasted disparate plans together and found all kinds of features and was able to look at the site's internal organisation and spatial variation (Wilcox 1981).

These examples show how new perceptions of the archaeological record have shifted to issues of how sites, features and artefacts are structured in relation to each other because of the interest in the behavioural facet of material culture. How is this contemporary approach characterised, though? In Chapter 2 we discussed in a historical perspective how things are found – the methods used and the concepts behind those methods. In this penultimate chapter, I want to return to the field and look more closely at the contemporary relationship between our methods and such broader concepts. In general, the nature of this relationship has a dual aspect. On the one hand lies a starting point of the archaeological remains themselves and a working up to the behaviour or events which produced them (e.g. stratigraphy, geomorphology, micromorphology) – what, in discussion of analogies, might be called subject-side studies. On the other hand there is research, working from observed human behaviour or natural processes to analogous material remains (e.g. ethnoarchaeology, experimental archaeology) – what might be called source-side or actualistic study. Rarely does any study of the archaeological record not involve both sides of this equation at some level, either explicitly or referentially. I want to discuss this equation and critically explore the nature of the bridge made between both sides. Ultimately, I will ask what status the source-side or actualistic studies have in relation to archaeology and, indeed, what status archaeology has as a discipline.

The formation of the archaeological record

The nature of the archaeological record

Madame de Staël's interpretation can be described as a classic example of the 'Pompeii Premise' – that is, reading events directly from remains as if they had just been left yesterday. It is worth briefly delving into the Binford–Schiffer debate about the 'Pompeii Premise' because I believe it has ramifications beyond the internal quarrels of processualists (Binford 1981; Schiffer 1977). Schiffer famously argued that the archaeological record is not a direct representation of past events but has undergone various changes which result from two broad kinds of process, called C- and N-transforms. C-transforms indicate cultural processes which affect the record such as re-use of objects, discard practices, reclamation and disturbance activities, while N-transforms refer to natural or environmental processes such as weathering or larger-scale climatic changes (Schiffer 1987). However, as Binford notes, the very idea of C-transforms does not make much sense – it implies that the archaeological record is *distorted* – and one can only uphold this if one views that record as, at the point of its formation, a kind of 'Pompeii', that is a fossilised record of a living cultural system (Binford 1981). How can a C-transform be distinguished from the cultural system on which it is supposed to act?

To give an example: a recently ploughed field might bring a scatter of artefacts to the surface. If we wanted to say anything about this, particularly about the composition of the finds, we need to understand that this scatter may be a product of natural processes such as slopewash rather than the residue of an *in situ* activity area. This much is fine, and one can legitimately talk of N-transforms; but if the artefact scatter is the result of middening, for example, then it is more problematic. On the one hand, the finds – say potsherds – are not in what we would call their usual context (for example as whole vessels in a domestic structure) but broken up and far away from the settlement core. To read off information about pottery use and vessel function, etc., we have to understand the processes which have affected the pottery and removed them from their 'normal' context into the field – in this case, breakage, deposition and middening. All examples of C-transforms. Yet, on the other hand, all these processes are equally part of the cultural or systemic context as vessel use, all equally 'normal' uses of pottery – to separate these C-transforms from the broader systemic context is very dubious indeed.

Binford's point is well made – and yet there is a sense in which he still retains a notion of the archaeological record as a 'fossil' – not necessarily as a Pompeii, but of the cultural system itself. Where Binford and Schiffer agree is on the notion of distinguishing the archaeological context from the systemic context (of the living culture), and for Binford in particular this means that the former is a static *representation* of something dynamic (Binford 1981). It is a representational model of the archaeological record, as something which stands for something else. Moreover it does appear that Binford would at least recognise with Schiffer that such representation is open to distortion – although not from the system which it supposedly represents (for how can the 'original' distort the 'copy' – this is what Schiffer's C-transforms amount to), but from external, natural/environmental processes – with which Binford has no problem (Binford 1981).

Binford's critique was very much directed at the concept of *transforms* and not formation processes in general, although Schiffer's later book *Formation Processes of the Archaeological Record* largely reaffirms the distinction between systemic and archaeological context and asserts that moving from one to the other requires the study of formation processes (Schiffer 1987: 3–7). In it he also criticises other views, in particular earlier and more simplistic formulations such as an entropy theory or sampling bias theory (ibid.: 8–11). In the former, propounded by Ascher, the older the site, the more affected it will be, three phases being defined: inhabited (i.e. occupation), ghost (i.e. abandonment) and archaeological (i.e. excavation) (Ascher 1968). The latter view (ascribed to Cowgill) appears as a slightly more sophisticated version of this, where an artefact population is said to undergo various processes which increasingly affect its composition so that the archaeological sample finally retrieved is not necessarily representative of the original population.

This view has been repeated in British archaeology, in particular through discussions of sampling theory and field survey techniques; for example Haselgrove gives a four-level structure to the archaeological record, where the target population refers to the *extant* remains and the sampled population, the *accessible* remains (Haselgrove 1985). In contrast, Schiffer argued for a *transformation theory* which rather than making probabilistic assumptions about how the systemic context differs from the archaeological one, actually studies analogous processes and attempts to make generalisations about these processes. A critical difference between this view and many of the others is that formation processes do not just degrade artefact patterns but might actually create them (ibid.).

There is little doubt that no other work has superseded Schiffer's for its detail and breadth, but it also seems true that the book has not generated as much debate as the original formulation. Much of this relates to the development of post-processualism and the shift towards a different issue. Discussion of the archaeological record since the 1980s has increasingly been focusing on the broader interpretation of cultural formation processes (CFP), having accepted Binford's rejection of the distinction between C-transforms and the living system/context (e.g. systems vs. texts/practices; see Patrik 1985). Thus all the examples Schiffer gives of CFP – re-use, deposition, reclamation and disturbance – can be seen as facets of a cultural context indistinguishable from production or primary use. In particular, his distinction of primary or *de facto* from secondary refuse is dubious. It is misleading and arbitrary to draw a line between any of these. Indeed the very linearity of the process – production $\rightarrow$ use $\rightarrow$ discard – is questionable; one can almost see this tripartite structure as a metaphor for the conventional archaeological process, but in reverse (see Table 6).

Ascher actually says as much in his entropic view: 'The path of disorganisation from "inhabited", through "ghost" and on to archaeological disturbance is irreversible, but it must be figuratively reversed when inferring past human behaviour' (Ascher 1968: 47). However, despite these criticisms, the debate seems to have ignored the question of natural formation processes

Table 6 Models of artefact cycle and the archaeological process compared

Life cycle	Study cycle
Production	Retrieval
Use	Contextual analysis
Discard	Artefact analysis

with the implication that the distinction between the archaeological and living/systemic context is still viable at a base level. Most field archaeologists, I believe, still tacitly accept this distinction albeit basing it solely on natural formation processes. Consequently, field interpretation of deposits and stratigraphy has largely been ignored by post-processualists, at least until very recently (e.g. Barrett 1995; Richards 1995; Hodder 1997). I think there is a strong reason for this, and that is the necessity to retain an aspect which is non-cultural against which the cultural formation processes can still be checked. Without a baseline in natural processes, one has no measure for cultural processes; in brief, the archaeological record becomes viewed as a natural phenomenon *in the first instance* (see Chapter 3).

I am not saying that archaeologists perceive the archaeological record as the *product* of natural processes, only that they view it as being constrained – and contained – by a larger natural system. Schiffer actually describes the archaeological context as totally part of an environmental system (Schiffer 1987: 3–4), as does Binford through the idea that the archaeological record is static. Schiffer in this respect seems a little more aware of the dynamic nature of the archaeological record, yet he still views it essentially *as* a natural system which is a transformation or distortion of an *original* cultural or behavioural system. However, even if we disagree with this, arguing for example for cases where an archaeological site might remain or be re-incorporated into cultural systems (e.g. monuments such as Stonehenge), there is still a sense in which we treat it as a natural phenomenon. When we study it, all the things we conventionally record on archaeological sites employ a naturalistic nomenclature, *as if* they were natural phenomena. We measure, we make soil descriptions – in short, we talk about features in terms of their *physical properties* – these provide the baseline of our archaeological interpretation.

We recognise that an archaeological site is primarily a human creation, the product of human presence and activity, and we may use the term 'anthropogenic' to identify any constituent of a site which has this character. But what does this actually translate into? How might our record of a feature differ if it was seen as the result of a human rather than non-human event? Of course we recognise a wall as a human product, an alluvial layer as a natural event, and perhaps a hollow as ambiguous – pit or solution hole? And of course the identification of something as anthropogenic or natural will have significant consequences for interpreting a site. But while we may point to certain details (constituents, spatial and stratigraphic boundaries) as helping to decide whether something is anthropogenic or not in more ambiguous situations, the fact that both natural and anthropogenic records are commensurable, use the very same parameters and categories of description, says a great deal about the way we conceptualise the archaeological record.

Although linked to the issue of objectivity, it is not simply a case of a solid objective recording used to construct more tentative subjective interpretations; most archaeologists today recognise that subjectivity enters into even these basic descriptions and that the distinction between objectivity and subjectivity is hard, if impossible, to identify. No, rather the point is that physical or naturalistic attributes are used rather than anything else, attributes deriving largely from the natural sciences and invariably conforming to a measurable scale. A typical deposit description on an archaeological site in Britain, for example, will include dimensions, colour, compactness, texture and inclusions, all of which are usually described according to standardised criteria. Of course herein lies the rejoinder – without standardisation one cannot compare, and without comparison one cannot analyse or interpret. But standardisation is not the issue; the issue is rather the naturalistic way in which we describe the archaeological record. I want now to move on and discuss some of the problems and debates surrounding this naturalistic view of formation processes and field descriptions, and then link them into the broader issue of interpretation and cultural formation processes.

A matter of form: the nature of archaeological deposits

There have been two broadly opposing views on the basic description of archaeological deposits and stratigraphy (Farrand 1984; Barham 1995). On the one hand there is the geoarchaeological or geological school which views archaeological deposits in terms of soil science/sedimentology, and on the other is the Harris matrix/unit and its variants. Archaeological work on soils and sediments only began in the 1950s with the work of Ian Cornwall and others, although this was largely focused on palaeosols and large-scale anthropogenic effects on the landscape (Macphail and Goldberg 1995: 2; Rapp and Hill 1998: 4–17). Earlier, most work was primarily geological and linked either to issues of human antiquity as in the later nineteenth century, or of broad environmental change as in the earlier twentieth century (Rapp and Hill 1998: 4–17). As a result, it does not appear to have had such a direct impact on the way deposits are routinely excavated and recorded in the field because of the scale. A similar concern for studying *in situ* sediments on archaeological sites is reflected in the USA from the same time, although directed much more to cave and rockshelter sites (Stein and Farrand 1985). Here, the work of such geoarchaeologists has had a much greater influence on field excavation and recording.

This approach appears to contain the basic premise that the archaeological record is primarily a *natural* datum which incorporates cultural material – for example Gasche and Tunca's classification of stratigraphic units in which the most fundamental unit is the lithologic while the chronostratigraphic and ethnostratigraphic units are lithologic units grouped by time or artefact type (Gasche and Tunca 1983; also see Courty *et al.* 1989: figure 3.3). Equally bold is Stein's belief that archaeological deposits are no different from geological sediments, for 'culture is only one of the many types of biological or mechanical agents of transport and deposition' (Stein 1987: 378; also see Harris 1991 for critique). It was not until the development of micro-morphology in the 1980s that more detailed work could be done on the kinds of features which are more like archaeological than geological deposits, such as floors, and it is in this area that the greatest clashes are likely to be met with, with the Harris method. Some of the major ramifications are discussed below, but it is important to note that micro-morphology is also adding to the older conventional soil studies such as ditch silting and the 'dark earths' as well as opening up new horizons (Courty *et al.* 1989; Macphail and Goldberg 1995).

In contrast to these geoarchaeological approaches is Harris's discussion of stratigraphic units and its descendants, now in common use throughout most of field archaeology in Britain and elsewhere (Harris 1989). Here, there is much less explicit reference to the natural basis to a deposit; rather the deposit is defined first and foremost as a topological entity. The event which produced it could be natural or cultural or a mixture, but this in itself is not directly relevant to the definition of a stratigraphic unit. What is relevant is the single quality of the interface, the edge, the surface (Harris 1989, 1991). The Harris unit is defined solely in terms of spatial extension (i.e. dimensions and co-ordinates within the site grid). Qualities such as the particular shape of a cut or the constituents of a deposit are *secondary* in so far as they describe the singular nature of the feature, but it is its spatial extension which defines it primarily as a unit *in itself*.

In a way, the differences between Harris and the geological school could be summed up by a distinction of form and content. Gasche and Tunca, for example, focus almost exclusively on the content (or lithologic homogeneity) of the deposit (Gasche and Tunca 1983), while for Harris it is the interface between units that is important *stratigraphically*, not the constitution of the units themselves (i.e. what they are composed of), especially as this above all is what identifies the possibility of negative units (Harris 1991). This, he sees, is the biggest failing of the 'geological' approach to stratigraphy – that it is focused solely on solids, on deposits, and more specifically the contents of those deposits rather than their topology (ibid.). A cut or levelling event removes material and as an event it leaves a negative trace – e.g. the hole in a deposit (what Harris calls 'feature interfaces'; Harris 1989: 59). For negative units, the interface *is* the unit – it has no depth or substance. A deposit, however, such as a floor, has both an interface (surface) and depth/substance (what Harris calls 'layer interfaces'; Harris 1989: 54–5).

This is perhaps a crude opposition, especially as others in the geological school such as Fedele and Stein also stress a deposit's form or boundaries (Stein 1987: 348). Fedele for example defines his elementary sediment unit (ESU) in terms of both discontinuities (boundaries) and lithological homogeneity (Fedele 1984), while Stein also argues for the significance of boundaries, both conformable (surface) and unconformable (cut) (Stein 1987). And yet although it may be an overstated opposition, the very distinction between form and content in interpreting stratigraphy and deposits does present serious problems. On the one hand, by ignoring form as Harris says, a whole type of stratigraphic event is ignored, namely negative events – cuts. Many archaeologists outside Britain simply do not recognise the cut as a significant stratigraphic entity – in a pit, for example, it is enough to distinguish the layers in the pit (i.e. the fill) from the surrounding layers through which it is cut. If one is only interested in positive events, solids, in soil, one just will not *see* a cut – for example I have heard one archaeologist describe a pit cut as the hole left by the archaeologist after removing the fill. On this perception, it seemed quite ludicrous to record it, although to most British archaeologists *this* seems ludicrous. I think the best example to illustrate the importance of the negative feature is not a pit but a levelling or terracing event.

Here one might see in section a whole series of layers one on top of the other – such as in a floor; now between any two floors there are two ways of seeing the interface or edge – one as the contiguity of two surfaces, an upper and lower of two adjacent deposits, the other as a levelling cut which truncates a lower layer and, resting on this, the lower surface of the upper layer. These two ways of seeing have quite different consequences for the interpretation of the stratigraphy. For example, at Çatalhöyük, floors near the centre of a room were noted as having many fewer floor layers than those at the edges of the room; either this means people replastered the edges of the room more frequently than the middle, or – more plausibly – that the middle received more wear and erosion, which could in itself account for the fewer floor layers; alternatively, because of this wear and resultant unevenness, it may have required levelling before replastering.

This example should be familiar to geologists through the law of unconformity, and certainly it seems strange that such negative events should be ignored by some in the geological school. However, an equal criticism can be made of Harris for ignoring the constitution of stratigraphic units; by divorcing content from form, problems of indistinct interfaces are brushed under the carpet as anomalous or unusual depositional properties. But every excavator knows that it can be difficult sometimes to follow an edge to a deposit; there are many reasons why edges may be unclear – such as the rapidity with which a deposit is laid, its constituent difference from contiguous deposits or the effects of post-depositional activities. Behind this issue of clarity or sharpness of a boundary between deposits is the general question of visibility and scale; a more common problem perhaps is not that a deposit may grade into another over a large distance (that might appear sharper for example if viewed from a larger scale/more distant perspective), but that the boundary may be too small to be seen by the naked eye. Micro-morphology, a relatively recent branch of soil science, is making huge contributions in the field of micro-stratigraphy and formation processes (Courty *et al.* 1989; Macphail and Goldberg 1995; Matthews *et al.* 1997). However, even when interfaces are visible macroscopically, they may be too small to excavate; for example at the late Bronze Age site of Runnymede in England such a deposit was excavated using an arbitrary strategy in order to identify patterning in the finds and thereby demonstrate a succession of discrete dumps (Needham and Sørensen 1988: 113–26). What might have been treated as a single unit of deposition was in fact comprised of multiple units.

Similarly, in recent excavations at Çatalhöyük in Turkey there were problems of how to excavate floors which might be no thicker than a millimetre and extend across several metres of space; one could see the differences, and over small areas even attempt to excavate them singly, but to do so systematically was impractical. On the other hand, it was crucial to have the stratigraphic information of these individual floors, particularly as large numbers of burials were associated with the room and it would be extremely informative to know exactly at what level a grave was cut. A compromise was to dig the floors in 'groups' divided by major packing/levelling episodes but to have running sections over the floor so some idea of the micro-stratigraphic sequence was not lost.

The problems at Çatalhöyük highlight a crucial issue – the relation of micro- to macro-stratigraphy. As Ian Hodder has suggested (pers. comm.), the scale at which one wishes to excavate or record something as a unit depends on the prior interpretation we have of it and the significance we see of bounding any finds (whether macro- or micro-artefacts) at a certain scale. It was because the excavators at Runnymede saw the deposit as potentially a midden or at least composed of sub-deposits, that they decided to impose an arbitrary control to recover any patterning that might demonstrate this. If they had regarded it solely as a single event such as alluviation in which everything was redeposited, such careful excavation would not have been justified. The same principle lies behind the excavation of midden deposits at Çatalhöyük. However, the question of scale is not simply one of space but of *visibility* – that is, some deposit boundaries may not be visible at 'normal' light wavelengths but only at greater (infrared, radar) or lesser (ultraviolet, X-ray) wavelengths (Barham 1995: 148–9). For example, micro-morphology might use UV light in studying thin-sections, while geoprospection or remote sensing can pick up larger-scale deposits (see Figure 16).

From this discussion it seems quite clear that a conception of archaeological deposits which focuses predominantly either on interfaces or composition presents problems for interpretation. On the one hand, not recognising negative events has serious consequences for understanding the stratigraphy, but perhaps more serious is ignoring the significance of invisibility and clarity of edges. Are there ways of trying to bring form and content closer together in our understanding of stratigraphy and deposit

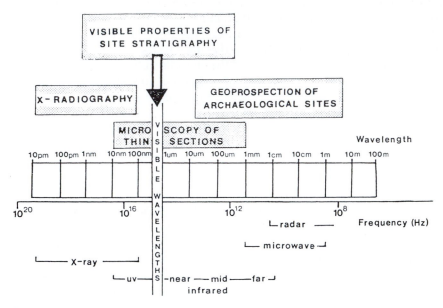

Figure 16   Visibility of stratigraphic/soil interfaces according to different electro-
magnetic wavelengths

formation in the field? Some ways have been explored, such as in the system used by the University of Durham field unit which explicitly tries to bring in a recognition of formation processes to the stratigraphic unit on its record sheet (Adams and Brooke 1995; also see Barham 1995: 162–4). Yet the problem of how to excavate a site stratigraphically with 'invisible stratigraphy' presents great difficulties. In such cases, a combined strategy of arbitrary and stratigraphic excavation has to be usefully employed, along with sampling of the deposits either of the disaggregated matrix or of an undisturbed column taken with monoliths or Kubiena tins (Barham 1995: 163). However, while such new information might aid understanding, there is a lurking worry that this route also increases the extent to which a unit is objectified through more complex recording criteria. We should perhaps be reconsidering the basic assumption of what the stratigraphic entity refers to: the event.

The construction site: contexts as objects

Consider the problem of surface discoloration, such as burning. For example, the firing or burning of a feature on a site might not necessarily be assigned as a separate unit under single-context recording (see Chapter 2). Rather, the burning would represent a secondary attribute of the unit – though clearly a difference has to be noted as to whether that burnt nature of the unit is actually part of it or whether it happened later. For example is a burnt fill burnt *in situ* or not? If it is, does the burning qualify as a separate unit? Surely it must and perhaps we can even delimit it, that is, fix it spatially – it may for example only cover a part of the deposit or it may cross over and affect other units. Fire or any surface modification should count, then, as a separate unit and in this sense it might be legitimate to talk of a surface as a separate unit, although the burning, no matter how slight, will always have depth and is not therefore just a surface (also see Harris 1989: 55).

This does, however, raise an important question about the meaning of such units – whatever they are (e.g. see Adams 1992; Clark 1992). Despite the difficulties surrounding the edges of more ambiguous units, there is the more intransigent issue of linking a bounded unit with a bounded event. One of the crucial assumptions of single-context recording as we have said is that each unit is representative of a single action or event – that its spatial limits also define temporal limits. Schiffer questions this equation of a single event to a single deposit; as he says, one depositional event can give rise to materials is different deposits, while conversely a single deposit can contain multiple depositional events (Schiffer 1987: 266). But even beyond this, do we in the field routinely relate an event at all to our stratigraphic unit or do we rather not just give it some shorthand term such as pit, ditch, etc. – in other words, *treat it like an object*? Why should this reduction of a feature from a human action to an object come about? Perhaps it is because we ignore or postpone the interpretation of how a deposit has formed and focus on its spatial extent. And yet, is there a conflict between the focus on the limits of a unit, that is treating it as a discrete entity or object, and its representation as an event?

Returning to the issue of treating surfaces as separate units to be included in a matrix, consider another problem: how does one distinguish the matrix of the floor and objects in it, from objects lying on its surface and associated with activities occurring on that surface? In this case, the actual material or floor matrix might be distinguished from its surface, one being associated with construction the other with use. But is this a legitimate distinction to make? Does the surface physically exist independently of the material to which it is associated? But, more pertinently, if a unit is supposed to represent an event, is it really the surface of the floor which signals events, or the objects and other deposits lying on that surface? This problem raises many issues regarding the relationship of events to units, but more significantly, I think, it exposes a deep dichotomy in the way archaeological events are conceptualised – between acts of production and acts of use.

Because the stratigraphic unit is invariably seen as part of a larger picture, the site stratigraphy, the 'event' nature of such units is dominated by the notion of their contribution to how the site is built up rather than how the deposit itself is formed. In other words, it is the formation process of the *site* rather than the *unit* which determines how we understand the unit as an event, the temporality of the site rather than the unit which is paramount. What this means is that the unit itself has no temporality, merely spatial extension – hence the emphasis on unit demarcation rather than formation. The site itself, through the matrix, has a rich temporality but its elements, its stratigraphic units, comprise homogeneous 'moments', equivalent and of no specific duration; their only temporality is their place in a sequence.

By actually thinking of units as objects, a whole series of connotations is drawn in, not just the notion of the cartesian extension, but capitalist notions of the object as a commodity, of its dual nature as product and consumable (see Chapter 3). What this seems to come down to is that the unit is a formation event defined primarily in terms of *production* – it is the temporal horizon of production that is employed to delimit it and in this it is almost identical to the conception of an artefact. Indeed the unit can be seen as the objectification of a person or people, the material product of their labour which then stands independent of them.

The notion that a site can be viewed in terms of production can be extended so that the formation process of a site is akin to building con-struction; the analogy reflects a deeper metaphor for the nature of the archaeological site, as a cultural site – a site of *culture*; the model of its formation derives from contemporary capitalist notions of what a cultural site is: the building, the city over against the field, the countryside. Wheeler, for example, explicitly recommends knowledge of building construction for the director in interpreting a site (Wheeler 1954: 72, 133). The work Harris quotes in his comparison of the matrix to critical path analysis (see p. 57), interestingly suggests that the 'builders of Stonehenge, Salisbury cathedral and the Empire State building presumably used some comparable procedure.' (Cole and King 1968: 570). This construction analogy is significant with its implication that the matrix is very much reflective of a constructional notion of a site, *as if it were a building*.

Perhaps more prevalent, however, than specific analogies with buildings is the notion that excavation is *destruction*. Pick up almost any field manual from the twentieth century and this idea will be repeated – from Petrie (1904: 48) to Coles (1972: 133). Here is Atkinson, for example:

> It is the excavator's task to remove all these deposits in the reverse order to that in which they were laid down, so that each successive stage in the history of the site may be revealed. . . . For excavation is, more than anything, destructive, and evidence not seen and recorded when first uncovered will be destroyed forever when digging proceeds.
>
> (Atkinson 1946: 16)

Offsetting this, as Atkinson implies, is the concomitant notion that *recording* negates this destructive element. The way he phrases it is that *unless* the evidence is recorded, excavation is destruction. Indeed the modern concept of excavation in Britain is imbued with the idea that it is *preservation by record* (in contrast to preservation *in situ*). The reasoning behind this was concisely summed up by Droop: 'An excavation should be so conducted that it would be possible in theory to build up the site again with every object replaced exactly in its original position' (Droop 1915: 7). This has remained the basic justification for all excavation ever since.

This reconstruction of the site is carried in the written, and particularly the graphic, record made. Indeed there is almost the idea that archaeologists are producing architectural plans in reverse, that the whole process of archaeology in the field is one which takes its metaphors from construction, but inverted. Taking off the layers in reverse order, working *from* the constructed site back *to* the plans and design, which are the end result and not the beginning of an archaeological project. One might even wish to explore ways in which the graphic representation of a site (plans, sections, elevations) mimics an architect's design. Of course this is not to argue that archaeologists regard the site as having been *actually* constructed this way, that is from plans etc.; but we do record it *as if* it had been.

As a result of this 'constructional' view of a unit, post-formation processes affecting that unit are separated from it, as is the post-formation temporality. Indeed one might say that the very distinction of formation from post-formation processes models itself on the notion of an original artefact or object, its primary production and secondary modifications and use. The problem this causes for identifying units in the field has been highlighted by Barham in the context of the geological perspective; he argues that three distinct properties of a unit have to be adequately assessed – properties inherited from pre-existing deposits (e.g. buried soil, natural geology), those acquired during deposition, and those acquired over time post-depositionally (e.g. bioturbation). One of the major flaws in the Harris system is the failure to distinguish these during recording, which might manifest itself in two particular ways: one, in identifying a stratigraphic boundary which is not primarily depositional at all but the product of post-depositional processes such as decalcification or bioturbation; the other, failing to identify a stratigraphic boundary because of its 'invisibility' (see p. 155; Barham 1995: 155–6).

This also brings us back to the question of burning – often it is merely given as a secondary characteristic of another unit, presumably because the event, the fire, only remains as a trace on another, earlier depositional event. The fire becomes, in effect, a post-depositional process of a unit and not a unit in its own right because it has no *clear* physical or spatial distinction from its associated deposit. This is a good example of how the perception of stratigraphic units is in fact not through an event but through an object – it is first interpreted as an object (though this process is usually called descriptive or identifying), and then interpreted as an event.

Temporalising the stratigraphic unit

How might we rethink the stratigraphic unit to get around this inherent tendency to objectify it? A good example to begin with is the ploughsoil. Ploughsoil archaeology is often regarded as a prospecting technique, particularly through fieldwalking, where it is used to detect 'sites' under the ploughsoil from the finds which are lifted out of sub-surface features through ploughing action – indeed it has even been shown that such finds exhibit very little lateral displacement, suggesting that densities of finds will more or less accurately overlie archaeological features (Hayfield 1980; Roper 1976). This approach, though entirely valid, is still a prospecting method and treats the ploughsoil as informative not in itself but of other contexts beneath it. A more significant recognition in many respects is of the ploughsoil itself as a meaningful context in terms of find associations – the crucial point in this recognition is the difference between ploughed-in and ploughed-out deposits (Haselgrove 1985). Many of the finds collected from the ploughsoil may derive from sub-surface features and have been ploughed out and are therefore useful prospecting material; however many other finds – and this is often the case with flints – do not come from any sub-surface features but have derived from once upstanding contexts such as middens or hearths.

The importance of treating the ploughsoil as informative in itself is a quite recent conception. Its implications are fairly widespread for it raises issues about the very nature of units, especially the distinction between 'open' and 'closed'. The distinction is a very significant one and is fundamental to modern fieldwork and analysis – the overburden of a site or the ploughsoil are commonly regarded as open contexts, that is contexts which are still active and therefore fluid in terms of their find associations, which is why one might find Roman pottery with mesolithic flints and asbestos fragments. Often such contexts are not regarded as at all informative and are often not even recorded during an excavation. Yet this is not always the case; many valuable studies have been done on such open contexts, particularly ploughsoils (e.g. Lewarch and O'Brien 1981; Haselgrove 1985; Schofield 1991; Sullivan 1998). Is it perhaps the case then that the degree of discreteness of a unit might be related to its degree of openness? And that what we call post-depositional effects, which might blur the edge, only denote that in fact the context is still being used/formed – that it is still open? An example may be of a ditch, the upper fill of which is continuous with a general layer which also seems to seal the ditch, a problem which also links to the question of clarity of edges (see p. 155).

Such examples are common on floodplains where periodic flooding leaves alluvial deposits which not only seal sites but will infill the tops of any features open at the time. To take this example further, we might consider a buried soil which in some instances, such as the Fenlands of eastern

England, is sealed by alluvium, thus representing an ancient or buried soil which might only otherwise be preserved in exceptional circumstances (e.g. under banks or mounds). This can then be sampled in a manner similar to the ploughsoil but requiring slightly different techniques, though strangely it has in one example actually been sampled in the same manner by stripping off the alluvium, then ploughing and fieldwalking it (Evans and Knight 1997). What buried soil archaeology suggests is that rather than treating units as either open or closed, we should perhaps think of every unit in terms of the degree of its 'openness' or 'closedness' – that is its duration – and this has a very clear relationship to the constitution of a deposit.

A ploughsoil or buried soil reveals its openness through our understanding of its soil matrix and morphology which would be very different from the backfill of a pit, for example. One needs to consider both form and content, and the concept of openness and temporality is a very useful one in bridging this distinction. Another way of studying openness is to look at artefact patterning within and between contexts; in contrast to the case of, say, Runnymede where such analyses were done to identify different deposits, one might look at attributes which would indicate longevity of formation such as the diversity or condition of an artefact assemblage (Schiffer 1987: 279–87; Gerrard 1991). For instance, an assemblage of a ditch fill may be more fragmented than that from a pit, which suggests greater weathering and therefore longer infilling.

There is no sense in a stratigraphic matrix of the duration or longevity of a unit, not only in terms of its formation but also in terms of its post-formation 'use' (see Carver 1990 for a similar critique). I mark the word 'use' because this is the word one is forced to employ to distinguish use from formation. What is perhaps needed is a supplement to the Harris matrix, a chart which shows the longevity of units not just their place in a sequence. How might this be done? Well Harris himself suggests a way, for the 'matrix diagram can be lengthened, shortened or otherwise reordered to give some indication of duration of deposits and interfaces' (Harris 1991: 19). The same procedure was first discussed by Dalland in his alternative matrix where the depth of the box could be used to indicate longevity of formation (Dalland 1984). However, there are problems with both of these solutions, problems caused by a *production* emphasis on stratigraphic units. For example, a ditch is cut; on a matrix the cutting is one unit, succeeded by others, its fills. The temporality of the ditch cut is reduced to its point in a sequence of other productive acts on the site. On this model, there is no sense that the ditch may have been open for so long, and that even while it was silting up, it was still active; nor that this fact may help to understand the development or use of a site. All this shows is the temporality of *production* and not use.

There is also the overwhelming practical problem of not being able to measure such longevity – one can guess or estimate, but not in all cases and not to the same degree. Here the solution must lie in not trying to provide absolute measures of longevity but rather in using the structured temporality of the matrix to produce a relative measure, which could be calibrated – much as one calibrates a traditional phase matrix. Such a chart has an advantage over the traditional phase matrix in that it does not require units or the site to fall neatly into phases, but rather produces a multi-layered temporality with both continuity and change expressed rather than the usual blocks of phase-time.

For example, consider the matrix in Figure 17 from a building recently excavated at Çatalhöyük; what we do is first create a chart with the necessary time zones derived from the number of steps on the matrix diagram; then we take each unit in turn for which we have a given inception in time zone N. What is now required is an evaluation of its longevity – that is, to isolate the latest point at which it could still function. For a ditch cut for example, the cut continues to function until either it is recut or its latest fill seals the top. This has close similarities to, but was reached independently of, Carver's 'matrix' which he developed in criticism of Harris's lack of temporality (Carver 1990). Moreover this representation is not intended to replace the Harris matrix but indeed actually utilises it in its construction. Consequently, one has a much more complex model of the site with something approaching a real-time development rather than phase-time. The importance of this is to bring to the fore the event-character of units rather than just seeing them as objects, conjoining the temporalities of succession and duration in understanding formation processes on archaeological sites.

This is not quite the end, however, because there is another problem, so far ignored in that neither the geological school nor Harris addresses it. This is the problem of events which do not correlate with a soil deposit or a cut; is there not a bias in the whole conception of seeing archaeological stratigraphy solely in terms of deposits and cuts, both of which ultimately derive from geology? For all Harris's discussion of the differences between archaeological and geological stratification, the basic units of stratification do derive from geology through the concepts of beds (layers), conformities (layer surfaces) and unconformities (cuts). The question I wish to ask is what the status of the object or find in relation to stratigraphic events is (also see Roskams 1992). Both Harris and the geological school only discuss them in so far as they relate to understanding the formation of sediments, soil and other deposits – for example from simple date fossils to more complex seriation and taphonomic studies (see p. 161). But can they be seen as something more?

Artefact patterning: objects as contexts

There are many ways in which excavation can be (and usefully) arbitrary, and there are two principal reasons why an arbitrary method might be employed. First, when there are no clear/visible differences in the deposit (e.g. a midden) and yet such are suspected – and might be demonstrated through micro-morphological sectioning (see p. 155); in such a case one might excavate in spits (vertically arbitrary). Second, where the limits to the unit are known (e.g. a floor), whether macroscopically or microscopically, but for sampling reasons (e.g. phosphates, artefact distribution) a grid is imposed to detect patterning (horizontally arbitrary). In both cases, arbitrary excavation is employed to reveal artefact/ecofact patterning within the deposit, but in one it is to demonstrate the existence of several different deposits while in the other it is to demonstrate the existence of different activities associated with a deposit (see Figure 18).

And yet if this is the case – that artefact/ecofact patterning can be used to differentiate deposits and activities within deposits, there is a certain problem with our definition of a stratigraphic unit/deposit as a single event; why not call all the activities identified within a deposit also stratigraphic units – events which take place on the floor, after the floor's construction (a point raised earlier)? Even considering the *post facto* nature of ascribing such units, how sharply can we delimit them? What if an event does not leave a *discrete* trace – a scatter of potsherds, micro-debitage, or charred seeds? How do these relate to the identification of stratigraphic units? Are there problems with the way the stratigraphic unit is defined – fundamental problems which have an effect on the way we interpret a site?

If we consider a site which consists primarily of artefacts in sedimentary deposits, such as on palaeolithic excavations, interpretation will invariably focus on the finds and their distribution. Indeed, the sub-field of intra-site spatial analysis largely developed from these contexts, especially in France (see Chapter 4). Throughout, there does seem to have been a strong bias in such studies towards earlier prehistoric sites, which undoubtedly relates to the relative paucity of features compared to later prehistory. In contrast, many of the spatial studies on later prehistoric or historic sites is based less on a 'pure' distribution across two- or three-dimensional space and more on a 'contextualised' association, using architectural and other features as a function of spatial variability. Among the earliest examples of these are studies of Pueblo villages in the American Southwest by Longacre and Hill during the 1960s (e.g. Longacre 1968; Hill 1968). For example, at the site of Broken K, Hill compared variability in room morphology with artefact patterning to identify three different types of room and associated activity (habitation, storage and ceremony).

Such studies have become perhaps the most commonly used type of interpretive analysis today, and the same methodology, although with different theoretical perspectives, lies at the heart of many post-processual and contextual studies. In Britain, the 1980s saw the development of many such studies on prehistoric sites, which are particularly associated with the concept of structured deposition, that is intentional, patterned associations

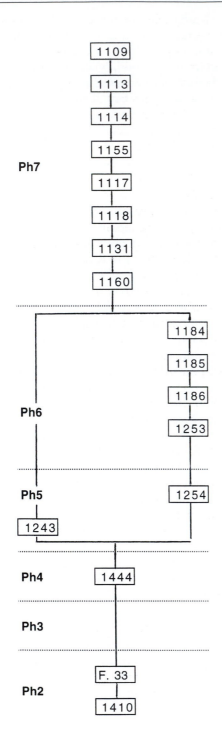

Figure 17a
Harris matrix (a) and
alternative graphic representation of site temporality
(b), based on a sequence at
Çatalhöyük, Turkey

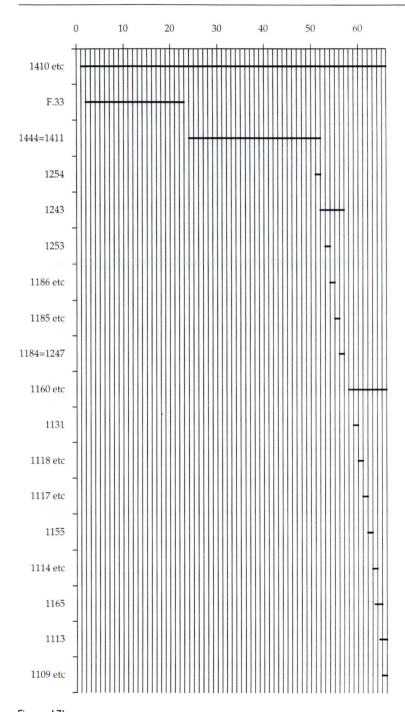

Figure 17b

Pottery

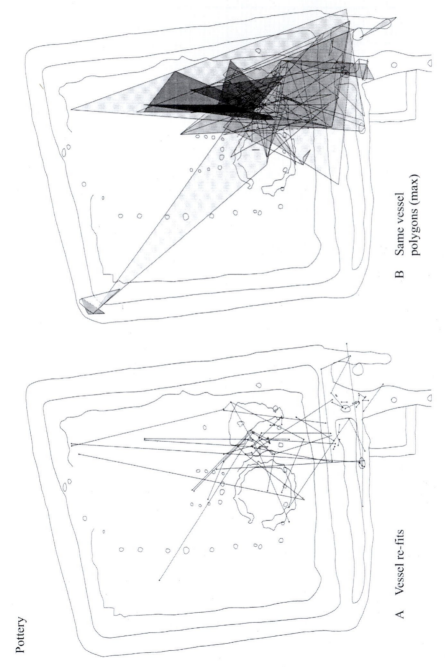

A Vessel re-fits

B Same vessel
   polygons (max)

Figure 18 Objects as contexts: pottery refits at the Romano-British site of Haddenham

of artefact assemblages with specific features or parts of features. A classic example is of high densities of cultural material in ditch terminals associated with a range of Neolithic monuments such as long barrows and henges, and usually interpreted as a ritual deposit linked to feasting (e.g. Thomas 1991). However, there are problems with the interpretation of such spatial analyses, both of point pattern distributions of artefacts and contextual associations of assemblages. For example, some of the original interpretations of spatial variability at Broken K have recently been compromised by a reassessment of the formation processes in the rooms (Schiffer 1987), while the earlier attempts to find correlations between artefact types ('tool kits') and spatial distribution in palaeolithic sites have rarely been successful (Kroll and Price 1991b: 304).

Nevertheless, the first thing to reiterate is that what the studies of intraspatial patterning do demonstrate, regardless of any methodological flaws, is that meaningful actions and events can and often do occur both above and below the level of depositional or stratigraphic units. In other words, the stratigraphic entity recorded in the field may be actually meaningless in terms of human behaviour and of understanding the site. Indeed, the very same issue arises over the question of the site itself, for human activity may be just as structured and meaningful over an even larger space, namely the landscape. The distribution of features or artefacts might occur on a much larger scale than on a site – for example, the distribution of prehistoric stone axes in Britain across the landscape reveals fluctuating densities which correlate with landscape features such as riversides or other wet places. Here, the 'site' is the whole landscape and it is only on this scale that we can begin to understand the distribution of material culture in terms of human activity – in this example, in terms of ritual deposition. The very concept of the site as the locus of human activity is therefore ambiguous.

At the same time as the new spatial archaeology emerged (see Chapter 4), archaeologists involved in field survey and sampling techniques were finding that the old view of sites as dots on a map was equally inadequate (Thomas 1975; Cherry et al. 1978: 11; Dunnell and Dancey 1983; Gaffney and Tingle 1984). Such a view was reinforced by the predominance of excavation as a field technique with its site-oriented perspective, but the increase in field surveys which occurred after the 1960s (integrated with earlier aerial photographic surveys) were producing an image of the archaeological record as a continuous landscape rather than isolated sites (Cherry and Shennan 1978: 17). The idea of treating sites as discrete entities was seen as very anachronistic, and it was thought that that intensive rather than extensive surveys were needed to better understand the archaeological record. Such surveys moreover ought to be coupled with a more explicit approach to sampling which is not simply a technique but integral to research design (Redman and Watson 1970; Flannery 1976: 51–62; Cherry et al. 1978: 4–6).

This approach led to a critique of the concept of the site, first by David Thomas but most extensively by Robert Dunnell in the USA (Thomas 1975; Dunnell and Dancy 1983; Dunnell 1992; also see Foley 1981). Dunnell argues that sites are nothing more than high densities or concentrations in an otherwise continuous distribution of artefacts over the landscape. Emphasising the site as the key concept in archaeological survey or excavation ignores this fact and misrepresents the nature of the archaeological record. There has been some reaction to Dunnell's view, particularly from Binford who seems to agree with Dunnell's conception of the archaeological record as a variable continuum, but does not see what harm there is in employing the concept of site to refer to concentrations within the continuum, on whatever scale (Binford 1992). The real disagreements between Dunnell and Binford are sometimes hard to see, but the primary one seems to be epistemological. Binford criticises Dunnell for a naive empiricism in trying to link spatial patterning directly to meaningful behaviour without independent theory in the form of middle range research. The notion of site, understood as 'place', is a very useful methodological concept in middle range research (e.g. Binford 1982). Dunnell on the other hand argues that there are theoretical implications in retaining the notion of 'site', even as an operational concept *contra* Binford; he thinks that a site is simply an inadequate unit of analysis to cover all examples of spatial activity. Dunnell does have a point – the site concept in emphasising 'place' as the spatial paradigm of human activity ignores other forms (such as journeys, for example). Indeed, it is a very fixed, non-mobile, *non-temporal* concept.

Concepts such as the site or the stratigraphic unit, through which archaeology works, are clearly problematic for the interpretation of human activity. While one might argue that many of the problems in identifying meaningful actions are due to an uncritical view of spatial distributions without consideration of 'distortions' from the cultural context to the archaeological context, I think this is only partially true. Certainly it is a question of considering formation processes, but equally it is a question of reconsidering the general nature of actions/events which are identified in the archaeological record and their relation to the archaeological concepts of object and context. I have shown how *distributions* of objects can spill over traditional concepts of analysis such as the stratigraphic unit or the site and mark events, but equally *single* objects can also denote events. Indeed, almost every artefact is a palimpsest of events – its manufacture, its use/wear, its breakage, etc. (see Chapter 3). Just as stratigraphic units such as a pit or a wall can be treated as objects/artefacts, so objects can be treated as eventful contexts; indeed, there are many instances where there are real overlaps between deposits and objects, for example where an artefact might contain deposits, such as cremation urns (see Figure 19). One could thus argue that the very distinction between objects and contextual units such as deposits, features and sites is ambiguous, and is certainly relative.

Figure 19   Objects as contexts: half-sectioned Bronze Age cremation urn

   The crucial point in the foregoing discussion is that without reflexivity, without a concern for how our concepts and practices affect interpretation, the routinised methodologies usually employed in the field can become very constraining. The key point is the importance of foregrounding the event nature of the archaeological record from a single artefact to a landscape – it is the product of temporal phenomena, whether cultural or natural. This is not to be confused with Binford's distinction between a dynamic past cultural system and a static archaeological record. Firstly, the archaeological record is not static, as Schiffer has demonstrated; but secondly, the temporality I am talking about affects methodological concepts such as object and context, not simply a general concept such as society. In the next section, I will address how such events or activity are theorised in terms of human action or behaviour, and then discuss how this compares with the conception of actions and events in actualistic studies such as ethnoarchaeology and experimental archaeology.

Archaeological events

Agency and material culture

The idea that, although archaeology deals with artefacts, it is always the people behind the artefacts who matter, is as old as archaeology. Pitt Rivers explicitly pointed this out, and what he understood by 'people' was chiefly their minds or rather the contents of their minds – ideas:

> Human ideas, as represented by the various products of human industry, are capable of classification into genera, species and varieties, in the same manner as the products of the vegetable and animal kingdoms, and in their development from the homogeneous to the heterogeneous they obey the same laws.
>
> (Pitt Rivers 1906: 18)

The relation between language and ideas is quite closely linked to this history so I shall make references to it. Pitt Rivers considered language as basically similar to artefacts, as both were outward signs of inner ideas. The chief difference is that language is better able to express complex ideas, and thus there will be an inverse relation between the degree of evolution and the importance of material culture:

> In endeavouring to trace back prehistoric culture to its root forms, we find that in proportion as the value of language and the ideas conveyed by language diminishes, that of ideas embodied in material forms increases in stability and permanence.
>
> (Pitt Rivers 1906: 13)

With Childe, however, a rather different view emerges, one which stresses a materialism rather than an idealism, where anything that is of real or lasting consequence has, by the nature of history, to be materially expressed:

> For all culture finds expression in action – action in the material world. It is indeed through action alone that culture is maintained and transmitted; a belief that exists only in somebody's head forms no part of culture and has no existence for history or anthropology. Some of the actions dictated by, and expressive of, culture effect durable changes

in the material world. All such fall within the purview of archaeology. It is indeed just these human actions that have provided the material out of which archaeological cultures are constructed.

(Childe 1951: 33)

For Childe, the absence of access to past language is then also not necessarily cause for despair. Both Pitt Rivers and Childe express the possibility of understanding past people in real ways through their material culture, though for different reasons; Pitt Rivers because prehistoric material culture was more expressive of their (simple) ideas than language (unlike today), Childe because all significant actions have material manifestation.

Both Pitt Rivers and Childe, however, saw material culture as ultimately referring to something else – ideas, thoughts, etc. Even Walter Taylor essentially expressed the same view when he regarded material culture as not really culture, but the material expression of culture. In his seminal text, he distinguished three orders of phenomena – culture, behaviour and objects; culture is first and foremost a mental phenomenon:

It also follows from this that the concept of material culture is fallacious. Culture is unobservable, is non-material . . . . Even behaviour, though observable, is non-material . . . . Therefore the term material culture is a misnomer and the dichotomy between material and non-material relates only to observable results of cultural behaviour, not to culture itself.

(Taylor 1948: 102)

Taylor's conception of culture as mental was similar to that of his contemporaries such as Kroeber (e.g. Watson 1995: 685), and it was clearly a notion which was shared on both sides of the Atlantic as the previous examples show. The importance of this understanding of culture lies not so much in the distinction between mental and material but in the notion that *ideas* formed the basis of culture – not behaviour, practices or objects, all of which were derivative of ideas. It is this which also explains why the concerns of the culture-historical period were heavily focused on classification and other expressions of normativism. It was not until the 1960s and the New Archaeology that a new turn was given to this conception, and behaviour in particular came to take on much greater significance – indeed, one might say that in Taylor's three orders the position of ideas and behaviour was reversed in terms of importance.

Binford's classic statement of the New Archaeology, 'Archaeology as anthropology', adopted Leslie White's definition of culture as 'man's extrasomatic means of adaption' (Binford 1962). Binford and New Archaeology in general paid very little attention to the mental realm, to ideas; his main focus was on behaviour and material culture and how they related through this conception of culture:

> Granted we cannot excavate a kinship terminology or a philosophy, but we can and do excavate the material items which functioned together with these more behavioural elements within the appropriate cultural subsystems. The formal structure of artifact assemblages together with the between element contextual relationships should and do present a systematic and understandable picture *of the total extinct* cultural system.
>
> (Binford 1962: 218)

Under this functional interpretation of material culture, interpretation of the archaeological record in terms of behaviour rather than normative ideas changed the whole perception of that record. By taking the 'mental' out of the equation, behaviour was no longer an expression of something else (i.e. beliefs) but a primary element in society, functioning to maintain the viability of that society. Beliefs were now in fact just one sub-system (ideological) among others (the social and the technological), each having quite different frames of reference but subordinate to the more basic concepts of behaviour and material culture. A classic example, and one I have introduced elsewhere in the book, is Binford's study of inter-assemblage variability among Mousterian stone tools (Binford 1973). Here variability of material culture which was previously interpreted in terms of mental templates (i.e. culture), is now re-interpreted in behavioural terms expressing different types of activities.

A major critique of the functional interpretation of material culture was precisely its failure to fully address the 'mental' dimension of culture (Johnson 1989: 191). The post-processual reaction pioneered by Hodder re-asserted its significance and, in particular, its relation to behaviour (e.g. Hodder 1985). For Binford, the mental realm or beliefs remain just a sub-system, and one largely irrelevant, as well as often dismissed as 'palaeopsychology' despite his early acceptance through the notion of 'ideotechnic subsystem' (cf. Binford 1962 and 1987). Yet for Hodder, ideas or beliefs are not just a sub-system but inextricably part of behaviour (and material culture) – you cannot justifiably ignore them. Whether it is making a pot or growing crops, the beliefs surrounding that action (e.g. about why it is being done) are not epiphenomenal but affect to the deepest level how the action is performed and therefore its consequences. Moreover, the action itself helps to reinforce that belief – thus while Hodder is partially restoring Taylor's tripartite scheme instead of Binford's reduced two, it is not a return to the hierarchical implications of that model. Hodder does not see behaviour or material culture as expressive or derivative of beliefs, but rather all form part of a whole, each constituting the other. Thus of prime importance is the *active* nature of human behaviour and material culture. Moreover, despite the behavioural emphasis in the New Archaeology, such behaviour was usually interpreted on a macro-level, in terms of how a society or a community behaved, with little importance attached to individuals. Post-processualism, in highlighting the active nature of individuals, also raised the question of agency, that individuals can make a difference (see Bell 1992 for an alternative view on these issues).

To give an example of the post-processual approach, I will describe Matthew Johnson's study on the transformation of English medieval housing in the sixteenth century (Johnson 1989). He argues that individual houses should not be seen merely as expressions of broad normative structures but the result of interplay between the individuals who constructed and/or lived in them and the wider social *habitus* they inherited. Comparing two houses, similarities and differences emerged, one expressive of the wider trends, the other of the individual nature of the site and people involved. Thus both houses were sited away from the main village and used similar reorganisation of architectural elements such as back-to-back fireplaces, staircases and ostentatious ceilings, but differed in that one was a new building, the other on the site of an older moated hall, and used different details associated with the fireplaces. It is this conjunction of shared and individual elements which can be linked to the theoretical articulation of social structures and agency, as exemplified in structuration theory.

Much post-processual archaeology has been criticised for espousing the active nature of human behaviour or agency in theory, but falling short in practice (Johnson 1989; Barrett 1988); the critics usually invoke Giddens' structuration theory as an attempt to overcome this problem and articulate in greater detail the role of action and agency in archaeology (Giddens 1984; Barrett 1988). Barrett's criticism in particular encapsulates a debate here between different notions of material culture, between regarding it as similar to a text (Hodder 1989a) or as practice (Barrett 1988). In many respects, though, the difference between Hodder's and Barrett's positions may be exaggerated; both use very similar language in describing the relation between individuals and society and both reference similar theorists (e.g. Giddens, Bourdieu).

Nevertheless, in the light of post-processual critique, archaeologists from within the processual mainstream began to rethink their views on behaviour, of which two main strands might be picked up: cognitive archaeology as presented by Renfrew and the behavioural archaeology of Earle and Preucel.[1] A growing range of studies under the name of cognitive archaeology sees itself as part of, and a continuation of, processualism (e.g. Renfrew 1994). Cognitive archaeology is concerned to understand 'how people used their minds, and formulated and utilised useful concepts' regardless of the philosophical standpoint (Renfrew 1994: 5). For Renfrew, cognitive archaeology is a science, the science of how humans have constructed and used symbols. Examples include the study of measuring systems (e.g. tally sticks, weights), representative or iconic art (e.g. rock carving/painting) or design templates for artefact production.

The kinds of studies included under cognitive archaeology vary and it may be misleading to give them a theoretical consensus, but it is quite clear that despite apparent convergence they differ quite radically from post-processual approaches (e.g. see 'Viewpoint' in *Cambridge Archaeological Journal* (1993) 3: 247–70). On the one hand, they adopt the importance of the mental as a key component alongside behaviour and material culture, instead of viewing it simply as a sub-system; on the other hand, however, cognitive archaeology seems to argue against any conflation of these, with beliefs, behaviour and material culture – although all interacting – still occupying discrete realms. Thus while Renfrew and others such as Flannery and Marcus argue for a holism where the cognitive realm affects behaviour or more specifically, where religious beliefs may affect subsistence practices, there is still a sense in which the two can be separated. In doing so, such an approach misunderstands the key point of post-processualism – that belief, behaviour and material culture are not just related but intertwined and mutually constitutive. The very idea of 'an archaeology of the mind' as a separate field is highly dubious under post-processualism.

A major problem seems to be a misunderstanding over the concept of 'meaning' – processual-cognitive approaches affirm an objective methodology and thus distinguish cognition as a process from its subjective experience – as Renfrew puts it, between *how* they thought and *what* they thought (Renfrew 1993: 249). But meaning is not about getting inside people's minds for it pervades all aspects of human existence. Renfrew seems to be conflating two issues here – the subjective and the objective with the mental and material – and regards meaning as somehow a subjective property of the mind, while thought processes and structures are somehow objective in so far as they manifest themselves in behaviour and material culture. Despite the recognition of the active nature of material culture, cognitive archaeology sustains a divide between the mental, behavioural and the material. As Hodder says, one cannot separate these out; the content and the structure of cognition are intertwined, a good example being the presumption of rationality in studies of decision-making which ignores the fact that such rationality may be culturally or socially specific (Hodder 1993b: 257).

This point leads directly on to the other development in processual archaeology, loosely termed 'behavioural', which has focused on decision-making processes (Earle and Preucel 1987; Earle 1991). Against earlier approaches which tended to view decision-making in 'rational' terms, Earle has proposed the addition of cultural rules (Earle 1991).[2] He thus distinguishes three types of rationality, all seen as mutually reinforcing rather than mutually exclusive: the first two, economic, and evolutionary, are those used normally in processualism and usually expressed through optimisation theory. Deriving from micro-economics, this theory assumes that decisions will be derived from optimising the results based on a weighing of the costs and benefits involved. As a specific theory it is weak and open to criticisms of ethnocentrism; as a general theory it might be described as trite. To refine it, the notion of cultural rationality is introduced which provides the relative measure of success – success being determined though group iden-tification or association. Essentially, the basis of this behavioural approach is the interplay of choices determined by pragmatics (economic/evolutionary rationality) and society (cultural rationality). Another version of this approach is in the use of operations research in archaeology, which looks at behaviour in terms of multi-linear event trees, mapping behav-ioural choices and consequences through a dendrogram (Bleed 1991). Again, while optimisation theory lies at the origin of this, it is claimed that such an approach can be modified through the inclusion of cultural factors influ-encing decisions.

While this might seem a fruitful union of processual and post-processual concerns, from a post-processual perspective the very distinction between pragmatic and cultural choices might be suspect. However, rather than focus on this distinction (which has partly been discussed in Chapter 3 under the topic of production), I want to draw back and recapitulate the main issues. For all their differences, processual and post-processual approaches focus on behaviour or actions as the critical concept to be articulated with material culture. Unlike the earlier part of the twentieth century in which culture was seen as primarily a *mental* phenomenon, since the New Archaeology it is seen as a *behavioural* one – whether we choose to define behaviour as rational/functional or as meaningfully constituted. To what extent is material culture, though, still supplemental to the concept of culture – not so much to ideas any more as to human behaviour or action?

The subject has been most widely addressed in post-processual discourse, partly because, under processualism, material culture patterning came to stand in for behavioural patterning – it represented or expressed it, just as earlier it expressed beliefs, ideas, etc. Indeed the very distinction of behav-iour and material culture lay at the basis of middle range theory (see p. 183). Thus the important shift for processualists was from ideas to behaviour. It is only under post-processualism that the *passivity* of this view *vis-à-vis* ma-terial culture has been criticised, although there are differences about how to articulate the relation between material culture and behaviour, as exem-plified in the views of Ian Hodder and John Barrett (also see p. 173). Barrett is quite specific about the importance of the material world for human agency: it acts as a locale, an arena within which practice takes place, yet the derivative role of material culture is quite explicit: 'The material world contains acculturated structures drawn upon and invested with meaning by human action' (Barrett 1988: 9). But the concern for looking at practices implies the primacy of the agent and the supplementarity of the artefact. After all, one can perform actions without artefacts – artefacts come after (both historically and logically) agents.[3] Is this acceptable? Indeed Hodder

makes just this kind of point in criticising Barrett for sustaining a distinction between practice and thought (Hodder 1989a),

Despite the significant development of Hodder's notion of an active material culture, there are still residual problems, and I think that ultimately
both he and Barrett perpetuate something of the idea of the person as the
'origin' of meaning, the absent presence in the archaeological record (see
Hodder 1989a). Even though the meaning of material culture does not
derive from ideas or thoughts, one sees in the position of both Hodder and
Barrett the tacit notion that it at least derives from *people*, and more particularly, agents. We tend to see the subject as the *origin* of material culture
– material culture as supplemental to the basic fact of the human person.
In this sense, the subject or agent is the fundamental datum of any social
science – meaning derives from this subject which transforms the world.
The agent as origin. But can we really privilege the agent in this way as
the origin of meaning? Is there not almost a contradiction in asserting both
a theory of agency (in the strong sense critiqued here) and the active nature
of material culture?

It is important to clear up what the concept of agency means. When
the issue arose in post-processual archaeology, proponents were quick to
point out that agency and the individual are not the same and thus objec-
tions to reinstating people were misguided. But consider what an agent is,
against an individual: it is an abstraction or reduction from the individual,
a person distilled into their essence (as Western philosophy teaches) – the
essence being freedom. What marks the essence of Man (*sic*) is his capacity
for free will, to act. The whole notion of agency is based on this Protestant-
capitalist notion of the individual as a *free agent*. Individuals like Julius
Caesar are generally not what archaeology is about, but it can take into
account the fact that Caesar, not in his particular being but his essential
being, is free and can alter history through this freedom, and in this he is
the same as every other individual, potentially. I do not need to dwell on
the essentialism and archaism of this view, but it is strange that the conception of agency has not been more critically examined.

If the individual is the source of meaning, where does this lie? What are
the limits of the individual and her action? Raising an arm to signal is a
meaningful gesture, but what makes it different from a pot? What makes
the action different from the artefact? Is it that an action relies on the
body, whereas an artefact is physically separate? Yet most actions clearly
incorporate physically separate things, such as opening a door, so do we
call such an action a combination of action and artefact or is it irreducible?
Or, if we have an armless person with an artificial limb who opens a door,
does she simply perform an action or is that a mixture of an action-plus-
artefact? What I am trying to draw out in these questions is the role the
body plays in this distinction between actions and artefacts. The tendency
is to implicitly use the body as the dividing line, yet explicitly deny the

body, in fact to focus on intentionality or other such things which use the body or manifest themselves in the body. Bodily alterations such as circumcision, ear or nose piercing, or a tattoo are revealing in this respect for they are both of the body and not of the body.

From the other angle one might ask whether the body is such a stable or bounded entity either. Lynn Meskell has written extensively on the issue of the body in relation to archaeology and, drawing on broader philosophical and feminist debates, convincingly argues for a fluidity to corporeality (Meskell 1999: ch. 1). Not only is the body open to modification in the ways mentioned above, but it is an 'open system' in so far as all kinds of material exchanges take place, substances both leaving and entering the body such as faeces, semen, food, etc. More generally, therefore, the body is not so much a given entity as a process, a materialising of social or cultural phenomena such as sex/gender.

Meskell's discussion of the body is tied in to the broader issue of identity and she eloquently discusses a whole range of terms such as the individual, agency and personhood, in relation to archaeology. As she rightly remarks, the key issue is to reconcile the multiplicity of social identities (i.e. gender, race, ethnicity, class, etc.) with the singularity of individual experience (Meskell 1999: 50). An important site for such a reconciliation lies in the body, or more accurately, perhaps, in embodiment or materialisation. The usefulness of this conception is evident if one considers the idea of material culture – what is it in distinction to? *Ideal* culture? What does the 'material' refer to? As Walter Taylor said – but from a different perspective – the term material culture is fallacious (see p. 171). It is an undiscussed concept, with both implications of physicality (Yates 1991), and extra-corporeality, that is, outside the body.

We can relate it to a very Hegelian conception of human agency which Daniel Miller has already made interesting use of in his discussion of the nature of material culture, particularly of the concept of objectification (*Entausserung*). Like Hegel he places the process of objectification between a subject and an object, and while he frequently states that each constitutes the other, that is neither is prior – the impression is that this process still has its ultimate origin in the subject. Thus the process of objectification is one in which 'a subject externalises itself in a creative act of differentiation, and in turn re-appropriates this externalisation through an act which Hegel terms sublation (aufhebung)' (Miller 1987: 28). What maintains this impression is the phrasing of the dialectics in terms of (human) subject and (material) object, a distinction which, I believe, is harmful – perhaps the concept of material culture should be put under erasure to signify this.

The critical point to come from this, is that if people are not agents but bodies, then actions cannot be viewed from a simplistic causal model which posits the agent as the cause of an event. Similar critiques have been levelled from within the sociology of technology which employs the term *actant* rather than agent to signify the fact that agency can be nonhuman as well as human (e.g. see Latour 1992; also Boast 1997 for its relevance to archaeology). Just as the material boundaries to an action cannot be split, nor can the causative links in history be split. Many of the concerns for presenting a more human narrative of the past may not necessarily be served by invoking agency, which is, as I have already said, a very abstract notion anyway. Indeed I think there are two separate issues here which have got conflated in the concept of agency – one being the particularity of history and social life, the other, the presence of a human dimension, archaeology with a face. Johnson's study of agency and structure in English housing related above could ultimately be seen as a conjunction of the particular and the general – the specific articulation of a more general set of concepts. The particulars in question which are subsumed under the concept of agency could just as easily be explained in terms of more local (i.e. family, village, parish) concepts or structures, as opposed to broader national or European concepts. The structure–agency dichotomy subsumes a great deal more variety of spatial and temporal scales which may be more informative. On the other hand, if the issue is 'humanising the past', then agency is a red herring; there are far more exciting ways, which focus more on an archaeology of the body and an archaeology of the senses – an archaeology which engages with emotion, for example. An excellent example of this is Sarah Tarlow's recent re-examination of death from the point of view of experience. Ironically, most archaeological work on death has looked at it in terms of everything except death itself – status, ideology, power. No one has actually studied what death means as a part of human experience (Tarlow 1999). Drawing on metaphors of death on tombstones, she introduces an emotional component to the interpretation of mortality. Approaches such as this offer a far more humanised presentation of the past than abstract agents.

From this discussion, I think it is important to reassert the interconnected nature of material culture, behaviour and belief; the question of agency is the last lingering vestige of a processual, even pre-processual notion of culture which is divided into separate realms. Belief, or the mental, was fully integrated with behaviour under post-processualism but behaviour in the guise of agency remained distinct as a concept from material culture, despite assertions on the active nature of material culture. All three of the Taylorian realms should be seen as merging into each other and it is misleading to try and separate them (as in cognitive archaeology, for example). This of course implies the need for a much more complex understanding of causality and events in the archaeological record that does not base itself on the notion that material culture is distinct from behaviour. And yet, there is a deep epistemological reason for keeping this distinction, which ties in to the role of actualistic studies. Before discussing this reason, I want to contrast the theoretical complexity presented here with a very simple model of causality and events used in such actualistic studies as well as site reports and other 'descriptions' of the archaeological record.

Ethnoarchaeology, experimental archaeology and the basic event

We often use the term 'palimpsest' to describe archaeological sites, but what does this really mean? At one level, in excavating a multi-phase or multi-period site, particularly present in urban contexts, the archaeology consists of several superimposed activity areas or 'sites' even. But the language we use is revealing, because we do tend to think in terms of phases of activity as if any one phase had a clear beginning and end. I have always thought that one of the best things about the Harris matrix is its multi-linearity, and yet at the end of the day its very virtue is often hidden through coarse-grained phasing as if the site consisted of a series of geological layers. Ironically, the image of the site presented in the final synthesis often shows little difference from pre-matrix days. At a more complex level, a palimpsest might be the superimposition of artefact distributions, each associated with a different activity; the resulting pattern is therefore not the product of a single event but of several, each potentially obscuring the other (e.g. see Carr 1987 for an interesting study of dissecting such palimpsests).

This situation is very analogous to the superimposion of features with all the concomitant disturbances and blurring it can effect. However, as in that case, here too the record is treated as if it was composed of several discrete actions, which, if only they could be dissected, would reveal their individual patterning. In both cases, the perception is of a simple sequence of discrete events which only needs to be pulled apart by careful strati-graphic excavation or spatial filtering, to produce an event chain. But if, as we have argued, such an image is overly simple and misleading, what is the alternative? One of the advantages in the supplementary chart to the Harris matrix I discussed earlier in the chapter is that it shows the duration as well as the sequence of stratigraphic entities, without separating produc-tion from use. Another advantage is that it shows a site as a palimpsest of activities occurring at different rates or scales of duration and that instead of having to phase a site, one can retain a sense of multi-temporality. At any one time or place on a site, a whole series of events may be taking place simultaneously, but not necessarily at the same rate or 'speed'.

For example, consider one feature on a site such as a compound ditch around a prehistoric farmstead; what a rich temporality it must have from when it was first cut, to the gradual weathering of the sides and the rain washing soil into its base, the windborne pollen which falls into the silts, a broken pot dumped one day. The throwing of the pot may take merely seconds, the cutting of the ditch a day, while the silting up takes years.

How can a matrix display this, and how should we separate the act of throwing away the pot from the cumulative silting up? Maybe such an act would never have been done on a freshly cut ditch; all these events are implicated with each other even though they take place at different scales of duration, and even the ditch itself does not contain these events. The same summer pollen also falls in a pit or a well, the same cutting of the ditch later sees a human burial, part of the same broken pot ends up as lid to another pot. It is the interconnectedness of events which are so repressed in conventional conceptions of the archaeological record, unless that interconnectedness is expressed merely in terms of a causal chain.

Traditional intra-site spatial analysis and stratigraphic recording have, by focusing on a single activity at any one time and following its depositional patterns, perpetuated the idea that life consists of a sequence of discrete events. This is not to say that we do not envisage different activities occurring contemporaneously in different locales on a site or even at the same locale, but rather that we envisage the activity itself as a discrete entity, which has its own space–time zone – as if it can and does exist independently of other activities. On such a perception, the overlapping of any activities will always be interpreted as interference, as pathological. It is as if we recognise that the archaeological record is a palimpsest but that the phenomenon of the palimpsest is something which distorts or obscures the original actions or events behind the record which exist as discrete entities. But maybe the palimpsest is in the very nature of actions and events – in history. Rather than treat it as a pathology to be dissected, we should embrace it as the heart of a living site.

Unfortunately, ethnoarchaeology and experimental archaeology have only exacerbated this perception and sustained the idea of simple event sequences in the archaeological record. This is due, as I will argue, to their role in epistemological issues of archaeology. The difference between the two sub-disciplines has been debated – for some, both are forms of experimental archaeology (e.g. Ingersoll *et al.* 1977), but generally a distinction is maintained (e.g. Skibo 1992: 24). In many ways, the distinction is relative to whether one is looking at the purposes of the study or the means; both sub-disciplines share a concern for material culture–behaviour correlates, although they use different means. Ethnoarchaeology, as distinct from ethnographic analogy (Hodder 1982c: 28; Kent 1987: 39–43) developed as a specific field of study with the New Archaeology in the late 1960s/1970s in order to aid understanding of the patterning found in the archaeological record. It also forms a core part of what is known as middle range theory or research (see p. 183). In this role, ethnoarchaeology is ultimately a field study which typically examines specific activities in terms of their material patterning so these can be contrasted with an analogous archaeological context, either directly or indirectly through generalising statements (cf. Skibo 1992: 16–17). Whether this comparison is formal, lawlike or relational, in either case the aim is to associate a *particular* behaviour with a *particular* material correlate. Of course, ethnoarchaeology can feed into more general theories of material culture, but then this might not be described as ethnoarchaeology but as archaeological anthropology (Hodder 1982c: 212). I do not want to get embroiled in a discussion of definitions since the point I want to make chiefly concerns the way studies of modern material culture (of Western or non-Western societies) are used in a direct way towards the archaeological record. As an example, I will choose a familiar case study, Binford's smudge pits (Binford 1967).

Binford's paper looked at the various attributes of a certain type of archaeological feature on Mississippian sites in the USA, a pit filled with carbonised corncobs (Binford 1967). He compares these to ethnographic examples of similar pits which are known to have been used for smoking hides, and then supports the analogy with a set of associated variables such as seasonality and female labour. Whether or not Binford's argument is convincing or sufficiently supported by explanatory links between the similarities, a key question must hang over the idea that it is valid to focus on a *specific activity*. Hodder raises the importance of the wider cultural context in which such an activity occurs (Hodder 1982c: 20–3). Indeed, this is the very heart of his critique and approach to analogy, but the point needs to be pushed; there is a difference between arguing that a certain material patterning/ activity is *related* to other patterns/activities and arguing that any material patterning/activity may not be so discrete or distinct. This notion of discrete activities can be seen in another classic ethnoarchaeological study, 'Millie's Camp' (Bonnichsen 1972).

In this study, Bonnichsen analysed the layout and distribution of objects in a recently abandoned Indian camp in the Canadian Rockies and then tested his inferences by consulting a former occupant, Millie. Central to his analysis was the concept of *activity area*, the site being divided up and numbered into different parts based on features, features with objects and clusters of objects (Bonnichsen 1972: 277). Now what is interesting about this study is not so much the testability of it, or that he got some things right and others wrong, but that in a way, by asking Millie about the site *in terms of activity areas*, the notion of discrete events relating to discrete material deposits is never in question – either the inference is right or wrong. Bonnichsen seems to recognise that activity areas did overlap, but in his list of four successive inferential errors, the idea that activities and the functions of objects are discrete is maintained.

If ethnoarchaeology overemphasises the discreteness of activities/patterns, then experimental archaeology is even more culpable. Experimental archaeology has as long a history as the use of ethnographic analogy – Pitt Rivers conducted various experiments in using prehistoric tools and the study of ditch weathering, but there have been many more studies, especially in the replication of ancient artefacts or structures (Ascher 1961a; Ingersoll *et al.*

1977; Coles 1979). Coles sees the basis of any experimental archaeology as a 'test of quality' for anything from sites to weapons; by quality he means any of three levels: basic appearance, production technology and function (Coles 1979: 35–41). It is quite clear that these levels are all framed by a certain conception of the archaeological record – that is, it is primarily a material or physical record which has certain basic, given, physical properties which both constrain and determine form and function. For Ascher, this fact restrained the scope of imitative experiments to aspects of technology and subsistence, yet to him this is more or less all that the archaeological record consists of anyway (Ascher 1961a: 793–4). Coles makes a similar point: 'Experimental archaeology has the virtue that it deals with the basic sources of archaeological data, the material remains of stone, bone, wood and metal' (Coles 1979: 243).

The idea of testing goes hand in hand with this concept; it is a question of evaluating the quality of form or function for a particular aspect of the archaeological record, and such tests can only make sense against universal, non-cultural criteria. The Scandinavian projects on clearance and cultivation by Steensberg and Iversen, or the British studies on earthwork erosion at Overton Down, or even 'living' experiments such as at Butser Farm, are all characterised by this belief. The problem is, what do they really tell us? Such objects, their form and function, are only meaningful in a cultural context. The fact that we can use Neolithic axes to chop down trees efficiently tells us nothing about the Neolithic; all it tells us is that we can chop down trees with such axes. Of course micro-wear comparisons might strengthen the claim that Neolithic axes *were* used to chop down trees but this still does not tell us why.

The problem with experimental archaeology is that it pulls an action or event out of any cultural context, and presents it as an isolated action as if it had meaning outside a cultural milieu. This is very misleading and helps to perpetuate notions we have of actions or events as discrete entities, which can be sub-divided or conjoined as an event chain. Cutting down a tree is never just that; it is not for the experimental archaeologist since they are doing it within the milieu of Western academic science, and nor was it for a Neolithic person. The danger here also is that one can assume there is a *basic action* which underlies both the archaeologist's experiment and the Neolithic person's forest clearance – but even this confuses the physical act involving a human body, an axe and a tree with an intentional and meaningful act. It is quite possible to envisage all kinds of intentions in someone hacking away at a tree which do not involve forest clearance or even tree-felling although this may be a consequence – the very experimental act is just one of them.

Both ethnoarchaeology and experimental archaeology rely on this atomistic view of human actions – indeed it is the basis for their use in middle range theory, for if one cannot separate out distinct sequences of behaviour from the wider cultural context, then all such patternings and studies cannot be applied to other cultural contexts such as the archaeological record. This is most obvious in Schiffer's behavioural archaeology which studies the relation of behaviour to material culture in terms of discrete behavioural chains; indeed it is a condition of his whole theoretical system that such behavioural chains are distinct and potentially separable from each other (Schiffer and Skibo 1997). A similar approach is used in operations research which, although it employs multi-linear sequences, still presumes that actions and events can be broken down naturally into discrete elements and decision forks (Bleed 1991). I want to finish with a recent example which illustrates this theme and the close relationship between ethnoarchaeology and experimental archaeology – Skibo's work on the use of temper in cooking pots (Skibo 1992: 28–30).

Beginning with controlled laboratory experiments, the heating effectiveness and performance of differently tempered vessels was tested to explain the transition from organic to sand-tempered pottery in the Late Archaic–Early Woodland period of the eastern USA. To strengthen this inference, ethnoarchaeological work was done to find out how people become aware of performance characteristics and which ones were noticed. It was found that in use (i.e. cooking, washing-up), features such as heat effectiveness and ease of cleaning were important in selecting different types of vessels. This study combines both approaches to unravel correlates between the use of pottery and its form – between behaviour and material culture. The trouble is, it assumes that a basic event or property (i.e. performativity) can be distilled from the particular context of the study – both in the experiment and the pottery-using group. The post-processual critique of behaviour in so far as it is viewed as situated in specific historical and cultural contexts clearly argues against this, and in doing so provides quite damaging consequences for the role of actualistic studies in archaeology. In the next section, I examine the whole question of middle range theory, its status in archaeology, and the consequences of its rejection.

Middle range theory and the identity of archaeology

Middle range theory and middle range research

Middle range theory developed directly out of the early theoretical writings of the New Archaeology in North America, in particular of Lewis Binford who argued for the development of a specifically archaeological theory distinct from general social theory (Binford 1977; Raab and Goodyear 1984: 258–62). A specifically archaeological theory was one which focused on the archaeological record and how to make inferences from it, or, as Binford characterised it, how to move from the *static* archaeological record to the past *dynamic* cultural system. He characterised MRT as a 'Rosetta Stone', a means of translating or decoding the static into the dynamic, and, elsewhere, as a tool for diagnosing the 'disease' from its 'symptoms' (Binford 1982: 130; 1981: 23–4). All these metaphors essentially capture the fact that, unlike most social sciences, archaeology has only *indirect* access to behaviour and therefore requires a method for inferring behaviour from material correlates. A good example and one commonly employed is the ascription of a certain function to a certain artefact, such as the use of a pointed stone as an arrowhead. Through experimental work, analogies and use–wear analysis, such an inference can be at least partially substantiated. All these studies are examples of middle range research. On this basis, MRT is a body of theory (or methodology – see p. 186) which bridges the gap between our observation of the archaeological record and our interpretation of it as a cultural system – it provides the middle ground between unreflective observation and general theory. It is middle range in a *procedural* sense, not in the sense (as originally used in sociology) of its *applicability* (e.g. Raab and Goodyear 1984; Kosso 1991: 622–3). Thus an MRT might have very general cross-cultural applicability, but its role in interpreting the past is as a bridge or methodological tool and is quite distinct from general social theory.

The distinction which Binford upholds is quite important for this discussion, but, ironically, much of what he says – in particular in terms of the debate with Schiffer on this subject – seems to contradict this distinction. I have already partially discussed the Binford–Schiffer debate at the beginning of this chapter, but one of the main differences is over the relation between MRT and general theory (Tschauner 1996: 8–10). For Binford, as I have said, MRT is distinct from general theory, but Schiffer tries to reclaim something of the original sociological meaning of the term as something occupying a middle ground of abstraction (Schiffer 1988: 462–3). Thus, while for Binford all of Schiffer's work constitutes middle range theory, Schiffer's main distinction is between general or social theory and reconstruction theory (ibid.). Is this simply a semantic difference or a different way of dividing up the same realms of theory (cf. Schiffer 1988: figure 1)? Partly, but there is a deeper issue emerging from the differences between Binford and Schiffer, particularly about the separation of social or general theory from middle range or reconstruction theory. The issue hinges on Binford's critique of Schiffer's notion of C-transforms.

Schiffer's transformational or reconstruction theory makes a similar distinction as MRT does between what he calls the archaeological context and the systemic (i.e. past cultural) context; but, importantly, Schiffer adds that archaeological theory needs to distinguish the *correlates* between behaviour and material residues, from those processes, or *transforms* which distort the residues, and which he divides into two types – natural and cultural (hence N-transforms and C-transforms). Until recently, Schiffer wrote much more on transforms, giving the impression that his behavioural archaeology is simply about formation processes (e.g. Schiffer 1976, 1987), but current work, particularly his latest text on material culture as a theory of communication, shows how formation processes are just one side of his theoretical perspective (Schiffer and Miller 1999). The disagreement between Binford and Schiffer would seem to revolve around this distinction between transforms and correlates – in short, Binford appears to see this distinction as spurious, or at the very least ambiguous, especially when it comes to C-transforms, as I discussed earlier in the chapter.

Thus, on this point Binford has a more integrated conception of formation processes, where the distinction between them and the systemic context or cultural system is more fluid. He criticises Schiffer's programme which detaches them and sets them up as 'absolute formation processes' (Binford 1983: 162); for Binford, they are necessarily limited in scope and generality because they are partially contingent on the cultural system. For Schiffer, on the other hand, this is not so – he regards the study of formation processes as providing independent, cross-cultural generalizations about the relationship between the archaeological and systemic context, separate from general theories about the systemic context. And, ironically, Schiffer's position is more consistent – for if Binford is right, and the distinction between transforms and systemic context is fluid, then so necessarily is the distinction between MRT and general theory (Tschauner 1996: 9). For the difference between MRT and general theory hinges on the one being concerned with the relation between the archaeological record and the cultural context, and the other with just the cultural context, and yet if the archaeological record is not distinct from the cultural context, then it follows that general theory cannot be that distinct from MRT. The consequences of this have a strong bearing on philosophical issues about the status of archaeological inference and generalisation. To show this it is necessary to go back a little and describe why, especially for Binford, it is so important to keep MRT distinct from general theory.

The role of MRT, you will recall, was to act as a bridge, a methodological tool to move from observation to interpretation – it helped to ground interpretation by providing an independent check against general theory. It marks the processual acceptance of the theory-ladenness of data. In themselves, therefore, middle range theories are as theoretical as any other theory and no more or less general than 'general' social theory – indeed in another context, say a study of middening practice, they might constitute interpretation and require their own, other middle range theory (e.g. Kosso 1991: 623). This is a critical epistemological point – because middle range theories are theories like any other, they can stand independently, and it is this independence which acts as a check on the interpretative process.

This however is precisely the point on which post-processual critique targets MRT: the assumption of independence:

> While the idea of Middle Range Theory in relation to physical processes (e.g. decay of C-14) is feasible, it is difficult to see how there can ever be universal laws of cultural process which are independent of one's higher-level cultural theories. Of course, within these high-level theories there is a great need for research on material culture, processes of deposition and the like – one can call this Middle Range research. What is quite different, and denied in this volume, is that the type of measuring device discussed by Binford and termed Middle Range Theory can exist independent of cultural context.
>
> (Hodder 1986: 103)

For Hodder and indeed most post-processualists, MRT is thus a misguided enterprise. Interestingly, however, in two recent publications MRT is redefined as the background knowledge or assumptions to more general interpretations of the past (Kosso 1991; Tschauner 1996; also see Saitta 1992 for a Marxist MRT). Comparisons are made between MRT and hermeneutics, arguing that in practice both processual and post-processual interpretations rely on the same kinds of independent, background assumptions or theory. Just as processual explanation uses MRT to bridge observation and theory, so post-processual interpretation makes use of a number of similar assumptions (such as analogies, formation processes). Tschauner's paper in particular goes through some examples in a very detailed way to demonstrate this.

Their arguments are very convincing and there is no doubt that both processual and post-processual studies do make use of a similar range of assumptions and background theory which we might call MRT. However, I find one problem here which has not been fully addressed and perhaps misses the central difference between processualists and post-processualists – that is, the status of middle range research and its distinction from middle range theory. If we accept Kosso's and Tschauner's arguments about MRT, then it must stand as quite independent from middle range research – the explicit study of formation processes, ethnoarchaeology, experimental archaeology, etc. MRT, as they describe it, is a *procedural* or epistemic title, something which refers not to the *content* of a theory but simply to its status in archaeological inference or generalisation. In the example quoted above from Kosso, a study of manuring does not constitute MRT, it only *becomes* MRT when it is incorporated into an interpretation of archaeological field systems for example. But this begs the question, what is it then prior to MRT?

The obvious answer is middle range research; indeed Hodder himself in the quote above suggests this. However, to call it middle range research is to imply that MRT is *not* simply a relative appellation but that *content does matter*. The very idea of conducting research specifically to resolve linking arguments suggests that MRT deriving from such sources has no other function but to be MRT, and in fact most research of this kind is conducted for this reason. And this is what is slightly troubling in Hodder's espousal of middle range research as distinct from MRT, for if middle-range research is conducted solely in order to act as middle-range theory, it implies that such research and MRT in general does not have the independent status claimed for it – MRT is not just a theory like any other, but one specifically designed as a methodological tool. The alternative is to redefine what such middle range research is – that it does stand alone as a separate enterprise, as many would now describe ethno-archaeology, for example, which has become largely an independent sub-discipline. Indeed, despite the earlier quote, Hodder does seem to uphold this view later on when he talks about ethnoarchaeology as 'the study of archaeology in ethnographic contexts in order to throw light on the ethnographic present' (Hodder 1986: 105). Ethnoarchaeology is more a part of anthropology or ethnohistory than archaeology, and certainly *not* a methodological field of research. This would also mean that the study of non-natural formation processes should really be part of ethnoarchaeology or an archaeology of the present rather than methodological research. Moreover, to continue calling any of these studies middle range research is thus a serious misnomer.

This is really the logical outcome of Binford's critique of Schiffer too, for it accepts the situated nature of formation processes (at least C-transforms), and rather a source of cross-cultural generalisations, their status becomes closer to that of analogies. Indeed, raising the question of analogy alongside middle range research goes to the heart of the issue. There is no question that middle range research forms a major part in archaeological inference, either explicitly or implicitly, but if its methodological status is challenged, what is left but its use analogically. But this of course begs the question of the status of analogy in archaeological interpretation. To conclude this section and at the same time broach some fundamental questions about what archaeology as a discipline is supposed to be, I will address this issue of analogy.

Analogy and archaeological generalisation

In the late nineteenth and early twentieth centuries, analogy – specifically ethnographic analogy – was central to cultural evolutionism. It provided the whole justification for cultural evolution in so far as non-Western societies were consistently used as examples of a certain type of society which throughout Europe had become extinct – or rather had evolved into modern Western civilisation:

> The existing races, in their respective stages of progression, may be taken as the bona fide representatives of the races of antiquity. . . . They thus afford us living illustrations of the social customs, forms of government,

laws and warlike practices, which belong to the ancient races from which they remotely sprang, whose implements, resembling, with but little difference, their own, are now found low down in the soil. . . .

(Pitt Rivers 1906: 53)

Such 'survivals' as they were often called were not simply illustrations of prehistoric communities but were themselves prehistoric, even though they existed as contemporaries of their Victorian observers. Works such as Sven Nilsson's *Primitive Inhabitants of Scandinavia* (1868), David Wilson's *Prehistoric Man* (1862), John Lubbock's *Prehistoric Times* (1865) and Lewis Henry Morgan's *Ancient Society* (1877) all worked on this premise. At the extreme is Sollas' *Ancient Hunters* (1911) where direct comparisons are made between palaeolithic cultures and contemporary societies with suggested historical connections: Mousterians became Tasmanians, Aurignacians became Bushmen and Magdalenians became the Eskimo (Sollas 1924: 591 ff.). The role of analogy is perhaps accentuated here if we remember that archaeology and anthropology, even in Europe, were for much of the nineteenth century effectively the same discipline with the same subject (Orme 1981: 15). With the divergence of these disciplines by the twentieth century and the rise of culture history in archaeology, the use of analogies in the explicit manner of nineteenth-century evolutionists was much more moderate and of less interest. Its role did not become a subject of discussion in archaeology until the 1950s and 1960s when more behavioural and functional interpretations of the archaeological record were starting to appear. The role of analogy in contemporary archaeology is thus very closely allied with this 'behavioural turn'.

In Britain, both Gordon Childe and Grahame Clark addressed the question of ethnographic analogies. Childe was generally sceptical and saw them as of primarily heuristic value unless some continuity could be demonstrated (Childe 1956: 48–9; Clark 1951; 1953). Clark made the same points in his paper 'Folk-culture and the study of European prehistory', and questioned the nineteenth-century notion of 'survivals', arguing that present non-Western societies have a history as long as ours and they have not simply remained 'stuck in time' (Clark 1951: 52). Like Childe, he initially preferred the use of analogies with some historical continuity over exotic ones, arguing that 'analogies between phenomena torn from their historical contexts may be very deceptive' (Clark 1951: 55). However, only two years later he goes a little further, arguing that 'it seems legitimate to attach greater significance to analogies drawn from societies existing under ecological conditions which approximate those reconstructed for the prehistoric culture under investigation than those adapted to markedly different environments' (Clark 1953: 355). However, he still qualifies this with a cautionary note, and prefaces this statement with the suggestion that its applicability is best confined to palaeolithic archaeology because of the lack of historical continuity.

The implicit idea that 'history' only really started in the Neolithic over-
lies a more tacit notion that the status of a society in terms of cultural
development is linked to our ability to comprehend it. Christopher Hawkes'
paper on the ladder of inference, a notion shared by many of his contemporaries including Childe, is highly informative in this respect (Hawkes
1954). Put briefly, the paper states that the extent to which we can know
about past societies is graded according to a scheme which places economy
and subsistence at the bottom (strongly grounded inference) to ideology at
the top (weakly grounded inference). But, and it is something we usually
forget, this ladder was shadowed by another, that of an evolutionary view
of prehistory (Wylie 1985: 74; Evans 1998). Significantly, this implied that
our ability to ascend the ladder of inference is directly related to the extent
to which the culture group had ascended the ladder of civilisation, for
which Hawkes proposed his own periodisation (Hawkes 1951). In other
words, we can understand the more ideological aspects of more developed
societies than less developed ones – Iron Age beliefs are more accessible
than palaeolithic ones. Another twist on this, though, is that the ecological and economic component of a society is stronger in a less developed
culture and therefore more important. I believe this is why Clark regards
the use of comparative analogies (as opposed to direct historical approaches)
for the Palaeolithic as more acceptable than for the Neolithic. To some
extent, the same prejudice continues today in so far as the distinction
between hot and cold societies is often overlain by differences in interpretation – for example the greater degree to which hunter-gatherers
are explained in functional/ecological terms while farming societies
receive much more in the way of social and ideological interpretations
(Duke 1991: 8–9).

In the USA, where the use of direct historical approaches had a longer
history, there was far more criticism of this – indeed, even where cultural
continuity and environmental continuity could be demonstrated, analogies
may be misleading (Wylie 1985: 75). However, such failures of analogy
were not necessarily viewed sceptically but rather seen as a challenge for
finding ways to strengthen their use. The first systematic study of analogy
and one which attempted to do just this was conducted by Ascher. In
'Analogy in archaeological interpretation' (1961b), as well as reviewing the
use of the concept and earlier literature, Ascher proposed a strategy for
strengthening the use of analogy in both its historical and comparative/cross-
cultural modes. Three suggestions were made: first, following Clark and
others, he suggested selecting analogies based on a similar economic or
subsistence level, and also on close historical continuity as well as close
formal similarity. Second, the stock of analogies needed to be expanded by
drawing more intensively from ethnographic sources. Third, and most importantly, the archaeologist should go out and study the processes which create
archaeological records first-hand (Ascher 1961b).

Ascher's last point is clearly a call for ethnoarchaeology and other actu-alistic studies discussed in the last section. Some work had already been done in this area by Thompson although he viewed it much more scepti-cally than Ascher (Thompson 1956). The main point of all these discussions of analogy in the 1950s, however, is the 'chronic ambivalence' surrounding the use of analogy: as Alison Wylie remarks in her critical study, 'analogy seems to be both indispensable to interpretation and always potentially misleading' (Wylie 1985: 81). She goes to the heart of the matter, which lies in the *ampliative* nature of analogy – that it necessarily goes beyond what we can be certain of; there is always a leap made. It was precisely this which caused the reaction to analogy she documents in the 1960s and 1970s, when the issue of securing inferences became of critical importance.

The reaction to analogy took three forms. In the first instance there was simply an informal reaction, often in the shape of cautionary tales, and mostly from Europe. Both Laming and Leroi-Gourhan, for example, argued that the use of analogies was on the whole unproductive for it stifled the archaeological imagination and made the past merely a shadow of the present (Orme 1974: 203–4). Ucko, in trying to recapture some use for analogies in the light of their critique, was still very cautious but argued for their use as an aid to interpretation (ibid.: 206–7; Ucko 1969). The other reactions from the USA were far more systematic in their presenta-tion. The second reaction, with the adoption of the hypothetico-deductive model of archaeological inference, argued that analogies could not be used to test the validity of an explanation although they could still inform the construction of hypotheses. Thus, against Ascher, Binford claimed that no amount of improvement could strengthen the reliability of analogies; what one could do, however, was to test a hypothesis which might be informed by an analogy (Binford 1968). This whole stance of course rested on the distinction between induction and deduction, between contexts of discovery or theory-construction and contexts of justification or theory-evaluation (Wylie 1985: 85–6).

Such distinctions are now regarded as untenable, even by Binford, and consequently he shifted ground towards the third position; this involves the use of actualistic research to construct generalisations which can then be applied to the archaeological record. Such a position was first fully artic-ulated by Gould who argued for the construction of uniformitarian principles, largely based on eco-utilitarian models of human behaviour, which could be derived from actualistic research (Gould 1980). Gould of course recognised that such principles would not cover all aspects of the archaeological record but their use could provide a baseline from which anomalies could be perceived; it was left to the archaeologist to explain these anomalies in similar eco-utilitarian terms as far as possible. Gould's work is effectively of the same order as middle range research and compa-rable to Binford's later studies as well as those of others such as Schiffer.

It is this third strand, exemplified through middle range research (see p. 183) which has remained the dominant model. Thus, while the first and second reactions retained analogy as a useful source of hypothesis construction, the third reaction abandoned it altogether in favour of generalisations.

However, as Wylie points out, the very nature of such generalisations made in actualistic research is itself analogical; the failure to see this was partly the result of a very simple understanding of what analogy means. For many, analogy was simply a formal point of resemblance between a source (ethnography) and a subject (archaeology), where similarities in some properties were taken to signify similarities in others. However, in distinction to such formal analogies, relational analogies stress that similar relations must hold between the properties, not just the presence or absence of such properties (Wylie 1985: 94–5). Clark's use of ecological or subsistence patterns as a dimension of relationality is a good example, even though he provides no explicit justification for it. To go forward, however, work is needed to strengthen such analogies, both on the source side and subject side through substantiating principles of connection (see also Stahl 1993 for a similar discussion in connection with historical analogies).

Wylie's own arguments for the use of analogy and in particular for strengthening their relevance actually seem to be exemplified in middle range research, although she does not make the association explicit. Indeed, the whole enterprise of trying to strengthen analogies can be seen as a facet of middle range theory as it is conventionally articulated. However, while I agree with her characterisation of the role of analogy and its relationship to the kind of inferences or generalisations made in actualistic and subject-side research, I find there is also an inherent contradiction between the whole endeavour to strengthen such analogies and the nature of analogy. Wylie herself points out that analogy is not just about similarities but also about differences – the fallacy of the 'perfect analogy' is that such a thing is not an analogy at all (Wylie 1985: 94). The point about an analogy in other words is that it does not mark an equivalence between two terms (source and subject) but merely a resemblance.

Yet the use of analogy in archaeology, especially in actualistic research, is to posit just such an equivalence; the whole issue of control over the ampliative or expansive nature of analogy through boundary conditions and connecting principles is a strategy for increasing the security of the analogy. Even granted, as Wylie argues, that total security or certainty is not possible, the attempt to strengthen analogies is done through the *subordination* of the analogy to equivalences – namely shared boundary conditions and connecting principles. Yet doing this, I believe, it takes the very heart out of analogy. While there is a recognition of differences, the very fact that the use of analogy in archaeology is accompanied by an obsessive need to increase the similarities over the differences through these equivalences is an attempt to suppress what is special about analogy. Indeed, one might suggest that the very relevance of an analogy comes from *positing* it – not from the quality or quantity of similarities. The distinction between formal and relational analogies pulls us away from what is really characteristic of analogy in contrast to other types of generalisation: that the subject is both the same and not the same as the source. The tension between these two terms is not open to qualification in terms of the *degree* of similarity, whether formal or relational. To become obsessed about such degrees of similarity, is to substitute analogy for equivalence. In many ways, I see analogies in archaeology as comparable to metaphors, and metaphors take their strength precisely from the fact that the similarity is in tension with the (often greater) difference.[4]

What are the implications of this for the role of analogy in archaeology? I would go so far as to say that there is nothing wrong with using analogies where the differences seem greater than the similarities; the important point is that analogy, as analogy, should not be prefigured by equivalances in the form of boundary connections or connecting principles, as this robs it of its very nature. It suggests moreover that our use of analogies does not *need* strengthening. This is not to say their use cannot be subject to critique, but their 'strength' as defined by Wylie should not be the focus of this critique, any more than actualistic studies should have any special epistemological status in archaeological arguments.

Where has this left us? I think it is important to return to the point we made at the end of the last section, namely that actualistic studies such as ethnoarchaeology can no longer be seen as methodological. First and foremost, an ethnoarchaeological study of butchery discard among a hunter-gatherer group, or mortuary ritual among horticulturalists, informs us only about the material culture among those groups. Any use of these studies in other contexts is purely analogical, and in the sense I have just tried to argue, and no amount of 'strengthening' will change this. If we recognise this, then this whole topic shifts ground quite dramatically – the issue is not about the internal, methodological status of middle range research but a much broader, external one about the boundaries and relations between different academic disciplines. If ethnoarchaeology is more ethnohistory or social anthropology than archaeology, the real question about its status moves into the realm of inter-disciplinary divisions.

Archaeology is . . .

In the North American system, archaeology is one of the four divisions of the broad science of anthropology (which also includes cultural anthropology, linguistics and physical anthropology) as outlined by Boas at the turn of the twentieth century. In European countries, the relation of archaeology to other disciplines is less closely defined and while in most cases it does share a common historical link with anthropology, over the course of the twentieth century this link has loosened as archaeology has pulled closer to history. However, regardless of the differences between North America and Europe over the disciplinary affinities of archaeology, there are some more general issues I would like to discuss. We can all recognise the differences between archaeology and other disciplines such as anthropology, sociology or history, yet we are also aware that they overlap, not only in terms of their subject matter but in terms of general theory. For example, archaeology overlaps with history when it deals with historic periods; with anthropology when it conducts ethnoarchaeology; and with sociology when it deals with the 'archaeology of us'. Similarly, however, archaeology also overlaps with these disciplines in sharing the same broad range of theories about culture, society or knowledge: post-modernism, Marxism, hermeneutics can all be found discussed and employed in these disciplines. There are thus two ways in which other disciplines can be seen to interact conventionally with archaeology: theoretically and substantively.

Theoretically, archaeology has a tradition of drawing on other disciplines – social anthropology for perhaps the longest because of the shared disciplinary origins – but the association with geography goes back to the early part of the twentieth century. Ecology was drawn upon from the mid-century on, and since the 1980s literary theory and sociology have provided a strong source of ideas. It is mostly in the theoretical realm that such interaction is actively sought, while substantive links usually seem to be downplayed in an attempt to distance archaeology from other disciplines in order to demonstrate its independence. A case in point is the relation between archaeology and history; theoretically, archaeologists have avidly drawn on historical theory such as from the *Annales* school or the narrativism of Hayden White, Paul Ricoeur or Paul Veyne, but the substantive association has been more often than not described as a millstone where archaeology is characterised as ancillary to history. One historian, for example, famously summed up archaeology as an expensive way of telling us what we already know.[5] Of course, to counter this, archaeologists draw on theoretical arguments to show how archaeology can provide quite different evidence and interpretation from history, indeed might even serve to critique certain historical orthodoxies.

There is then a tension between these two relations which is rarely if ever explored. The question of middle range research, however, lies right at this juncture, because it deals with both substantive and theoretical issues. One way of articulating the tension is to argue from a methodological stance, which is what MRT does – it mediates between general social theory and substantive research. But if we deny this role, middle range research is perforce either ejected from archaeology or becomes a sub-specialism as an archaeology of the contemporary world. We are then forced to rethink the tension as one which expands to cover the relationship between sub-specialisms within archaeology and also between archaeology and other disciplines in general. The issue relates to the nature of specialisms within archaeology as well as to archaeology itself as a disciplinary specialisation, in the sense of being distinct from history, sociology, geography etc. Indeed, how coherent is archaeology? To begin answering this, I think it is important to question the distinction between theoretical and substantive work – is it viable?

The distinction in many ways is tied in to a positivist philosophy of science which distinguishes theory from data, interpretation or explanation from observation or description. Given the critique of positivism, accepted by processualists and post-processualists alike, is it not ironic then that such a distinction between methodological and substantive research is still used in archaeology? It is interesting – and ironic – to consider that in the same breath as cultural taxonomies were being rejected in North America, the same kind of classificatory thinking was applied to the archaeological process and its relation to other disciplines by the same critics of those taxonomic methods. Most of the new approaches espoused in the late 1940s/1950s, from Walter Taylor, Irving Rouse and Gordon Willey and Philip Phillips maintained the need for cultural-historical or descriptive synthesis, which they sustained within an epistemological hierarchy resting between observation (fieldwork) and explanation (evolutionary or processual interpretation). Indeed, such hierarchies played on broader disciplinary divisions made very explicit by Taylor and, later on, Rouse; for both, archaeology was a fact-gathering exercise at the bottom of a procedural and epistemological ladder which culminated in the unifying discipline and enterprise of anthropology (Taylor 1948: ch. 6; Rouse 1972: ch. 1).

David Clarke, in response to such disciplinary definitions, wrote that 'archaeology is archaeology is archaeology', to affirm its holistic status against these views (Clarke 1978: 11). The same point has been re-asserted by Hodder in the wake of a perceived divide between theoretical and 'practical' archaeology (Hodder 1992: 1–6). For granted that few archaeologists today might construct such a hierarchy as that of Taylor or Rouse, there still remains an implicit sub-disciplinary division between theoretical archaeology on the one hand and, on the other, the whole range of specific area and period researches which constitute its material, the very 'stuff' of archaeology. We might legitimately ask whether the concept of theoretical archaeology (especially since post-processualism) is not something of a contradiction? Hodder of course tackles the issue from the other side and questions whether there can be such a thing as an a-theoretical archaeology. Either way, the implication is that archaeology should be viewed as a holistic discipline in terms of its substantive and theoretical realms.

If we accept this, though, on what basis do we distinguish archaeology from other disciplines such as science? Should we perhaps not see all disciplines as holistic enterprises? At first glance this might seem to be nothing more than a question about the unity of the sciences, and many would no doubt say that in this sense archaeology is part of a wider endeavour. But the issue is really not that all the disciplines are united – or even divided (e.g. into arts and sciences) – but the question is the grounds on which they are carved up – on what grounds does each have its separate identity? This is a major historical and theoretical issue which I cannot pretend to deal with here (cf. Foucault 1970); but we can at least ask this of archaeology. Indeed, this is an often forgotten link between archaeological epistemology and disciplinary history – as archaeology changes its theoretical and philosophical perspectives, its shape and definition will also change.

Yet, ironically, conventional archaeological histories often consolidate an identity for our discipline. If you pick up most texts today on archaeological methods or general introductions to the discipline, there is usually always a historical background which places these methods in perspective (e.g. Greene 1983; Renfrew and Bahn 1991). While this is undoubtedly important, there is something slightly unsettling about these presentations; it is almost as if a historical sketch is sufficient to justify the way we do things and it is usually implicit in such presentations that the relation between archaeology's history and its contemporary practice is one of progression. This may not always be explicitly stated, but then it is a tricky thing to state in these postmodern times: is it simply a case of better techniques and knowledge today compared with a hundred years ago or is there perhaps something a little more complex occurring, a question of different ways of seeing? It may seem rather perverse to argue for totally different perceptions, as if Pitt Rivers for example belonged to an alien discipline, yet can archaeological historiography paint a simple picture of progress in methods and techniques without risk of ridicule?

Usually the issue is sidestepped in favour of generalising statements such that studying a discipline's history puts it in perspective, helps to clarify why we do things in this way and this of course is undeniable (e.g. Meltzer 1989: 12). Sometimes the implication is bolder, that the history of archaeology is a history of improvement, although even here it is not directly stated but suggested. Whether it is too obvious to state or too provocative, though, is it adequate? Surely we must demand that looking at the history of archaeology itself requires some justification? Meltzer discusses the view of Glyn Daniel, perhaps the first historian of archaeology in English, who regarded a historiographic perspective as useful in so far as it increased our knowledge of the discipline – the more we know, the less we are likely to repeat the errors of the past (Daniel 1981; Meltzer 1989). This view sounds just like the schoolbook view of history in general and is of course naive in the extreme. Meltzer's own view is more general and is referred to at the start of this paragraph: 'the best way to understand why we do what we do is to unfold the beliefs that have structured, and continue to structure, our work' (Meltzer 1989: 12). Why *this* is important is not as explicitly addressed but Meltzer

does appear to believe that progress is better served by being able to tran-
scend one's own history through self-knowledge (ibid.: 19).

If we turn to Bruce Trigger who is one of the major living writers in
English of the history of the discipline, he too asks what a history of the
discipline serves:

> A final question is whether a historical study can measure progress in
> interpretation of archaeological data. Are steady advances being made
> towards a more objective and comprehensive understanding of archae-
> ological findings, as many archaeologists assume? Or is the interpretation
> of such data largely a matter of fashion and the accomplishments of a
> later period not necessarily more comprehensive or objective than those
> of an earlier one?
>
> (Trigger 1989: 25)

Trigger's answer is essentially for the former, and his reason also serves to
explain why studying history is so important. Because he sees the problem
as one of recognising social bias in interpretation, only history can offer
the perspective which disentangles enduring truth from the historically/
socially contingent; even if it cannot erase all bias, 'it almost certainly
increases the chances of gaining more rounded insights into what has
happened in the past' (Trigger 1989: 4).

Trigger essentially states more explicitly what Meltzer alluded to, and in
the end such histories validate current practice in terms of scientific progress;
regarding this, Hinsley makes an important point:

> most [histories] still look inward for a logic of progress in data gathering
> and in theoretical modelling. However one modifies such history – intro-
> ducing notions of paradigmatic structures, admitting occasional wrong
> turns or even the exclusive nature of the scientific community under
> conditions of 'normal science' – it still remains essentially Whig history,
> an Enlightenment legacy that assumes what it purports to illustrate: an
> upward trajectory toward more accurate, cumulative knowledge.
>
> (Hinsley 1989: 80)

If presenting the history of the discipline has become almost synonymous
with justifying the status quo (but cf. Taylor 1948 and more recently, Kehoe
1998), theory has taken almost the inverse role, standing for the critique
of contemporary practice. Major theoretical texts of the past twenty to
thirty years have typically looked at the broad spectrum of archaeological
work as it is done today and showed ways in which it is lacking and ways
in which it can be developed. The epithet 'new' has commonly been linked
to changes in archaeological perspective, especially in the USA – the new
stratigraphic methods developed in the second decade of the twentieth

century announced a 'New Archaeology' in a paper of that title by Clark Wissler in 1917, while a collection of papers which drew on evolutionary and environmental themes espoused by Steward or White were published in 1955 as *New Interpretations of Aboriginal American Culture History* (Anthropological Society of Washington). All this before Binford and his students proclaimed their New Archaeology.

However such critique and 'newness' can only go so far without undermining the very existence of archaeology. As Wylie says, remarking on this recurrent phenomenon of 'new archaeologies', each time a break is urged with the past, there has been an equally vociferous opposition and support for traditional approaches (Wylie 1993: 20). Thus today it has been argued the New Archaeology is not really 'new' at all. Kent Flannery was an early detractor (Flannery 1973, 1982), but the French archaeologist Paul Courbin has written what is probably the most extensive and scathing critique, arguing that there is very little in it which is in fact new:

> In reality, the real progress made in the past three decades has not been in theory, as the New Archaeology would have us believe: it has been in techniques, whether it be contributions of the 'sciences' to archaeology or the help of statistics, and especially computer studies. These advances are very real. But they are completely independent of the New Archaeology. . . .
>
> (Courbin 1988: 159)

Courbin's critiques may be too extreme, but they represent the same fundamental view of history and theory in the end, simply stressing continuity over change. Since, for all the critique theory offers, it still needs to preserve the integrity of the discipline or else it becomes self-defeating, I doubt any theoretical archaeologist, however radical, would deny all links with the past of their discipline. Theoretical archaeology is never simply pursued as critique but also as productive development; in questioning current ways of interpreting the past, alternative ways are offered in the process. The same dual aspect to theory is brought out in the relatively new field of *metaarchaeology*, a term coined by the philosopher Lester Embree in the USA, and which he defines as a 'critical reflection upon the science of archaeology' (Embree 1992a: 3). Much of his work has looked specifically at the sub-discipline of theoretical archaeology, which he sees as a rather loose term to cover broadly any kind of reflexive or critical archaeology, some of which may reflect on archaeology as a whole (therefore falling under what he calls metaarchaeology), some of which is more methodological/ problem oriented (therefore falling under what he calls substantive research) (Embree 1989: 68).

Embree raises a number of significant questions which metaarchaeology can address, including the status of archaeology as a science, and its relation to society, to the historiography of archaeology and to philosophy (Embree 1992a, ff.41). However, much of his emphasis lies on how (theoretical) archaeology is done rather than on its value. In his analysis of Gordon Willey's work on the Virú valley in Peru, for example, he separates out the question of whether Willey's work was an improvement or not, from the question of whether or not it effected a change in how archaeology was done, and only gives the former question a few sentences at the end of the paper (Embree 1992b: 191). Tellingly, he says that the question can also be historiographic, and indeed the very framing of it in terms of 'improvement' merely confirms that he sees the value of theoretical archaeology ultimately in progressive terms – progress being defined by 'a new mode of evidencing', that is, new ways of collecting, analysing and synthesising data. Quite how this is assessed though is left rather vague.

From a bold perspective, theory/critique is part of the same process of progression presented in history; without it, there would be no advances, no developments – no history in effect. In this view, history and theory are interlinked in the grand narrative of scientific progress. An alternative view might simply highlight the importance of change, with the critical term not being theory or history but practice; practice lies between them, supported by history, undermined by theory; but in keeping them apart, it also enables them to complement each other through an ongoing hermeneutic. Histories of archaeology do not have to affirm any progress, or even any disciplinary identity – especially as history and theory are integrated through practice. I hope that this book has demonstrated this. But whatever archaeology is, it is not static. The very processes of archaeological interpretation which seem to represent a 'new consensus' (e.g. Preucel 1991; Wylie 1992), namely the interdependency of interpretation and data, must also affect the shape of the discipline as well as the shape of our representations of the past. The power of this dialectic is reflexive as well as dynamic – its effects rebound back on the discipline, how it is constituted, as well as articulating its focus, its subject matter.

Another way of characterising this is to say that archaeology is not just a mental or theoretical exercise – it is a practice as well. Hodder discusses this in terms of the concept of *praxis*, a term used to denote the socially and historically situated nature of archaeology – it is not passively contemplative but active and creative (Hodder 1992: 3; also see Hodder 1984). The notion that archaeology is a social practice has been a recurrent theme, especially but not exclusively, of post-processualism (e.g. Shanks and Tilley 1987a; Gero 1995). But I think there is still something missing from this equation – something which archaeology itself is all about: material culture. Recall Taylor's three orders of phenomena – ideas, behaviour and material culture. I argued that one of the major innovations of post-processual theory was how it integrated these previously disjunctive categories into a whole – each constituted the other. The stress on praxis as the conjunction of theory and practice could be seen as incomplete in the light of post-processualists' own formulation of their subject matter. If material culture is so important and active, equally constituting as constituted by beliefs/theory and behaviour/practice, then we need to include this in our conception of archaeology. Archaeology is not just contemplative, nor is it just a social practice, it is also a material praxis.

Chapter 6

Conclusion
Material archaeologies

In reflecting on what has been written so far, I would like to try and reiterate the directions in which this book has travelled. I began by establishing the theme as an investigation into several key historical and conceptual issues in archaeological practice. The development of practice was studied initially through the changes in fieldwork, and three major conceptual trends were identified: a focus on finds or artefacts, a focus on assemblages of finds and finally the concern for the social or behavioural context of finds/assemblages. It was argued that these foci are not necessarily exclusive to any one particular point in the history of archaeology but rather that, as foci, they provided a major orientation on the nature of the archaeological record and one which was linked in to the ways in which archaeological fieldwork was conducted. These foci in turn became the basis for discussion in subsequent chapters – on finds analysis, culture classification and middle range theory. From the discussion of these foci, both from a historical and conceptual perspective, it was seen that they exhibited a practical dimension in the form of disciplinary specialisations. In the case of finds analysis, such issues were tied back into finds specialisms; similarly, in the case of culture classification, the issue of area/period specialisms was questioned; and finally for middle range theory, the status of archaeology itself as a 'specialised' discipline distinct from others such as anthropology or history was highlighted.

In this book, therefore, I hope I have raised what I think are relevant issues about the nature of archaeology, issues which have clear consequences for the way we do archaeology both theoretically and practically. They affect not just our interpretations of the past but the structure of our discipline. In many ways, this book is a study of archaeology which embraces the hermeneutic discussed at the end of the last chapter between theory and practice and applies it to the way archaeology itself functions – to the archaeological process. In conclusion, I would like, unfortunately all too briefly, to take up the issue left hanging at the end of the last chapter – the relation between this hermeneutic of theory and practice, and materiality.

In the summer of 1998 I was excavating a Viking period farmstead called Hofstaðir in northeast Iceland, of which the main turf longhouse had been excavated previously in 1908 by a Danish archaeologist called Daniel Bruun. It took several people several days to remove the backfill of Bruun's trench by hand, using spades and shovels, the weather was variable and there were blackflies in abundance, crawling into every open part of the face – eyes, nose, ears and mouth. At the beginning, the edge of the earlier trench cut was not always very clear and it took some time before we realised how the trench had been cut. As we moved down, we also had to be careful to stop at the level of the earlier cut since we knew that the excavator had stopped at the floor but that he might have cut through it too and its survival could be patchy. Another thing we were looking for was traces of a wall which the earlier excavator said was missing. As we cleaned up the trench, we found indeed that the floors were patchy and that the exca-vator had gone too deep, and that there was in fact a wall, a very clear wall. The excavator had cut quite a way into it, as on other walls but had still missed it, and yet by all accounts he was good for his day. There was much speculation on why he excavated the way he did and why he did not see the things we could . . .

In re-excavating the 1908 trench at Hofstaðir, the questions were always in terms of what Bruun or his workmen were doing, or why they had dug like this. When I compare this with my thoughts on, for example, another feature on the site such as a silo pit, they are similar but there is also a difference. Throughout the process of excavation of the silo pit, the same questions recurred but were always being posed in term of what the *pit* was doing, how the edges were behaving. And this is my more typical reaction to archaeological features, to see them as purely material objects which generate problems of interpretation – they have no face, no person, they are anonymous. One can easily see why this happens. With most archae-ology we have no personal associations with features, and even if we can link some historical person with a site, it is unlikely we can actually join that person with any particular feature, let alone its production. But this difference is misleading for it is not really about attaching a face or person to a particular feature – it is about attaching an intention. This means understanding the feature in terms of some purpose; understanding what the edges were doing with the pit was all part of my understanding of it – in the first instance as a pit dug by a person deliberately; and in the second, as a pit dug for a particular purpose, in this case hay storage. If I had started to see it as a different kind of pit, I might have had different expectations of what the edges would do.

This story provides a way into an alternative view of the relationship between history, theory and practice. Excavating Bruun's trench and the interpretive process involved is in a way like using archaeological methods to understand the history of archaeology. Encountering the trenches of earlier excavators is not uncommon, especially on famous sites, and one may learn things about the previous excavator and his or her record which could not be gleaned from any written sources. An Icelandic friend, and the person who initiated the project on the Viking farm mentioned in the story, once told me that he wanted to do just this (Adolf Fridriksson, pers. comm.). What could it mean to turn our methods back on to ourselves? I find this a tantalising possibility – it offers a reflexivity which is not simply a questioning of why and how we do things, but a questioning that employs the very methods we seek to interrogate. Putting it like this is interesting because it brings out the *material* nature of archaeological practice – it not only studies material culture but uses and produces material culture in this process. From this perspective, archaeology and its object begin to merge (Figure 20).

Excavating an excavation might seem like a special case, and in most cases archaeology and its object remain distinct. Are they though? What if we see excavation as part of the archaeology of the site – and not just any earlier excavation, but the one happening now. Thus as we uncover the site we also add to it. The dominant ethos sees excavation as destruction, the 'unrepeatable experiment' at Barker once put it (Barker 1982: 11–12). Now, it may be that we remove features, but this does not necessarily have to be viewed as a subtractive process but rather as a transformative one. An excavation trench is part of the history or archaeology of the site, as much as anything else there. History does not stop – it is ongoing, and when we come to a site we should not see ourselves as coming to something halted but as being part of something continuous. It is a little too obvious that we write ourselves out of the sequence of events on a site, that the top of a stratigraphic matrix is not our trenches and excavations but the topsoil. It is very telling of our perception of the site as something separate from us and our actions, pulling ourselves out of its history. To this extent, we are perhaps not being as true to the linearity of time we portray, either in the past or in the development of archaeology.

But excavation is more than just another part of the history of a site – it is special in the sense that it is reflexive, it reiterates everything that has left a trace on the site. Inasmuch as excavating an excavation can be called repetitive, all archaeological practice could be ascribed the same character; it is an encounter which has taken place before. A friend once expressed it this way – that every time we excavate a ditch or pit on a site, we are in fact re-excavating it, we are repeating an act performed maybe thousands of years ago, in exactly the same place (M. Knight, pers. comm.). This event is so commonplace in archaeology, yet it is an experience I had never before heard expressed in this way and it makes the physical process of excavation extremely significant. It is very common, on the other hand, to hear how holding an artefact that has not seen the light of day for thousands of years brings the past alive, is maybe even the closest one can get in

Figure 20 Excavation at a Viking farmstead in Iceland in 1908 (a) and 1995 (b)

experiencing the past. But the mere holding of something, the touch and the gaze it involves surely does not come anywhere close to the act of re-excavation, an act involving the whole body, a productive act, not simply a contemplative one.

Of course this perception of excavation only applies in a very restricted sense since we are not removing the same kind of soil when excavating the ditch, nor are we repeating the events of its filling up which may not even be the result of human but of natural processes. But in a way, the relevance here is not in faithful reproduction or duplication but in repetition; it is through repetition that a sense of difference is generated. Excavating Bruun's trench was also an act of repetition, yet while he was trying to understand the edges of walls and floors, we were trying to understand his attempt at understanding. What is this, if not an archaeology of archaeology? Or just archaeology for that matter? In the rest of this chapter I want to explore ways in which archaeology is a material practice, or rather, shall we say, a *materialising* practice. In so doing, this is perhaps less of a conclusion, a closure, as an opening, a looking forward. By materialising, I mean the ways in which we produce or create physical products in the course of doing archaeology, two of which dominate – texts and images. Thus I will not be discussing the management of museums or heritage sites here, which although they are certainly material practices, do not in themselves routinely create new objects. They are not materialising, although they are linked to materialising practices such as the production of display boards and captions, guidebooks, etc. It is this general field of textual and graphic production that I want to examine.

Writing archaeology

The theme of archaeology as a textual practice has of course received much attention recently, especially in the wake of a similar turn in anthropology (Clifford and Marcus 1986; Baker and Thomas 1990; Tilley 1993; Pluciennik 1999). Hodder in particular has questioned narrative styles in site reports and more general syntheses (Hodder 1989b, 1993a). To paraphrase Marcus, textualisation is at the heart of archaeology. How does this manifest itself? Right at the beginning, if we can use such a term, we textualise archaeology in field notebooks and context sheets. I discussed in the introduction the ways in which context sheets affect practice through a system of checks, controls and standardisation. The adoption of sheets, particularly in replacing the field notebook (as in Britain) where there were no prompts but just blank pages, is very telling of how perceptions of textualisation have changed, particularly as this shift occurred alongside the New Archaeology. Not that writing in notebooks was, or is, necessarily a free or undisciplined affair – students learn what should and should not be placed in notebooks.

Hodder's study of the narrative form of site reports takes us into another realm of textual production (Hodder 1989b). He shows how early reports of excavations were often in the form of letters, and only later gradually shifted to articles, many of which were read at some meeting or other. The use of the first person and the construction of the narrative around the act of discovery was a predominant feature again, until by the end of the nineteenth century and the beginning of the twentieth, a form more familiar to us emerged: writing in the passive voice, descriptive rather than narrative. Hodder links these changes to broader shifts in the way science is conducted and authority established, away from individuals to institutions. Indeed it is not hard to see how the form of textualisation in archaeology relates to wider historical trends, especially in the shift from letters to articles (also see Hamilton 1999 for a similar, more recent critique). To some extent, Hodder's reservations against the dryness of modern site reports have received a new twist, as journals become less and less willing to publish site reports at all, unless they are framed within a suitably academic, research agenda (C. Evans, pers. comm.).

Turning finally to more general works, in light of Hodder's comments we can interestingly compare his most influential theoretical text, *Reading the Past*, with David Clarke's *Analytical Archaeology* in terms of textual style. Clarke's is a massive text, the second edition cut down to over 500 pages with justified text, highly structured chapters and numbered sections reflecting the philosophy he is putting forward: a very *systematic* book. By contrast, Hodder has written a fairly brief work of under 200 pages with unjustified text, each chapter treating an almost separate theme, themes which are, nevertheless, interwoven by various connecting ideas. The differences in the two styles are clearly linked to their authors' theoretical outlook, their perspectives clearly affecting the mode of textualisation.

The three examples of textualisation – fieldnotes, site reports and general works – all show how the process of textual production is mediated by and influences the way we perceive archaeology. Moreover, just as we can think about the rhetoric or poetics of texts, it is equally important to think of them as material products – as books or digital displays. Indeed, the widespread adoption of computers and word-processing software has undoubtedly altered the way we write – the ease with which we can self-edit our texts on computers compared with written or typed manuscripts may have affected the whole process of textual production. Perhaps of equal interest, however, is to consider the form of a text – its structure in terms of layout and typography. We can all instantly tell the difference between a serious academic text and a coffee-table book for lay consumption – format size, text to image ratio, layout of the text and images and so on. Would a site report look more interesting if it was in the style of the fashion magazine *Vogue* I wonder? More importantly, perhaps, what would thinking about using this format do to the way we write the site report?

Imaging archaeology

If textual production pervades all areas of the archaeological process, the same is true of image production through drawings and photographs. Just as forms of textual production have altered, so archaeological illustration has seen some interesting changes over the past century (Piggott 1965). In 1828 E. T. Artis excavated a series of Roman sites near Peterborough in eastern England, which he published as a series of plates (Artis 1828). It is an interesting example because it reveals something of how archaeological sites were perceived in the early nineteenth century – as part of a Historical/Romantic landscape. It is worth quoting Piggott at length on this issue, because he reinforces this observation:

> One cannot say that any discernible archaeological style of draughts-manship came into being in the eighteenth, or really the nineteenth century, and one would be surprised if it had. . . . Not unnaturally, the delineation of antiquities, sites or architecture conformed to the conventions of non-specialised draughtsmanship at large. Perspective views of field monuments – 'prospects', the equivalent of modern photographs – fell naturally within the developing traditions of the topographical artists of the day, and indeed the depiction of antiquities played an important part with almost all the early landscape painters. . . . Plans were drawn and engraved according to the prescriptions of estate surveyors and cartographers; small antiquities were illustrated as if they were butterflies or petrifactions or prodigies of nature which might well have accompanied them in the cabinet of curiosities of an ingenious gentlemen.
>
> (Piggott 1965: 171)

However, such a series of 'prospects', is not what Petrie or Pitt Rivers would have had in mind. Their concern was more abstract – to represent an object, not a view. It is the visual equivalent of Hodder's example of the passive voice – while the view retains a sense of a viewer, the plan and section erase it.

This even spills over into the finds; earlier depictions were usually perspective figures, often painted, much in the style of curios as Piggott remarks. One might also venture that such depictions could have been influenced by contemporary retail catalogues of goods (see Figure 21). However, with Pitt Rivers there is great concern for scale and accuracy and each sherd is accompanied by its section, which anticipated present-day illustrations; here the standard half-section of pottery so familiar today derives from Dragendorff's famous typology of Samian (1895), which became widely adopted by the early part of the twentieth century (Piggott 1965: 175). Such representations have, however, come to be contested recently – for example,

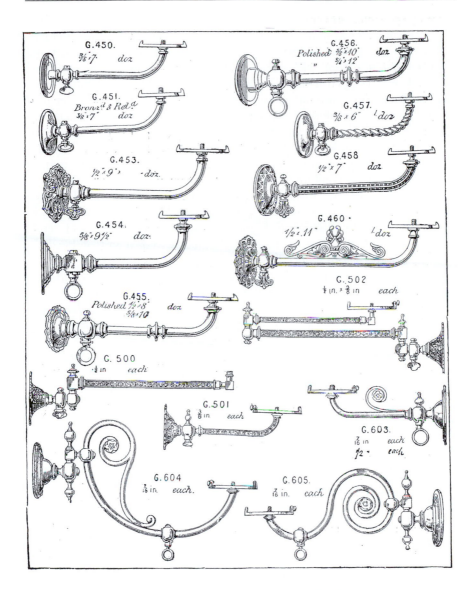

Figure 21 Late nineteenth-century advertisement for gas brackets

many of the conventions derive from nineteenth- and early twentieth-century reproduction technology (e.g. engraving, lithography), while the scope of contemporary computer-aided design is only just beginning to be exploited (Hughes 1999).

With the establishment of scale drawings, new concerns emerged over what was the best way to draw the site. The most famous debate about graphics in British field archaeology was over field drawings and between those who favoured a 'naturalistic' approach after Bersu or a more schematic one after Wheeler (Piggott 1965: 175–6; Bradley 1997: 68–70). While Bersu's sections (and plans) attempted to show a pit fill 'as it was', Wheeler used more stylistic conventions, most importantly a hard or sharp line to distinguish different layers and cuts (Figure 22). In general, Wheeler's approach has dominated because of the way British field archaeology adopted the idea of discrete stratigraphic units in its excavation procedure. Again, the current use of computers in combination with total-stations changes the whole way the graphic record on site is made – potentially, one does not need to draw any plans at all as the whole process is automated and can be linked in to find spots, etc. (e.g. Biswell et al. 1995). However, such a method, while increasing speed and accuracy, loses in its inability to deal with ambiguity – it is the graphic record reduced to a series of lines and dots.

Other forms of imaging include mathematical figures – graphs, charts and tables. As Clark and Stafford (1982) showed with respect to North American archaeology, simple descriptive quantification is as old as the discipline. The same undoubtedly applies to British archaeology – basic tabular presentation of data can be seen in many studies from the later nineteenth century onwards (e.g. Greenwell's *British Barrows*, published in 1877, or Pitt Rivers' *Relic Tables*), and it is still a commonly used representation of quantitative data. The use of charts or graphs is more recent – in an interesting study of graphic representation of seriation between the 1920s and 1960s it was shown how there was a gradual shift from the use of tables to charts, but more significantly, perhaps, many of the early charts were effectively intuitive depictions of the data rather than accurate representations (Lyman *et al.* 1998). Indeed, good graphs are far more persuasive rhetorical devices than tables, which are now frequently confined to appendices or microfiche. As the 1960s ushered in a new wave of more complex, inferential statistics based on probability theory and testing, a whole new range of graphic images was introduced into archaeological texts to aid arguments – indeed, one might say that in many instances they are an essential component of any data analysis.

A common assumption of much of the imaging discussed here – particularly drawings and photography – is the importance of objectivity. While their selective nature is recognised, there is still a strong sense that accuracy and precision are critical – the use of scales and proper measuring equipment is an important component in the materialisation of such images. The objectivity of these kinds of images is accentuated when they are juxtaposed with artistic reconstructions. In archaeology, the question of reconstructions of past life has recently received considerable attention, particularly

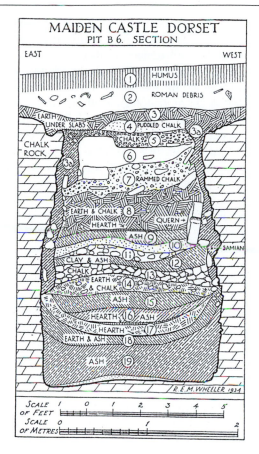

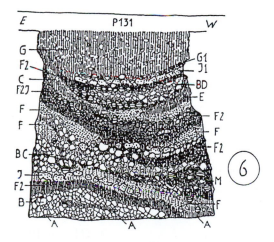

Figure 22   Wheeler's and Bersu's section drawings

in the realm of early hominids and how gender stereotypes are represented (Moser 1992; Moser and Gamble 1997; Wiber 1998). While this issue is about the political and social nature of such images, it also raises the question of their objectivity. Alongside these critiques lie internal debates about how to reconstruct an image without going too far beyond the evidence (e.g. James 1997). A recent textbook on archaeological illustration recommends that the artist use the archaeological evidence to the full, and exploit devices such as obstacles of perspective which can cover up any gaps in our knowledge (Adkins and Adkins 1989: 145–7). Thus although their status as artistic impressions is recognised, there is still an important ethic of constraint. However, the history of models illustrates how such reconstructions can shift in meaning.

The use of models today is generally as museum pieces showing the site as it might have looked in the past, a kind of three-dimensional version of artistic impressions. However, it was not always like this (Evans n.d.). Pitt Rivers' use of models for example was quite different. He employed a carpenter to render many of his sites in this form; these models were not simply artistic recreations, but a part of his actual excavation archive, a record of the archaeology in three dimensions instead of the usual two. It cannot be too far-fetched to suggest that he perceived these as being the *best representation* he had of the sites he excavated. From the 1930s and 1940s full-scale models or re-creations of structures were also considered an important part of understanding the archaeology, but not as a record so much as an experiment revealing information on the constructional properties of, say, roundhouses, allowing for guided interpretation on things such as the pitch of a roof. This kind of work too has more or less gone out of vogue, and models today have a status similar to that of artistic impressions.

This tension over objectivity in imaging is evocatively illustrated in Cook's voyage to the Pacific:

> [C]onsidering that such expeditions left Europe each time with an anticipation of confronting the unknown, one can readily imagine the difficulties inherent in having to decide, in advance, what one's criteria might be for representing something of which, at present, one has no experience – that is, for apprehending the exotic. When Joseph Banks was charged by the Royal Society to find illustrators for Cook's first voyage to the Pacific in 1768, he resolved the problem as both the scientist and the gentleman that he was. He would have one illustrator, Sidney Parkinson, provide faithful copies of plants and animals, and another artist, Alexander Buchan, provide him pictures of savages and scenery that would delight his friends back home.
>
> (Napier 1992: 9)

Archaeology reproduces this dilemma, not just between the site plan and the artist's reconstruction, but even within these modes. The same tension is played up by Shanks in a recent paper concerning photography (Shanks 1997). Shanks argues for viewing photography as photowork, in which it mediates between its role as a record and as a creation through techniques of collage and montage (Shanks 1997: 83–4). I find his discussion here extremely useful when thinking about the nature of imaging, in that through the selectivity of the frame and the juxtaposition of fragments, photography makes a new reality, one which does not refer outside of itself as suggested in the record or the artistic impression. It is particularly in the idea that photoworks create their own reality that they circumvent the whole tension of objectivity in representation, and it seems to me that they do this because they are viewed as materialising practices, not simply as passive representations. A good example is the use of photography with computer-designed images to make 'reconstructions' – much like the technology used in films to juxtapose actors with computer-generated dinosaurs (Lamb 1999).

Materialising archaeology

Despite the production of texts and images having been discussed separately, they have always been used together in archaeology. However, the relationship between the two has changed, just as each mode of materialisation has changed. In Chapter 2, we discussed the esteem in which Pitt Rivers was held by later archaeologists (especially Wheeler) for his recording. What is really interesting about his record, especially the four volumes on Cranbourne Chase, is that they are all arranged around the plates. All the text is (albeit often extended) annotations to the figures, and this includes not just the finds but also the site features. It is as if, in his conception, the site was *best* represented by drawings and only *secondarily by text*. This is supported by a saying attributed to him: 'Describe your illustrations, do not illustrate your descriptions' (Piggott 1965: 174). This is almost the inverse of today's approach which is heavily textually dominated. Is Pitt Rivers unusual, though? Not really, for Petrie felt the same and indeed actually spelt it out: 'the text is to show the meaning and relation of the facts already expressed by form' (Petrie 1904: 115). For Petrie, it was the lack of figures in older archaeological work that was their chief failing – Greenwell's *British Barrows*, for example, he felt could be reduced almost entirely to a series of plans – it was too text-laden (ibid.: 114).

The visual record was thus perhaps seen as the most important part of the archaeological record in the latter part of the nineteenth century, as that which most accurately represents it. To further support this, one might cite Petrie's effusive recommendation on the use of photography and, perhaps even more tellingly, Pitt Rivers' use of scale models. Despite the preference for seeing the visual record as the best way of representing the archaeology, Petrie's ideal of a site report consisting solely of figures was never realised. Instead, by the 1920s and 1930s the standard site report was established and has changed little up to the present except in detail. In effect, a balance of interlinked graphic and textual representation is offered. However, with the advent of computer-aided publication, this balance may be about to change. The very boundaries between text and image can be broken down, through the use of annotated and 'cartoon' style graphics in conventional publications (e.g. Hamilton 1996), but even more so in the field of hypermedia. This will certainly have consequences for the way archaeology is presented and, ultimately perhaps, feed back into the way it is practised – certainly the use of hypertext can be linked to non-linear types of narrative for example (Hodder 1999).

I want to close with a reminder as to what is perhaps the most basic materialising practice in archaeology – the creation of the archaeological record. By this, I am saying nothing more than that we actually have to go out and actively find our data – primarily by digging, but also through surface, aerial and geophysical survey. What perhaps distinguishes archaeology from other disciplines such as history, anthropology or even other material culture studies, is that it involves an operation of materialisation. In all these other disciplines, the material or data is already there – only in archaeology is there a performance of presencing, materialising the data.[1] Beyond this, of course, all disciplines create their data in the qualified sense of data being theory-dependent, but this other aspect, of materialisation, is something rarely raised. I am not so sure it is unique to archaeology, but I will leave this for the moment; instead, I want to ask what relationship this mode of materialisation in archaeology has to those of textualisation and imaging already discussed.

To answer this, I will use as an example a formulation of the archaeological record made in Britain in the 1970s, which employed a hierarchy of different levels distilling a process of representation (see Table 7; Frere 1975). First there is the Level I archive, the site itself, which exists independently of and prior to any investigation. Beyond Level I lie the various representations we make of that site: the primary archive, analyses and finally publication. Critically, the flow is reversible in most cases except usually between Levels I and II – we can go back to the primary archive or the analyses, but we can never re-excavate. Fundamentally, the reversibility of the lowest levels justifies the irreversibility of the upper, that is, excavation. That the hierarchy permits iteration, repeatability, is a fundamental axiom of scientific 'fieldwork', and in a way this barrier between Level I and the others validates the whole schema, because if it was not there, there would be no stopping point or point of rest. This point is Level I, archaeological reality, Archaeology Degree Zero.

Table 7 Levels of archaeological data as proposed by the Frere and Cunliffe report (Frere, 1975)

Level	Site description	Loose material
I	The site itself and general notes, old letters, previous accounts, etc.	Excavated finds
II	Site notebooks, recording forms, drawings, sound-recorded tapes	Finds records, X-rays, photographs, negatives, colour transparencies
III	Full illustration and description of all structural relationships	Classified finds – lists and finds – drawings, all analyses
IV	Synthesis of descriptions with supporting data	Selected finds and specialist reports relevant to synthesis

But consider a geophysical survey. It might show perhaps an enclosure ditch, without us ever having seen or felt it. The enclosure exists only in the greyscale plot and we can read it precisely because we have seen this kind of representation a thousand times before on site plans of excavated features. How does the geophysical plot differ from the measured plan? Both are representations – in the former of something which has never been seen and in the latter of something which can never be seen again. What is the difference? With excavation, we might argue that the site is real, was actually there, and we can claim to make a distinction between the record we make of it and the site itself – but with the geophysical survey, the site remains a virtual site, the record and the site itself are *no longer distinct.* How could you argue that the site exists independently of your record in a geophysical survey, when the only proof you have of its existence is that survey? This is an interesting paradox but it perhaps also confuses another issue – our use of material culture in materialising the past. The resistivity meter is an 'artificial eye'; it sees where we cannot. I think the important point here is that the proof of a geophysical survey would come through repetition – either through comparison with another survey or with an excavation plan. In this it highlights an important point which in fact goes against the whole ethos of this model: that the very validity of archaeological interpretation is *not* based on the independence of an archaeological reality (Level I, the site or objects themselves), but on the *iterability* of the representations we give it.

For example, even in those cases where old sites can be re-excavated, it is the comparison of plans that assesses the validity of the first interpretation – we can never compare their perception directly with our own, only the materialisations of that perception. It is these materialisa-tions – of texts and images – which guarantee the validity of archaeological interpretation, not the site itself. These materialising practices are not simply representations but materialising strategies for enabling the archaeological record to be subject to repeated investigation. They create the possibility of iterability. And, like any materialisation, they have a certain independence, a certain life of their own – indeed this is a cornerstone of post-structuralist theory in relation to texts. This is why archaeologists can re-examine old sites and come up with new interpretations, as in the examples given in the last chapter of Glastonbury or Snaketown.

Image and textual materialisation enable comparison, but, more significantly, *repeatable* comparison. The records we make in archaeology are our answer to the scientific experiment – it is a way of re-excavating a site, re-analysing an object over and over again. This is why we call excavation destruction – we have to, otherwise the record we make is of no value. Without these materialising practices, there would be no archaeology – they allow its discourse to develop. Indeed, the archaeologists' facts are primarily not sites or artefacts, but the textual and graphic materialisations which stand in for them – from fieldnotes to site reports, from drawings to photographs (see Duke 1991). In this way, the concept of materiality and material culture is introduced into the previously closed dualism of theory and practice. It is this materiality which actually enables the hermeneutic to function as an iterable process.

Notes

1 Introduction: archaeology and the field

1   In Britain, the term 'fieldwork' is sometimes used to denote specifically non-excavation types of archaeological investigation (for example surveying, fieldwalking). Throughout this book however, I use the term more broadly to cover all types of investigation in the field.

3 Splitting objects

1   Although it must be said that much of the basic analytical work on ceramics from sites was often conducted by anonymous or forgotten practitioners, frequently women.

4 The measure of culture

1   Unfortunately I have not been able to pinpoint this statement of Bataille's but it comes from his major work *The Accursed Share*.

5 Eventful contexts

1   To be distinguished from Schiffer's behavioural archaeology which is primarily about the relationship between the archaeological record and behaviour.
2   Preucel has now distanced himself from behavioural archeology since his paper with Earle (pers.comm.).
3   The comparison to Derrida's critique of phonocentrism should not be missed (Derrida 1976), for it is exactly the same process, a privileging of the natural resources of meaning (the agent, speech) over artificial resources (writing, artefacts).
4   I owe this point to Deleuze's discussion of the nature of generalisation (Deleuze 1997). Also see Ricoeur's discussion of metaphor as analogy (Ricoeur 1984).
5   The reference for this escapes me but I believe the person in question has subsequently recanted.

6 Conclusion: material archaeologies

1   I am indebted to Victor Buchli for this point.

References

Abercromby, J. (1912) *A Study of the Bronze Age Pottery of Great Britain and Ireland*, Oxford: Clarendon Press.

Adams, M. (1991) 'A logic of archaeological inference', *Journal of Theoretical Archaeology* 2: 1–11.

Adams, M. (1992) 'Stratigraphy after Harris: Some questions', in K. Steane (ed.), *Interpretation of Stratigraphy: A Review of the Art*, pp. 13–16, Lincoln: City of Lincoln Archaeology Unit.

Adams, M. and Brooke, C. (1995) 'Unmanaging the past: truth, data and the human being', *Norwegian Archaeology Review* 28: 93–104.

Adams, W. (1988) 'Archaeological classification: theory versus practice', *Antiquity* 61: 40–56.

Adams, W. and Adams, E. (1991) *Archaeological Typology and Practical Reality*, Cambridge: Cambridge University Press.

Adkins, L. and Adkins, R. (1989) *Archaeological Illustration*, Cambridge: Cambridge University Press.

Aldenderfer, M. S. (1987a) 'Assessing the impact of quantitative thinking on archaeological research: historical and evolutionary insights', in M. S. Aldenderfer (ed.), *Quantitative Research in Archaeology. Progress and Prospects*, Thousand Oaks, CA: Sage Publications.

Aldenderfer, M. S. (1987b) 'On the structure of archaeological data', in M. S. Aldenderfer (ed.), *Quantitative Research in Archaeology. Progress and Prospects*, Thousand Oaks, CA: Sage Publications.

Alexander, M. (1970) *The Directing of Archaeological Excavations*, London: John Baker Ltd.

Allen, K. M. S., Green, S. W. and Zubrow, E. B. W. (eds) (1989) *Interpreting Space: GIS and Archaeology*, London: Taylor & Francis.

Almgren, B. (1995) 'The development of the typological theory in connection with the Exhibition in the Museum of National Antiquities in Stockholm', in P. Åström (ed.), *Oscar Montelius. 150 Years*, pp. 23–39, Stockholm: Kungl Vitterhets Historie och Antikvilets Akademien.

Andah, B. (1995) 'Studying African societies in cultural context', in P. R. Schmidt and T. C. Patterson (eds) (1995) *Making Alternative Histories. The Practice of Archaeology and History in Non-Western Settings*, pp. 149–82, Santa Fe, NM: School of American Research Press.

Andrefsky, W. (1998) *Lithics*, Cambridge: Cambridge University Press.

Andresen, J., Madsen, T. and Scollar, I. (eds) (1993) *Computing the Past*, Aarhus: Aarhus University Press.

Appadurai, A. (ed.) (1986) *The Social Life of Things*, Cambridge: Cambridge University Press.

Arnold, D. (1985) *Ceramic Theory and Cultural Process*, Cambridge: Cambridge University Press.

Artis, E. T. (1828) *The Durobrivae of Antoninus*, London.

Ascher, R. (1961a) 'Experimental archaeology', *American Anthropologist* 63: 793–816.

Ascher, R. (1961b) 'Analogy in archaeological interpretation', *Southwestern Journal of Anthropology* 17: 317–25.

Ascher, R. (1968) 'Time's arrow and the archaeology of a contemporary community', in K. C. Chang (ed.), *Settlement Archaeology*, pp. 43–52, Palo Alto, CA: National Press Books.

Ashbee, P. (1972) 'Field archaeology: its origins and development', in P. J. Fowler (ed.), *Archaeology and the Landscape*, pp. 38–74, London: John Baker.

Ashmore, W. and Knapp, B. (eds) (1999) *Archaeologies of Landscape*, Oxford: Blackwell.

Atkinson, R. J. C. (1946) *Field Archaeology*, London: Methuen & Co. Ltd.

Baker, F. and Thomas, J. (eds) (1990) *Writing the Past*, Lampeter: St David's College, University of Wales.

Barham, A. (1995) 'Methodological approaches to archaeological recording: X-radiography as an example of a supportive recording, assessment and interpretive technique', in A. Barham and R. Macphail (eds), *Archaeological Sediments and Soils: Analysis, Interpretation and Management*, London: Institute of Archaeology, UCL.

Barker, P. (1969) 'Some aspects of the excavation of timber buildings', *World Archaeology* 1: 220–35.

Barker, P. (1977) *Techniques of Archaeological Excavation* (1st edn), London: Batsford.

Barker, P. (1982) *Techniques of Archaeological Excavation* (2nd edn), London: Batsford.

Barrett, J. C. (1987) 'The Glastonbury Lake Village: models and source criticism', *Archaeological Journal* 144: 409–23.

Barrett J. C. (1988) 'Fields of discourse. Reconstituting a social archaeology', *Critique of Anthropology* 7: 5–16.

Barrett J. C. (1992) 'Bronze Age pottery and the problem of classification', in J. Barrett, R. Bradley and M. Hall (eds) *Papers on the Prehistoric Archaeology of Cranborne Chase*, pp. 201–30, Oxford: Oxbow Monograph 11.

Barrett, J. C. (1995) *Some Challenges in Contemporary Archaeology*, Oxford: Oxbow Lecture 2.

Barrett, J. C., Bradley, R.J. and Green, M. (1991) *Landscapes, Monuments and Society. The Prehistory of Cranborne Chase*, Cambridge: Cambridge University Press.

Barrett, J. C., Bradley, R. J., Bowden, M. C. B. and Mead, B. (1983) 'South Lodge after Pitt Rivers', *Antiquity* 57: 193–204.

Barton, C. M. and Clark, G. A. (eds) (1997) *Rediscovering Darwin: Evolutionary Theory and Archaeological Explanation*, Archaeological Papers of the American Anthropological Association, no. 7.

Bataille, G. (1988) *The Accursed Share* (vol. I), New York: Zone Books.

Baudrillard, J. (1981) *For a Critique of the Political Economy of the Sign*, St Louis, MO: Telos.

Bell, J. (1992) 'On capturing agency in theories about prehistory', in J.-C. Gardin and C. Peebles (eds), *Representations in Archaeology*, pp. 30–55, Bloomington, IN: Indiana University Press.

Bender, B. (1992) 'Theorising landscapes and the prehistoric landscapes of Stonehenge', *Man* 27: 735–55.

Bender, B. (ed.) (1993) *Landscape, Politics and Perspectives*, Oxford: Berg.

Bender, B., Hamilton, S. and Tilley, C. (1997) 'Leskernick: stone worlds; alternative narratives; nested landscapes', *Proceedings of the Prehistoric Society* 63: 147–78.

Bennett, J. W. (1943) 'Recent developments in the functional interpretation of archaeological data', *American Antiquity* 9: 208–19.

Bersu, G. (1938) 'The excavation at Woodbury, Wiltshire during 1938', *Proceedings of the Prehistoric Society* 4: 308–13.

Bersu, G. (1940) 'Excavations at Little Woodbury, Wiltshire', *Proceedings of the Prehistoric Society* 6: 30–111.

Biddle, M. (1994), *What Future for British Archaeology?* Oxford: Oxbow Lecture 1.

Biddle, M. and Kjølbye-Biddle, B. (1967) 'Some new ideas on excavation', unpublished paper delivered at a research seminar at the Institute of Archaeology, London.

Biddle, M. and Kjølbye-Biddle, B. (1969) 'Metres, areas and robbing', *World Archaeology* 1: 208–19.

Binford, L. (1962) 'Archaeology as anthropology', *American Antiquity* 28: 217–25.

Binford, L. (1964) 'A consideration of archaeological research design', *American Antiquity* 29: 425–41.

Binford, L. (1967) 'Smudge pits and hide smoking: the use of analogy in archaeological reasoning', *American Antiquity* 32: 1–12.

Binford, L. (1968) 'Methodological considerations of the archaeological use of ethnographic data', in R. B. Lee and I. Devore, *Man the Hunter*, pp. 268–73, Chicago: University of Chicago Press.

Binford, L. (1973) 'Interassemblage variability: the Mousterian and the "functional" argument', in C. Renfrew (ed.), *The Explanation of Culture Change: Models in Prehistory*, London: Duckworth.

Bindford, L. (1977) 'General introduction' in L. Binford (ed.), *For Theory Building in Archaeology. Essays on Found Remains, Aquatic Resources, Spatial Analysis and Systemic Modeling*, pp. 1–13, New York: Academic Press.

Binford, L. (1981), 'Behavioural archaeology and the Pompeii premise', *Journal of Anthropological Research* 37 (3): 195–208.

Binford, L. (1982) 'The archaeology of place', *Journal of Anthropological Archaeology* 1: 1–31.

Binford, L. (1983) *In Pursuit of the Past*, London: Thames & Hudson.

Binford, L. (1987) 'Data, relativism and archaeological Science', *Man* 22: 391–404.

Binford, L. (1992) 'Seeing the present and interpreting the past – and keeping things straight', in J. Rossignol and L. Wandsnider (eds), *Space, Time and Archaeological Landscapes*, pp. 43–59, New York: Plenum Press.

Binford, L. R. and Binford, S. R. (1968) *New Perspectives in Archaeology*, Chicago: Aldine Publishing Company.

Bintliff, J. (ed.) (1991a) *The Annales School and Archaeology*, Leicester: Leicester University Press.

Bintliff, J. (1991b) 'The contribution of an Annaliste/structural history approach to archaeology', in Bintliff, J. (ed.) *The Annales School and Archaeology*, pp. 1–33, Leicester: Leicester University Press.

Biswell, S., Cropper, L., Evans, J., Gaffney, V. and Leach, P. (1995) 'GIS and excavation: a cautionary tale from Shepton Mallet, Somerset, England', in G. Lock and Z. Stančič, (eds) *Archaeology and GIS*, 269–85, London: Taylor & Francis Ltd.

Bleed, P. (1991) 'Operations research in archaeology', *American Antiquity* 56: 19–35.

Boas, F. (1915) 'Summary of the work of the International School of American Archaeology and Ethnology in Mexico 1910–1914', *American Anthropologist* 17: 384–91.

Boast, R. (1990) 'The categorisation and design systematics of British beakers: a re-examination', unpublished PhD Thesis, University of Cambridge.

Boast, R. (1995) 'Fine pots, pure pots, Beaker pots', in I. Kinnes and G. Varndell (eds), *'Unbaked Urns of Rudely Shape'. Essays on British and Irish Pottery for Ian Longworth*, pp. 69–80, Oxford: Oxbow Monograph.

Boast, R. (1997) 'A small company of actors. A critique of style', *Journal of Material Culture* 2 (2): 173–98.

Bonnichsen, R. (1972) 'Millie's Camp: an experiment in archaeology', *World Archaeology* 4: 277–91.

Boone, E. H. (1993) 'Collecting the pre-Columbian past: historical trends and the process of reception and use', in E. H. Boone (ed.), *Collecting the Pre-Columbian Past*, pp. 315–50, Washington, DC: Dumbarton Oaks.

Boone, J. L. and Smith, E. A. (1998) 'Is it evolution yet? A critique of evolutionary archaeology', *Current Anthropology* 39: 141–73.

Bowden, M. (1991) *Pitt Rivers*, Cambridge: Cambridge University Press.

Bradley, R. (1975) 'Maumbury Rings, Dorchester – the excavations of 1908–13', *Archaeologia* 105: 1–97.

Bradley, R. (1983) 'Archaeology, evolution and the public good: the intellectual development of General Pitt Rivers', *Archaeological Journal* 140: 1–9.

Bradley, R. (1990) *The Passage of Arms*, Cambridge: Cambridge University Press.

Bradley, R. (1997) ' 'To see is to have seen'. Craft traditions in British field archaeology', in B. L. Molyneaux (ed.), *The Cultural Life of Images. Visual Representation in Archaeology*, pp. 62–72, London: Routledge.

Braudel, F. (1980) *On History*, London: Weidenfeld & Nicolson.

Braun, D. P. (1983) 'Pots as tools', in J. Moore and A. Keene (eds), *Archaeological Hammers and Theories*, pp. 107–34, New York: Academic Press.

Brew, J. O. (1946) *The Archaeology of Alkali Ridge, Southeastern Utah* (Papers of the Peabody Museum 21), Cambridge, MA: Peabody Museum.

Browman, D. L. and Givens, D. R. (1996) 'Stratigraphic excavation: the first "New Archaeology"', *American Anthropologist* 98: 80–95.

Brown, J. (1982) 'On the structure of artifact typologies', in R. Whallon and J. Brown (eds), *Essays in Archaeological Typology*, pp. 176–89, Evanston, IL: Center for American Archaeological Press.

Brumfiel, E. M. (1994), 'Ethnic groups and political development in ancient Mexico', in E. M. Brumfiel and J.W. Fox (eds), *Factional Competition and Political Development in the New World*, pp. 89–102, Cambridge: Cambridge University Press.

Buchli, V. and Lucas, G. (forthcoming) 'The archaeology of alienation: a late twentieth century British council flat', in V. Buchli and G. Lucas (eds), *Archaeologies of the Contemporary Past*, London: Routledge.

Bulleid, A. and Gray, H. St G. (1911/1917) *The Glastonbury Lake Village*, Taunton: Glastonbury Antiquarian Society.

Burleigh, R. and Clutton-Brock, J. (1982) 'Pitt Rivers and Petrie in Egypt', *Antiquity* 56: 208–9.

Bushe-Fox, J. P. (1912) 'The Roman pottery', in R. H. Forster and W. H. Knowles, 'Corstopitum: report on the excavations in 1911', *Archaeologia Aeliana* (3rd series) 8: 137–263.

Bushe-Fox, J. P. (1913) *Excavations on the Site of the Roman town of Wroxeter, Shropshire in 1912*, London: Report of the Research Committee of the Society of Antiquaries.

Bushe-Fox, J. P. (1916) *Third Report on the Excavations on the Site of the Roman Town at Wroxeter, Shropshire, 1914*, RRCSA 4, Oxford: Society of Antiquaries.

Cameron, C. M. and Tomkin, S. A. (eds) (1993) *Abandonment of Settlements and Regions*, Cambridge: Cambridge University Press.

Carr, C. (1984) 'The nature of organization of intrasite archaeological records and spatial analysis. Approaches to their investigation', *Advances in Archaeological Method and Theory* 7: 103–222.

Carr, C. (1987) 'Dissecting intrasite artifact palimpsests using Fourier methods', in S. Kent (ed.), *Method and Theory for Activity Area Research*, pp. 236–291, New York: Columbia University Press.

Carver, M. (1988) 'In the steps of a master: Philip Barker and the future of archaeological excavation', in A. Burl (ed.), *From Roman Town to Norman Castle. Essays in Honour of Philip Barker*, Birmingham: University of Birmingham.

Carver, M. (1990) 'Digging for data: archaeological approaches to data definition, acquisition and analysis', in R. Francovich and D. Manacorda (eds), *Lo scavo archeologico: dalla diagnosi all'edizione*, pp. 45–120, Firenze: All'Insegna del Giglio S.A.S.

Castleford, J. (1992) 'Archaeology, GIS, and the time dimension: an overview', in G. Lock and J. Moffett (eds), *Computer Applications and Quantitative Methods in Archaeology 1991*, Oxford: BAR S577.

Chadwick, A. (1997) 'Archaeology at the edge of chaos – further towards reflexive excavation methodologies', *Assemblage* 2, http://www.shef.ac.uk/assem/3/3chad.htm

Champion, T., Gamble, C., Shennan, S. and Whittle, A. (1984) *Prehistoric Europe*, London: Academic Press.

Chang, K. C. (1958) 'Study of the Neolithic social grouping. Examples from the New World', *American Anthropologist* 60: 298–334.

Chang, K. C. (1968) 'Toward a science of prehistoric society', in K. C. Chang (ed.), *Settlement Archaeology*, pp. 1–9, Palo Alto, CA: National Press Books.

Chapman, W. R. (1985) 'Arranging ethnology. A.H.L.F. Pitt Rivers and the typological tradition', in G. W. Stocking (ed.) *Objects and Others. Essays on Museums and Material Culture*, pp. 15–48, Madison, WI: University of Wisconsin Press.

Chapman, W. R. (1989) 'Toward an institutional history of archaeology: British archaeologists and allied interests in the 1860s', in A. Christenson (ed.), *Tracing Archaeology's Past. The Historiography of Archaeology*, pp. 151–62, Carbondale, IL: Southern Illinois University Press.

Cherry, J. and Shennan, S. J. (1978) 'Sampling cultural systems: some perspectives on the application of probabilistic regional survey in Britain', in J. Cherry, C. Gamble and S. J. Shennan (eds), *Sampling in Contemporary British Archaeology*, pp. 17–48, Oxford: BAR 50.

Cherry, J., Gamble, C. and Shennan, S. J. (1978) *Sampling in Contemporary British Archaeology*, Oxford: BAR 50.

Childe, V. G. (1925) *The Dawn of European Civilization*, London: Kegan Paul.

Childe, V. G. (1929) *The Danube in Prehistory*, Oxford: Oxford University Press.

Childe, V. G. (1935) 'Changing methods and aims in prehistory', *Proceedings of the Prehistoric Society* 1: 1–15.

Childe, V. G. (1936) *Man Makes Himself*, London: Collins.

Childe, V. G. (1951) *Social Evolution*, London: Watts & Co.

Childe, V. G. (1956) *Piecing Together the Past*, London: Routledge & Kegan Paul.

Childe, V. G. (1964) *What Happened in History*, Harmondsworth: Penguin.

Christensen, A. L. and Read, D. W. (1977) 'Numerical taxonomy, R-mode factor analysis and archaeological classification', *American Antiquity* 42: 163–79.

Clark, G. A. and Stafford, C. R. (1982) 'Quantification in American archaeology: a historical perspective', *World Archaeology* 14: 98–119.

Clark, J. G. D. (1951) 'Folk-culture and the study of European prehistory', in W. F. Grimes (ed.), *Aspects of Archaeology in Britain and Beyond*, 49–65, London: H. W. Edwards.

Clark, J. G. D. (1952) *Prehistoric Europe: The Economic Basis*, London: Methuen.

Clark, J. G. D. (1953) 'Archaeological theories and interpretation: Old World', in A. L. Kroeber (ed.), *Anthropology Today*, pp. 343–60, Chicago: University of Chicago Press.

Clark, J. G. D. (1954) *Excavations at Star Carr*, Cambridge: Cambridge University Press.

Clark, J. G. D. (1957) *Archaeology and Society*, London: Methuen.

Clark, P. R. (1992) 'Contrasts in the recording and interpretation of 'rural' and 'urban' stratification', in K. Steane (ed.), *Interpretation of Stratigraphy: A Review of the Art*, pp. 17–19, Lincoln: City of Lincoln Archaeology Unit.

Clarke, D. L. (1968) *Analytical Archaeology* (1st edn), London: Methuen.

Clarke, D. L. (1970) *The Beaker Pottery of Great Britain and Ireland*, Cambridge: Cambridge University Press.

Clarke, D. L. (1972) 'A provisional model of an Iron Age society and its settlement system', in D. L. Clarke (ed.), *Models in Archaeology*, pp. 801–69, London: Methuen.

Clarke, D. L. (1973) 'Archeology: the loss of innocence', *Antiquity* 47: 6–18.

Clarke, D. L. (ed.) (1977) *Spatial Archaeology*, New York: Academic Press.

Clarke, D. L. (1978) *Analytical Archaeology*, (2nd edn), London: Methuen.

Clifford, J. (1990), 'Notes on (field)notes', in R. Sanjek (ed.), *Fieldnotes. The Makings of Anthropology*, pp. 47–70, Ithaca, NY: Cornell University Press.

Clifford, J. and Marcus, G. (1986) *Writing Culture: The Poetics and Politics of Ethnography*, Berkeley, CA: University of California Press.

Cole, Fay-Cooper (1951) *Kincaid. A Prehistoric Illinois Metropolis*. Chicago: University of Chicago Press.

Cole, J. P. and King, C. A. M. (1968), *Quantitative Geography*, London: John Wiley & Sons Ltd.

Cole, J. R. (1974) 'Nineteenth century fieldwork, archaeology and museum studies: their role in the four-field definition of American anthropology', in J. V. Murra (ed.), 'American Anthropology: The Early Years', *Proceedings of the American Ethnological Society*, pp. 111–25.

Coles, J. (1972) *Field Archaeology in Britain*, London: Methuen & Co. Ltd.

Coles, J. (1979) *Experimental Archaeology*, London: Academic Press.

Collingwood, R. (1927) 'Oswald Spengler and the theory of historical cycles', *Antiquity* 1: 311–25, 435–46.

Colton, H. S. (1942) 'Archaeology and the reconstruction of history', *American Antiquity* 7: 33–40.

Conkey, M. (1990) 'Experimenting with style in archaeology: some historical and theoretical issues', in M. Conkey and C. Hastorf (eds), *The Uses of Style in Archaeology*, pp. 5–17. Cambridge: Cambridge University Press.

Connolly, R. and Anderson, R. (1987), *First Contact*, New York: Viking.

Cottrell, L. (1953), *The Bull of Minos*, London: Pan Books.

Courbin, P. (1988) *What is Archaeology?* Chicago: University of Chicago Press.

Courty, M.-A., Goldberg, P. and Macphail, R. (1989), *Soils and Micromorphology in Archaeology*, Cambridge: Cambridge University Press.

Crawford, O. G. S. (1912) 'The distribution of Early Bronze Age settlements in Britain', *Geographical Journal* 40: 183–217.

Crawford, O. G. S (1921) *Man and his Past*, Oxford: Oxford University Press.

Crumley, C. (ed.) (1994) *Historical Ecology. Cultural Knowledge and Changing Landscapes*. Santa Fe, NM: School of American Research Press.

Crumley, C. and Marquardt, W. H. (1990) 'Landscape. A unifying concept in regional analysis', in K. Allen *et al.*, *Interpreting Space: GIS and Archaeology*, pp. 73–9, London: Taylor and Francis.

Cuming, H. S. (1891), 'On vessels of samian ware', *Journal of the British Archaeological Association* 47: 277–85.

Dalland, M. (1984) 'A procedure for use in stratigraphic analysis', *Scottish Archaeological Review* 3: 116–27.

Daniel, G. (1975) *A Hundred and Fifty Years of Archaeology*, London: Methuen.

Daniel, G. (1981) 'Introduction: The necessity for an historical approach to archaeology', in G. Daniel (ed.), *Towards a History of Archaeology*, pp. 9–13. London: Thames & Hudson.

David, N. (1972) 'On the lifespan of pottery, type frequencies and archaeological inference', *American Antiquity* 37: 141–2.

Davis, S. (1987) *The Archaeology of Animals*, London: Batsford.

DeBoer, W. R. and Lathrap, D. W. (1979) 'The making and breaking of Shipibo-Conibo ceramics', in C. Kramer (ed.), *Ethnoarchaeology: Implications of Ethnography for Archaeology*, pp. 102–38, New York: Columbia University Press.

Deetz, J. (1971) 'Must archaeologists dig?' in J. Deetz (ed.), *Man's Imprint from the Past*, pp. 2–9, Boston: Little Brown & Co.

Deetz, J. (1988) 'Material culture and worldview in colonial Anglo-America', in M. Leone and P. Potter (eds), *The Recovery of Meaning*, pp. 219–34, Washington: Smithsonian Institution Press.

Deleaze, G. (1977) *Difference and Repetition*, London: Athlone Press.

Derrida, J. (1976) *Of Grammatology*, Baltimore: Johns Hopkins University Press.

Descartes, R. (1968) *Meditations/Discourse on Method*, Harmondsworth: Penguin.

Deuel, L. (1978) *Memoirs of Heinrich Schliemann*, London: Hutchinson.

Díaz-Andreu, M. (1996) 'Constructing identities through culture. The past in the forging of Europe', in P. Graves-Brown *et al.* (eds), *Cultural Identity and Archaeology*, pp. 48–61, London: Routledge.

Díaz-Andreu, M. and Champion, T. (eds) (1996) *Nationalism and Archaeology in Europe*, London: UCL Press.

Díaz-Andreu, M. and Stig Sørensen, M. L. (1997) 'Excavating women. Towards an engendered history of archaeology', in M. Díaz-Andreu and M. L. Stig Sørensen (eds) *Excavating Women. A History of Women in European Archaeology*, pp. 1–28, London: Routledge.

Dincauze, D. F. (1992) 'Exploring career styles in archaeology', in J. E. Reyman (ed.), *Rediscovering Our Past: Essays on the History of American Archaeology*, pp. 131–6, Aldershot: Avebury.

Dixon, R. B. (1913) 'Some aspects of North American archaeology', *American Anthropologist* 15: 549–77.

Doran, J. E. and Hodson, F. R. (1975) *Mathematics and Computers in Archaeology*, Edinburgh: Edinburgh University Press.

Dragendorff, H. (1895) 'Terra Sigillata', *Bonner Jahrbücher* 96: 18–155.

Droop, J. P. (1915) *Archaeological Excavation*, Cambridge: Cambridge University Press.

Duke, P. (1991) *Points in Time. Structure and Event in a late Northwestern Plains Hunting Society*, Colorado: Colorado University Press.

Dunnell, R. C. (1978) 'Style and function: a fundamental dichotomy', *American Antiquity* 43: 192–202.

Dunnell, R. C. (1980) 'Evolutionary theory and archaeology', *Advances in Archaeological Method and Theory* 3: 35–99.

Dunnell, R. C. (1986a) 'Methodological issues in Americanist artifact classification', *Advances in Archaeological Method and Theory* 9: 149–207.

Dunnell, R. C. (1986b) 'Five decades of American archaeology', in D. J. Meltzer, D. D. Fowler and J.A. Sabloff (eds), *American Archaeology Past and Future*, pp. 23–49, Washington: Smithsonian Institution Press.

Dunnell, R. C. (1992) 'The notion site', in J. Rossignol and L. Wandsnider (eds), *Space, Time and Archaeological Landscapes*, pp. 21–41, New York: Plenum Press.

Dunnell, R. C. and Dancey, W. S. (1983) 'The siteless survey: a regional scale data collection strategy', *Advances in Archaeological Method and Theory* 6: 267–87.

Earle, T. K. (1991) 'Toward a behavioural archaeology', in R. Preucel (ed.), *Processual and Postprocessual Archaeologies. Multiple Ways of Knowing the Past*, pp. 83–95, Southern Illinois University at Carbondale, Occasional Paper no. 10.

Earle, T. K. and Preucel, R. (1987) 'Processual archaeology and the radical critique', *Current Anthropology* 28: 501–38.

Edgeworth, M. (1990) 'Analogy as practical reason: the perception of objects in excavation practice', *Archaeological Review from Cambridge* 9 (2): 243–51.

Edmonds, M. (1990) 'Description, understanding and the chaîne opérataire', *Archaeological Review from Cambridge* 9 (1): 55–70.

Eighmy, J. L. (1981), 'The use of material culture in diachronic anthropology', in R. Gould and M. Schiffer (eds), *Modern Material Culture: the Archaeology of us*, pp. 31–49, New York: Academic Press.

Embree, L. (1989) 'Contacting the theoretical archaeologists', in A. Christenson (ed.), *Tracing Archaeology's Past. The Historiography of Archaeology*, pp. 62–74, Carbonale, IL: Southern Illinois University Press.

Embree, L. (1992a) 'Introductory essay: The future and past of metaarchaeology', in L. Embree (ed.), 'Metaarchaeology. Reflections by archaeologists and philosophers', *Boston Studies in the Philosophy of Science* 147: 3–50.

Embree, L. (1992b) 'Phenomenology of a change in archaeological observation', in L. Embree (ed.), 'Metaarchaeology. Reflections by archaeologists and philosophers', *Boston Studies in the Philosophy of Science* 147: 165–93.

Evans, C. (1989) 'Archaeology and modern times: Bersu's Woodbury 1938 and 1939', *Antiquity* 63: 436–50.

Evans, C. (1998) 'Historicism, chronology and straw men: situating Hawkes' ladder of inference', *Antiquity* 72: 398–404.

Evans, C. (n.d.) 'Model excavations: presentation, textuality and graphic literacy', unpublished paper.

Evans, C. and Knight, M. (1997) 'The Barleycroft Paddocks excavations, Cambridgeshire', unpublished Cambridge Archaeology Unit Report, no. 218.

Evans, J. (1872) *The Ancient Stone Implements, weapons and ornaments of Great Britain*, Longman, Green & Co.

Evans, J. (1881), *Ancient Bronze Implements*.

Farrand, W. R. (1984) 'Stratigraphic classification: living within the law', *Quarterly Review of Archaeology* 5 (1): 1–5

Fedele, F. (1984) 'Toward an analytical stratigraphy: stratigraphy, reasoning and excavation', *Stratigraphica Archaeologica* 1: 7–15.

Fewkes, J. W. (1904) 'Two summers' work in pueblo ruins' *22nd Annual Report of the Bureau of American Ethnology, 1900–1901*: 1–96

Flannery, K. (1973) 'Archaeology with a capital "S"', in C. Redman (ed.), *Research and Theory in Current Archaeology*, pp. 47–53, New York: Wiley.

Flannery, K. (1976) *The Early Mesoamerican Village*, New York: Academic Press.

Flannery, K. (1982) 'The Golden Marshalltown: a parable for the archaeology of the 1980s', *American Anthropologist* 84: 265–78.

Fletcher, R. (1989) 'The messages of material behaviour: a preliminary discussion of non-verbal meaning', in I. Hodder (ed.), *The Meanings of Things*, pp. 33–40, London: Unwin (One World Archaeology).

Foley, R. (1981) 'Off-site archaeology: an alternative approach for the short-sited', in I. Hodder, G. Isaac and N. Hammond (eds), *Pattern of the Past: Studies in Honour of David Clarke*, pp. 157–83, Cambridge: Cambridge University Press.

Ford, J. A. (1952) *Measurements of some prehistoric design developments in the southeastern states*, New York: Anthropological Papers of the American Museum of Natural History 43.

Ford, J. A. (1954) 'The type concept revisited', *American Anthropologist* 56: 42–53.

Fortier, A. C., Lacampagne, R. B. and Finney, E. A. (1984) *The Fish Lake Site* (American Bottom Archaeology FAI-270 Report No. 8), Illinois: University of Illinois Press.

Forty, A. (1986) *Objects of Desire. Design and Society since 1750*, London: Thames & Hudson.

Foucault, M. (1970) *The Order of Things*, London: Tavistock.

Foucault, M. (1984) 'On the genealogy of ethics: an overview of work in progress', in P. Rabinow (ed.), *The Foucault Reader*, pp. 340–72, Harmondsworth: Penguin.

Fowler, D. (1987) 'Uses of the past: archaeology in the service of the state', *American Antiquity* 52: 229–48.

Fox, A. H. L. (1869) 'Further remarks on the hill forts of Sussex: being an account of excavation in the forts of Cissbury and Highdown', *Archaeologia* 42: 53–76.

Frere, S. (1975) *Principles of Publication in Rescue Archaeology*, London: HMSO: DoE.

Friedman, J. and Rowlands, M. (eds) (1977) *The Evolution of Social Systems*, London: Duckworth.

Gadamer, H.-G. (1989) *Truth and Method*, London: Sheed & Ward.

Gaffney, V. and Tingle, M. (1984) 'The tyranny of the site: method and theory in field survey', *Scottish Archaeological Review* 3: 134–40.

Gaffney, V. and van Leusen, M. (1995) 'Postscript – GIS, environmental determinism and archaeology: a parallel text', in G. Lock and Z. Stančič (eds), *Archaeology and GIS*, pp. 367–82, London: Taylor & Francis.

Gamio, M. (1913) 'Arqueologia de Atzcapotzalco, D.F. Mexico', *Proceedings, Eighteenth International Congress of Americanists*, pp. 180–7.

Gasche, H. and Tunca, Ö. (1983) 'Guide to archaeostratigraphic classification and terminology: definitions and principles', *Journal of Field Archaeology* 10: 325–35.

Gero, J. M. (1985) 'Socio-politics and the woman-at-home ideology', *American Antiquity* 50: 342–50.

Gero, J. M. (1991) 'Who experienced what in prehistory? A narrative explanation from Queyash, Peru', in R. Preucel (ed.), *Processual and Postprocessual Archaeologies. Multiple Ways of Knowing the Past*, pp. 126–39, Carbondale, IL: Southern Illinois University at Carbondale Occasional Paper no. 10.

Gero, J. (1995) 'Railroading epistemology. Palaeoindians and women', in I. Hodder, M. Shanks, A. Alexander, V. Buchli, J. Carman, J. Last and G. Lucas (eds), *Interpreting Archaeology: Finding Meaning in the Past*, pp. 175–8, London: Routledge.

Gero, J. M. (1996) 'Archaeological practice and gendered encounters with field data', in R. P. Wright (ed.), *Gender and Archaeology*, pp. 251–80, Philadelphia: University of Pennsylvania Press.

Gerrard, R. (1991) 'Beyond Crossmends: stratigraphic analysis and the content of historic artefact assemblages on urban sites', in C. Harris (ed.) *Practices of Archaeological Stratigraphy*, pp. 229–49, London: Academic Press.

Giddens, A. (1984) *The Constitution of Society*, Cambridge: Polity.

Gifford, J. C. (1960) 'The type-variety method of ceramic classification as an indicator of cultural phenomena', *American Antiquity* 25: 341–7.

Gilman, A. (1984) 'Explaining the Upper Palaeolithic Revolution', in M. Spriggs (ed.), *Marxist Perspectives in Archaeology*, pp. 115–26, Cambridge: Cambridge University Press.

Gladwin, W. and Gladwin, H. S. (1934) *A Method for the Designation of Cultures and their Variations* (Medallion Papers no. 15), Pasadena: Globe.

Goodman, M. (1999) 'Temporalities of prehistoric life: household development and community continuity', in J. Brück and M. Goodman (eds), *Making Places in the Prehistoric World. Themes in Settlement Archaeology*, London: UCL Press.

Gorodozov, V. A. (1933) 'The typological method in archaeology', *American Anthropologist* 35: 95–102.

Gould, R. A. (1980) *Living Archaeology*, Cambridge: Cambridge University Press.

Gräslund, B. (1976) 'Relative dating methods in Scandinavian archaeology', *Norwegian Archaeological Review* 9: 69–83.

Gräslund, B. (1981) 'The background to C. J. Thomsen's three age system', in G. Daniel (ed.), *Towards a History of Archaeology*, pp. 45–50, London: Thames & Hudson.

Gräslund, B. (1987) *The Birth of Prehistoric Chronology*, Cambridge: Cambridge University Press.

Graves-Brown, P., Jones, S. and Gamble, C. (eds) (1996) *Cultural Identity and Archaeology*, London: Routledge.

Gray, H. St G. (1905) *Excavations at Cranborne Chase: Index* (Volume V), privately printed.

Greene, K. (1983) *Introduction to Archaeology*, London: Batsford.

Greenwell, Rev. W. (1877) *British Barrows*, Oxford: Clarendon Press.

Greenwell, W. and Brewis, W. P. (1909) 'The origin, evolution and classification of the bronze spearhead in Great Britain and Ireland', *Archaeologia* LXI: 439–72.

Grinsell L., Rahtz, P. and Williams, D. P. (1974) *The Preparation of Archaeological Reports*, London: John Baker.

Gupta, A. and Ferguson, J. (1997) 'Discipline and practice: "the field" as site, method, and location in anthropology', in A. Gupta and J. Ferguson (eds), *Anthropological Locations. Boundaries and Grounds of a Science*, pp. 1–46, Berkeley, CA: University of California Press.

Haag, W. G. (1986) 'Field methods in archaeology', in D. J. Meltzer, D. D. Fowler and J. A. Sabloff (eds), *American Archaeology Past and Future*, pp. 63–76, Washington: Smithsonian Institute Press.

Hamilton, C. (1996) 'Faultlines', unpublished paper presented at TAG, Liverpool.

Hamilton, S. (1996) 'Reassessing archaeological illustrations: breaking the mould', *Graphic Archaeology*: 20–7.

Hamilton, S. (1999) 'Lost in translation? A comment on the excavation report', *Papers from the Institute of Archaeology* 10: 1–8.

Handsman, R. G. and Richmond, T. L. (1995) 'Confronting colonialism. The Mahican and Schaghticoke peoples and us', in P. R. Schmidt and T. C. Patterson (eds) (1995) *Making Alternative Histories. The Practice of Archaeology and History in Non-Western Settings*, pp. 87–118, Santa Fe, NM: School of American Research Press.

Hargrave, L. L. (1932) *Guide to Forty Pottery Types from Hopi Country and the San Francisco Mountains, Arizona*, Flagstaff, AZ: Museum of Northern Arizona Bulletin 1.

Härke, H. (1991) 'All Quiet on the Western Front? Paradigms, methods and approches in West German Archaeology', in I. Hodder (ed.), *Archaeological Theory in Europe: The Last Three Decades*, pp. 187–222, London: Routledge.

Harris, E. C. (1975) 'A stratigraphic sequence: A question of time', *World Archaeology* 7: 109–21.

Harris, E. C. (1977) 'Units of archaeological stratification', *Norwegian Archaeological Review* 10: 84–94.

Harris, E. C. (1984) 'The analysis of multi-linear stratigraphic sequences', *Scottish Archaeological Review* 3: 127–33.

Harris, E. C. (1989 [1979]) *Principles of Archaeological Stratigraphy* (2nd edition), London: Academic Press.

Harris, E. C. (1991) 'Interfaces in archaeological stratigraphy', in E. C. Harris (ed.), *Practices of Archaeological Stratigraphy*, pp. 7–20, London: Academic Press.

Harris, E. C. and Ottoway, P. J. (1976) 'A recording experiment on a rescue site', *Rescue Archaeology* 10: 6–7.

Haselgrove, C. (1985) 'Inference from ploughsoil artefact samples', in C. Haselgrove, M. Millett and I. Smith (eds), *Archaeology from the Ploughsoil. Studies in the Collection and Interpretation of Field Survey Data*. pp. 7–30, Sheffield: University of Sheffield.

Hawkes, C. (1951) 'British prehistory halfway through the century', *Proceedings of the Prehistoric Society* 17: 1–15.

Hawkes, C. (1954) 'Archaeological theory and method: some suggestions from the Old World', *American Anthropologist* 56: 155–68.

Hawkes J. and Hawkes, C. (1947) *Prehistoric Britain*, London: Chatto & Windus.

Hayfield, C. (ed.) (1980) *Fieldwalking as a Method of Archaeological Research*, London: DoE Occasional Papers 2.

Heidegger, M. (1962) *Being and Time*, Oxford: Blackwell.

Heizer, R. F. (1958) *A Guide to Archaeological Field Methods* (3rd revised edition), Palo Alto, CA: The National Press.

Heizer R. F. and Graham, J. A. (1968) *A Guide to Field Methods in Archaeology*, Berkeley, CA: University of California.

Herne, A. (1988) 'A time and a place for the Grimston Bowl', in J. Barrett and I. Kinnes (eds), *The Archaeology of Context in the Neolithic and Bronze Age: Recent Trends*, pp. 9–29, Sheffield: University of Sheffield.

Hester, T., Shafer, H. J. and Feder, K. L. (1997) *Field Methods in Archaeology*, Mayfield Publishing Co.

Hietala, H. (ed.) (1984) *Intra-site Spatial Analysis*, Cambridge: Cambridge University Press.

Higgs, E. S. (ed.) (1972) *Papers in Economic Prehistory*, Cambridge: Cambridge University Press.

Higgs, E. S. (ed.) (1975) *Palaeoeconomy*, Cambridge: Cambridge University Press.

Hill, J. N. (1968) 'Broken K Pueblo: Patterns of Form and Function', in L. R. Binford and S. R. Binford (eds), *New Perspectives in Archaeology*, pp. 103–43, Chicago: Aldine Publishing Company.

Hill, J. N. and Evans, R. K. (1972) 'A model for classification and typology', in D. L. Clarke (ed.), *Models in Archaeology*, pp. 231–73, London: Methuen & Co.

Hinsley, C. M. (1974) 'Amateurs and professionals in Washington anthropology, 1879 to 1903', in J. V. Murra (ed.), *American Anthropology: The Early Years*, *Proceedings of the American Ethnological Society*, pp. 36–68.

Hinsley, C. M. (1985) 'From shell-heaps to stelae. Early anthropology at the Peabody Museum', in G. W. Stocking (ed.), *Objects and Others. Essays on Museums and Material Culture* (HOA3), pp. 49–74, Madison, WI: University of Wisconsin Press.

Hinsley, C. M. (1989) 'Revising and revisioning the history of archaeology: reflections on region and context', in A. L. Christenson (ed.), *Tracing Archaeology's Past. The Historiography of Archaeology*, pp. 79–96, Carbondale, IL: Southern Illinois University Press.

Hodder, I. (ed.) (1978) *The Spatial Organization of Culture*, London: Duckworth.

Hodder, I. (1982a) *Symbols in Action*. Cambridge: Cambridge University Press.

Hodder, I. (ed.) (1982b) *Symbolic and Structural Archaeology*, Cambridge: Cambridge University Press.

Hodder, I. (1982c) *The Present Past*, London: Batsford.

Hodder, I. (1982d) 'Sequences of structural change in the Dutch Neolithic', in I. Hodder (ed.), *Symbolic and Structural Archaeology*, pp. 162–77, Cambridge: Cambridge University Press.

Hodder, I. (1984) 'Archaeology in 1984', *Antiquity* 58: 25–32.

Hodder, I. (1985) 'Post-processual archaeology', *Advances in Archaeological Method and Theory* 8: 1–26.

Hodder, I. (1986) *Reading the Past*, Cambridge: Cambridge University Press.

Hodder, I. (ed.) (1987a) *The Archaeology of Contextual Meanings*, Cambridge: Cambridge University Press.

Hodder, I. (ed.) (1987b) *Archaeology as Long-term History*, Cambridge: Cambridge University Press.

Hodder, I. (1989a) 'This is not an article about material culture as text', *Journal of Anthropological Archaeology* 8: 250–69.

Hodder, I. (1989b) 'Writing archaeology: site reports in context', *Antiquity* 63: 268–74.

Hodder, I. (1990) 'Style as historical quality', in M. Conkey and C. Hastorf (eds), *The Uses of Style in Archaeology*, pp. 44–51, Cambridge: Cambridge University Press.

Hodder, I. (1991) 'Interpretive archaeology and its role', *American Antiquity* 56: 7–18.

Hodder, I. (1992) *Theory and Practice in Archaeology*, London: Routledge.

Hodder, I. (1993a), 'The narrative and rhetoric of material culture sequences', *World Archaeology* 25: 268–82.

Hodder, I. (1993b) 'Social cognition', *Cambridge Archaeological Journal* 3: 253–7.

Hodder, I. (1997) '"Always momentary, fluid and flexible": towards a reflexive excavation methodology', *Antiquity* 71: 691–700.

Hodder, I. (1999) *The Archaeological Process*, Oxford: Blackwell.

Hodder, I. and Orton, C. (1976) *Spatial Analysis in Archaeology*, Cambridge: Cambridge University Press.

Hodson, F. R. (1982) 'Some aspects of archaeological classification', in R. Whallon and J. Brown (eds), *Essays in Archaeological Typology*, pp. 21–9, Evanston, IL: Center for American Archaeological Press.

Holmes, W. H. (1903) 'Aboriginal pottery of the Eastern United States', *Bureau of American Ethnology, Twentieth Annual Report*, Washington D.C.

Holmes, W. H. (1914) 'Areas of American culture characterization tentatively outlined as an aid in the study of the antiquities', *American Anthropologist* 16: 413–46.

Hughes, P. (1999) 'Archaeological drawings are in black and white', *Association of Archaeological Illustrators and Surveyors Newsletter*.

Ingersoll, D., Yellen, J. E. and MacDonald, W. (eds) (1977) *Experimental Archaeology*, New York: Columbia University Press.

Jacknis, I. (1985) 'Franz Boas and exhibits. On the limitations of the museum method of anthropology', in G. W. Stocking (ed.), *Objects and Others. Essays on Museums and Material Culture* (HOA3), pp. 75–111, Madison, WI: University of Wisconsin Press.

Jarman, H. N., Legge, A. J. and Charles, J. A. (1971) 'Retrieval of plant remains from archaeological sites by froth flotation', in E. Higgs (ed.), *Papers in Economic Prehistory*, pp. 39–48, Cambridge: Cambridge University Press.

Johnson, A. and Earle, T. (1987) *The Evolution of Human Societies*, Stanford: Stanford University Press.

Johnson, G. (1977) 'Aspects of regional analysis in archaeology', *Annual Review of Anthropology* 6: 479–508.

Johnson, M. (1989) 'Conceptions of agency in archaeological interpretation', *Journal of Anthropological Archaeology* 8: 189–211.

Jones, B. (1984), *Past Imperfect. The Story of Rescue Archaeology*, London: Heinemann.

Jones, M. K. (1991) 'Sampling in palaeoethnobotany', in van Zeist, K. Wasylikowa and K. E. Behre (eds), *Progress in Old World Palaeoethnobotany*, pp. 55–61, Rotterdam: A. A. Balkema.

Jones, S. (1997) *The Archaeology of Ethnicity. Constructing Identities in the Past and Present*, London: Routledge.

Joukowsky, M. (1980) *A Complete Manual of Field Archaeology*, Englewood Cliffs, NJ: Prentice-Hall.

Kehoe, A. (1998) *The Land of Prehistory. A Critical History of American Archaeology*, London: Routledge.

Kent, S. (1987) 'Understading the use of space: an ethnoarchaeological approach', in S. Kent (ed.), *Method and Theory for Activity Area Research*, pp. 1–60, New York; Columbia University Press.

Kenyon, K. (1953) *Beginning in Archaeology*, London: Phoenix House Ltd.

Kidder, A. V. (1927) 'Southwestern archaeological conference', *Science* 66: 486–91.

Kidder, A.V. (1962 [1924]) *An Introduction to the Study of Southwestern Archaeology*. New Haven, CT: Yale University Press.

Kidder, M. A. and Kidder, A. V. (1917) 'Notes on the pottery of Pecos', *American Anthropologist* 19: 325–60.

Kinnes, I., Gibson, A., Ambers, J., Bowman, S., Leese, M. and Boast, R. (1991) 'Radiocarbon dating and British Beakers: the British Museum programme', *Scottish Archaeological Review* 8: 35–68.

Kirch, P. V. (1980) 'The archaeological study of adaptation: theoretical and methodological issues', *Advances in Archaeological Method and Theory* 3: 101–56.

Klejn, L. S. (1982) *Archaeological Typology*, Oxford: BAR S153.

Klindt-Jensen, O. (1975) *A History of Scandinavian Archaeology*, London: Thames & Hudson.

Knapp, B. (1992) *Archaeology, Annales and Ethnohistory*, Cambridge: Cambridge University Press.

Kohl, P. L. and Fawcett, C. (eds) (1995) *Nationalism, Politics and the Practice of Archaeology*, London: Routledge.

Kopytoff, I. (1986) 'The cultural biography of things: commoditization as a process', in A. Appadurai (ed.), *The Social Life of Things*, pp. 64–91, Cambridge: Cambridge University Press.

Kosso, P. (1991) 'Method in archeology: middle-range theory as hermeneutics', *American Antiquity* 56: 621–7.

Kovacik, J. J. (1998) 'Collective memory and Pueblo space', *Norwegian Archaeological Review* 31: 141–52.

Krieger, A. D. (1944) 'The typological concept', *American Antiquity* 9: 271–88.

Kroeber, A. L. (1916) 'Zuñi potsherds', *Anthropological Papers of the American Museum of Natural History* 18: 7–37.

Kroeber, A. L. (1952 [1919]) 'Order in changes of fashion', in A. L. Kroeber, *The Nature of Culture*, pp. 332–6, Chicago: University of Chicago Press.

Kroeber, A. L. and Kluckhohn, C. (1952) *Culture – A Critical Review of Concepts and Definitions* (Papers of the Peabody Museum of American Archaeology and Ethnology no. 47), Cambridge, MA: Harvard University.

Kroll E. M. and Price, T. D. (eds) (1991a) *The Interpretation of Archaeological Spatial Patterning*, New York: Plenum Press.

Kroll E. M. and Price, T. D. (1991b) 'Introduction and postscript: the end of spatial analysis', in E. M. Kroll and T. D. Price (eds), *The Interpretation of Archaeological Spatial Patterning*, pp. 1–6 and 301–5, New York: Plenum Press.

Kubler, G. (1962) *The Shape of Time. Remarks on the History of Things*, New Haven, CT: Yale University Press.

Kuklick, H. (1997) 'After Ishmael: the fieldwork tradition and its future', in A. Gupta and J. Ferguson (eds), *Anthropological Locations. Boundaries and Grounds of a Science*, pp. 47–65, Berkeley, CA: University of California Press.

Kus, S. (1984) 'The spirit and its burden: archaeology and symbolic activity', in M. Spriggs (ed.), *Marxist Perspectives in Archaeology*, pp. 101–7, Cambridge: Cambridge University Press.

Kvamme, K. (1999) 'Recent directions and developments in GIS', *Journal of Archaeological Research* 7: 153–201.

Lamb, L. (1999) 'Visualising past landscapes', *Association of Archaeological Illustrators and Surveyors Newsletter.*

Lane, P. (1987) 'Reordering residues of the past', in I. Hodder (ed.), *Archaeology as Long-term History*, pp. 54–62, Cambridge: Cambridge University Press.

Latour, B. (1992) 'Where are the missing masses? The sociology of a few mundane artefacts', in W. E. Bijker and J. Law (eds), *Shaping Technology/Building Society: Studies in Sociotechnical Change*, pp. 225–58, Cambridge, MA: MIT Press.

Lemonnier, P. (1986) 'The study of material culture today: toward an anthropology of technical systems', *Journal of Anthropological Archaeology* 5: 147–86.

Lemonnier, P. (1990) 'Topsy turvy techniques. Remarks on the social representation of techniques', *Archaeological Review from Cambridge* 9 (1): 27–37.

Lemonnier, P. (1993) 'Introduction', in P. Lemonnier (ed.), *Technological Choices. Transformations in Material Cultures since the Neolithic*, pp. 1–35, London: Routledge.

Leone, M. (1978) 'Time in American archaeology', in C. Redman *et al., Social Archaeology: Beyond Subsistence and Dating*, pp. 25–36, New York: Academic Press.

Leone, M. (1988) 'The Georgian order as the order of merchant capitalism in Annapolis, Maryland', in M. Leone and P. Potter (eds), *The Recovery of Meaning*, pp. 235–62, Washington: Smithsonian Institution Press.

Leppmann, W. (1966) *Pompeii in Fact and Fiction*, London.

Leroi-Gourhan, A. and Brézillon, M. (1966) 'L'habitation Magdalénienne', *Gallia Préhistoire* 9: 263–385.

Levinas, E. (1996) 'Meaning and sense', in *Basic Philosophical Writings*, Bloomington, IN: Indiana University Press.

Levine, P. (1986) *The Amateur and the Professional. Antiquarians, Historians and Archaeologists in Victorian England, 1836–1886*, Cambridge: Cambridge University Press.

Lewarch, D. E. and O'Brien, M. J. (1981) 'The expanding role of surface assemblages in archaeological research', *Advances in Archaeological Method and Theory* 4: 297–342.

Lock, G. and Moffett, J. (eds) (1992) *Computer Applications and Quantitative Methods in Archaeology 1991*, Oxford: BAR S577.

Lock, G. and Z. Stančič (eds) (1995) *Archaeology and GIS*. London: Taylor & Francis Ltd.

Longacre, W. A. (1968) 'Some aspects of prehistoric society in East-Central Arizona', in L. R. Binford and S. R. Binford (eds), *New Perspectives in Archaeology*, pp. 89–102, Chicago: Aldine Publishing Company.

Loomes, B. (1978) *Complete British Clocks*, London: David & Charles.

Loomes, B. (1991) *Antique British Clocks*, Robert Hale.

Lubbock, J. (1865) *Prehistoric Times*, London: Williams & Norgate.

Lucas, G. (1995a) 'The changing face of time. English domestic clocks from the seventeenth to nineteenth centuries', *Journal of Design History* 8: 1–9.

Lucas, G. (1995b) 'Genealogies. Classification, narrative and time: an archaeological study of eastern Yorkshire, 3700–1300 BC', unpublished PhD, University of Cambridge.

Lucas, G. (1997) 'Forgetting the past', *Anthropology Today* 13 (1): 8–14.

Lyman, R. L. and O'Brien, M. J. (1998) 'The goals of evolutionary archaeology', *Current Anthropology* 39: 615–52.

Lyman, R. L., Wolverton, S. and O'Brien, M. J. (1998) 'Seriation, superposition and interdigitation: a history of Americanist graphic depictions of culture change', *American Antiquity* 63: 239–61.

McFadyen, L. (1997) 'Body imagery', unpublished MA thesis, University of Southampton.

McFadyen, L., Lewis, H., Challands, N., Challands, A., Garrow, D., Poole, S., Knight, M., Dodwell, N., Mackay, D., Denny, L., Whitaker, P., Breach, P., Lloyd-Smith, L., Gibson D. and White, P. (1997) 'Gossiping on people's bodies', unpublished paper presented at TAG 1997, Bournemouth.

McGovern, T. H. (1994) 'Management for extinction in Norse Greenland', in C. Crumley (ed.), *Historical Ecology. Cultural Knowledge and Changing Landscapes*, pp. 127–54, Santa Fe, NM: School of American Research Press.

McGuire, R. H. (1982) 'Ethnicity in historical archaeology', *Journal of Anthropological Archaeology* 1: 159–78.

McGuire, R. H. (1992) *A Marxist Archaeology*, San Diego, CA: Academic Press.

McGuire, R. H. and Paynter, R. (eds) (1991) *The Archaeology of Inequality*, Oxford: Blackwell.

McGuire, R. H. and Saitta, D. (1996) 'Although they have petty captains, they obey them badly: the dialectics of prehispanic western Peublo social organization', *American Antiquity* 61: 197–216.

McKern, W. C. (1939) 'The Midwestern taxonomic method as an aid to archaeological study', *American Antiquity* 4: 301–13.

McKern, W. C. (1942) 'Taxonomy and the direct historical approach', *American Antiquity* 7: 337–43.

McMillon, B. (1991) *The Archaeology Handbook*, John Wiley & Sons Inc.: New York.

McNairn, B. (1980) *The Method and Theory of V. Gordon Childe*, Edinburgh: Edinburgh University Press.

Macphail R. and Goldberg, P. (1995) 'Recent advances in micromorphological interpretation of soils and sediments from archaeological sites', in A. Barham and R. Macphail (eds), *Archaeological Sediments and Soils: Analysis, Interpretation and Management*, pp. 1–24, London: Institute of Archaeology, UCL.

McVicker, D. E. (1992) 'The matter of Saville: Franz Boas and the anthropological definition of archaeology', in J. E. Reyman (ed.), *Rediscovering Our Past: Essays on the History of American Archaeology*, pp. 145–60, Aldershot: Avebury.

Malina, J. and Z. Vašíček (1990) *Archaeology Yesterday and Today. The Development of Archaeology in the Sciences and Humanities*. Cambridge: Cambridge University Press.

Malmer, M. P. (1995) 'Montelius on types and find-combinations', in P. Åström (ed.), *Oscar Montelius. 150 years*, pp. 15–22, Stockholm: Kungl Vitterhets Historie och Antikvitets Akademien.

Marsden, B. M. (1971) *The Early Barrow Diggers*, Princes Risborough: Shire Publications.

Martin, P., Quimby, G. and Collier, D. (1947) *Indians before Columbus*, Chicago: University of Chicago Press.

Maschner, H. D. G. (ed.) (1996) *Darwinian Archaeologies*, New York: Plenum Press.

Mason, C. I. (1992) 'From the other side of the looking glass: women in American archaeology in the 1950s', in J. E. Reyman (ed.), *Rediscovering Our Past: Essays on the History of American Archaeology*, pp. 91–101, Aldershot: Avebury.

Mason, O. T. (1895) 'Influence of environment upon human industries or arts', *Annual Report of the Smithsonian Institution for 1895*, Washington DC: 639–65.

Matthews, W., French, C. A. I., Lawrence, T., Cutter, D. F. and Jones, M. K. (1997) 'Microstratigraphic traces of site formation processes and human activities', *World Archaeology* 29: 281–308.

Meggers, B. (1954) 'Environmental limitation on the development of culture', *American Anthropologist* 56: 801–24.

Meggers, B. (1955) 'The coming of age of American archaeology', in *New Interpretations of Aboriginal American Culture History*, pp. 116–29, Washington: Anthropological Society of Washington DC.

Meltzer, D. J. (1985) 'North American archaeology and archaeologists, 1879–1934', *American Antiquity* 50: 249–60.

Meltzer, D. J. (1989) 'A question of relevance', in A. L. Christenson (ed.), *Tracing Archaeology's Past. The Historiography of Archaeology*, pp. 5–20, Carbondale, IL: Southern Illinois University Press.

Meskell, L. (ed.) (1998) *Archaeology Under Fire. Nationalism, Politics and Heritage in the Eastern Mediterranean and the Middle East*, London: Routledge.

Meskell, L. (1999) *Archaeologies of Social Life*. Oxford: Blackwell.

Miller, D. (1982) 'Artefacts as products of human categorisation processes', in I. Hodder (ed.), *Symbolic and Structural Archaeology*, pp. 17–25, Cambridge: Cambridge University Press.

Miller, D. (1985) *Artefacts as Categories*, Cambridge: Cambridge University Press.

Miller, D. (1987) *Material Culture and Mass Consumption*, London: Blackwell.

Miller, D. and Tilley, C. (eds) (1984) *Ideology, Power and Prehistory*, Cambridge: Cambridge University Press.

Minnis, P. and LeBlanc, S. (1976) 'An efficient, inexpensive arid lands flotation system', *American Antiquity* 41: 491–3.

Mizoguchi, K. (1993) 'Time in the reproduction of mortuary practices', *World Archaeology* 25: 223–5.

Molyneaux, B. L. (ed.) (1997a) *The Cultural Life of Images. Visual Representation in Archaeology*, London: Routledge.

Molyneaux, B. L. (1997b) 'Introduction: the cultural life of images', in B. L. Molyneaux (ed.), *The Cultural Life of Images. Visual Representation in Archaeology*, pp. 1–10, London: Routledge.

Montelius, O. (1908) 'The chronology of the British Bronze Age', *Archaeologia* LXI: 97–162.

Montelius, O. (1986 [1885]) *Dating in the Bronze Age*, Stockholm: Kungl. Vitterhets Historie och Antikvitets Akademien.

Mortillet, G. (1897) *Formation de la nation Française*, Paris: Alian.

Mortimer, J. R. (1905) *Forty Years Researches in British and Saxon Burial Mounds of East Yorkshire*, London.

Moser, S. (1992) 'The visual language of archaeology: a case study of the Neanderthals', *Antiquity* 66: 831–44.

Moser, S. and Gamble, C. (1997) 'Revolutionary images: the iconic vocabulary for representing human antiquity', in B. L. Molyneaux (ed.), *The Cultural Life of Images. Visual Representation in Archaeology*, pp. 184–212, London: Routledge.

Mueller, J. W. (ed.) (1975) *Sampling in Archaeology*, Tucson: University of Arizona Press.

Nadaillac, Marquis de (1885) *Pre-historic America* (trans. N. D'Anvers), London: John Murray.

Napier, A. D. (1992) *Foreign Bodies. Performance, Art, and Symbolic Anthropology*, Berkeley, CA: University of California Press.

Needham, S. P. and Sørensen, M. L. S. (1988) 'Runnymede refuse tip: a consideration of midden deposits and their formation', in J. Barrett and I. Kinnes (eds), *The Archaeology of Context in the Neolithic and Bronze Age: Recent Trends*, pp. 113–26, Sheffield: University of Sheffield.

Nelson, N. (1916) 'Chronology of the Tano ruins, New Mexico', *American Anthropologist* 18: 159–80.

Noel Hume, I. (1969) *Historical Archaeology*, New York: Alfred Knopf.

O'Brien, M. J. (1996) 'The historical development of evolutionary archaeology', in H. D. G. Maschner (ed.), *Darwinian Archaeologies*, pp. 17–32, New York: Plenum Press.

O'Brien, M. J. and Holland, T. D. (1992) 'The role of adaptation in archaeological explanation', *American Antiquity* 57: 36–59.

Olsen, B. (1991) 'Metropolises and satellites in archaeology: on power and asymmetry in global archaeological Discourse', in R. W. Preucel (ed.), *Processual and Postprocessual Archaeologies: Multiple Ways of Knowing the Past*, pp. 211–24, Carbondale IL: Southern Illinois University.

Orme, B. (1974) 'Twentieth century prehistorians and the idea of ethnographic parallels', *Man* 9: 199–212.

Orme, B. (1981) *Anthropology for Archaeologists: An Introduction*, London: Duckworth.

Orton, C. (1980) *Mathematics and Archaeology*, Cambridge: Cambridge University Press.

Orton, C., Tyers, P. and Vince, A. (1993) *Pottery in Archaeology*, Cambridge: Cambridge University Press.

Parker-Pearson, M. (1996) 'Food, fertility and front doors in the first millennium BC', in T. C. Champion and J. R. Collis (eds), *The Iron Age in Britain and Ireland: Recent Trends*, pp. 117–31, Sheffield: University of Sheffield.

Parker-Pearson, M. and Richards, C. (eds) (1994) *Architecture and Order. Approaches to Social Space*, London: Routledge.

Patrik, L. (1985) 'Is there an archaeological record?', *Advances in Archaeological Method and Theory* 8: 27–62.

Payne, S. (1975) 'Partial recovery and sample bias', in A. T. Clason (ed.), *Archaeological Studies*, pp. 7–17, Amsterdam.

Pearson, N. and Williams, T. (1991) 'Single-Context Planning: its role in on-site recording procedures and in post-excavation analysis at York', in E. C. Harris (ed.), *Practices of Archaeological Stratigraphy*, pp. 89–103, London: Academic Press.

Peebles, C. S. (1991) '*Annalistes*, hermeneutics and positivists: squaring circles or dissolving problems', in J. Bintliff (ed.), *The Annales School and Archaeology*, pp. 108–24, Leicester: Leicester University Press.

Petrie, W. M. F. (1899) 'Sequences in prehistoric remains', *Journal of the Anthropological Institute* XXIX: 295–301.

Petrie, W. M. F. (1904) *Methods and Aims in Archaeology*. London: Macmillan and Co Ltd.

Piggott, S. (1932) 'The Neolithic pottery of the British Isles', *Archaeological Journal* LXXXVIII: 67–158.

Piggott, S. (1959) *Approach to Archaeology*, Harmondsworth: Penguin.

Piggott, S. (1965) 'Archaeological draughtmanship: principles and practice. Part I: Principles and retrospect', *Antiquity* 39: 165–76.

Piggott, S. (1976) *Ruins in a Landscape: Essays in Antiquarianism*, Edinburgh: Edinburgh University Press.

Pinsky, V. (1992) 'Archaeology, politics, and boundary-formation: the Boas censure (1919) and the development of American archaeology during the inter-war years', in J. E. Reyman (ed.), *Rediscovering our Past: Essays on the History of American Archaeology*, pp. 161–90, Aldershot: Avebury.

Pitt Rivers, A. H. L. F. (1875) 'Principles of classification', *Journal of the Anthropological Institute* IV: 293–308.

Pitt Rivers, A. H. L. F. (1887) *Excavations in Cranborne Chase* (vol. I), privately printed.

Pitt Rivers, A. H. L. F (1898) *Excavations in Cranborne Chase* (vol. IV), privately printed.

Pitt Rivers A. H. L. F. (1906) *The Evolution of Culture and Other Essays*, Oxford: Clarendon Press.

Pluciennik, M. (1999) 'Archaeological narratives and other ways of telling', *Current Anthropology* 40: 653–78.

Preucel, R. (1991) 'The philosophy of archaeology' in R. Preucel (ed.), *Processual and Postprocessual Archaeologies: Multiple Ways of Knowing the Past*, pp. 17–29, Carbondale, IL: Southern Illinois University Press.

Putnam, F. W. (1973 [1886]) 'On methods of archaeological research in America', in S. Williams (ed.), *The Selected Archaeological Papers of Frederic Ward Putnam*, New York: AMS Press Inc.

Pyddoke, E. (1961) *Stratification for the Archaeologist*, London: Phoenix House.

Raab, L. M. and Goodyear, A. C. (1984), 'Middle-range theory in Archaeology: a critical review of origins and applications', *American Antiquity* 49: 255–68.

Rapp, G. and Hill, C. (1998) *Geoarchaeology*, New Haven, CT: Yale University Press.

Read, D. W. (1982) 'Toward a theory of archaeological classification', in R. Whallon and J. Brown (eds), *Essays in Archaeological Typology*, pp. 56–92, Evanston, IL: Center for American Archaeological Press.

Redman, C. and Watson, P. J. (1970) 'Systematic intensive surface collection', *American Antiquity* 35: 279–91.

Reitz, E. J. and Wing, E. S. (1999) *Zooarchaeology*, Cambridge: Cambridge University Press.

Renfrew, C. (1969) 'Trade and culture process in European prehistory', *Current Anthropology* 10: 151–69.

Renfrew, C. (ed.) (1973) *The Explanation of Culture Change: Models in Prehistory*, London: Duckworth.

Renfrew, C. (1976) *Before Civilization*, Harmondsworth: Penguin.

Renfrew, C. (1977) 'Space, time and polity', in J. Friedman and M. Rowlands (eds), *The Evolution of Social Systems*, pp. 89–112, London: Duckworth.

Renfrew, C. (1982) 'Discussion: contrasting paradigms', in C. Renfrew and S. Shennan (eds), *Ranking, Resource and Exchange*, Cambridge: Cambridge University Press.

Renfrew, C. (1984) 'Transformations', in C. Renfrew and K. L. Cooke (eds), *Transformations. Mathematical Approaches to Culture Change*, pp. 3–44, London: Academic Press.

Renfrew, C. (1993) 'Cognitive archaeology: some thoughts on the archaeology of thought', *Cambridge Archaeological Journal* 3: 248–50.

Renfrew, C. (1994) 'Towards a cognitive archaeology', in C. Renfrew and E. Zubrow (eds), *The Ancient Mind. Elements of Cognitive Archaeology*, pp. 3–12, Cambridge: Cambridge University Press.

Renfrew, C. and Bahn, P. (1991) *Archaeology. Methods, Theory and Practice*, London: Thames & Hudson.

Renfrew, J. (1973) *Palaeoethnobotany*, London: Methuen & Co.

Reyman, J. E. (1989) 'The history of archaeology and the archaeological history of Chaco Canyon, New Mexico', in A. L. Christenson (ed.), *Tracing Archaeology's Past. The Historiography of Archaeology*, pp. 41–53, Carbondale, IL: Southern Illinois University Press.

Reyman, J. E. (1992) 'Women in American archaeology: some historical notes and comments', in J. E. Reyman (ed.), *Rediscovering our Past: Essays on the History of American Archaeology*, pp. 69–80, Aldershot: Avebury.

Richards, C. (1995) 'Knowing about the past', in I. Hodder *et al.* (eds), *Interpreting Archaeology*, pp. 216–19, London: Routledge.

Richardson, J. and Kroeber, A. L. (1952 [1940]) 'Three centuries of women's dress fashions: a quantitative analysis', in A. L. Kroeber, *The Nature of Culture*, pp. 358–72, Chicago: University of Chicago Press.

Ricoeur, P. (1984) *The Rule of Metaphor*, Chicago: University of Chicago Press.

Ricoeur, P. (1988) *Time and Narrative* (vol. 3), Chicago: University of Chicago Press.

Roper, D. C. (1976) 'Lateral displacement of artefacts due to plowing', *American Antiquity* 41: 372–4.

Roskams, S. (1992) 'Finds context and deposit status', in K. Steane (ed.), *Interpretation of Stratigraphy: A Review of the Art*, pp. 27–9, Lincoln: City of Lincoln Archaeology Unit.

Rossignol, J. and Wandsnider, L. (eds) (1992) *Space, Time and Archaeological Landscapes*, New York: Plenum Press.

Rouse, I. (1939) *Prehistory in Haiti, A Study in Method*, New Haven, CT: Yale University Publications in Anthropology 21.

Rouse, I. (1955) 'On the correlation of phases of culture', *American Anthropologist* 57: 713–21.

Rouse, I. (1960) 'The classification of artifacts in archaeology', *American Antiquity* 25: 313–23.

Rouse, I. (1968) 'Prehistory, typology, and the study of society', in K. C. Chang (ed.), *Settlement Archaeology*, pp. 10–30, Palo Alto, CA: National Press Books.

Rouse, I. (1972) *Introduction to Prehistory. A Systematic Approach*, New York: McGraw Hill.

Ruberstone, P. E. (1989) 'Archaeology, colonialism and seventeenth-century native America: towards an alternative interpretation', in R. Layton (ed.), *Conflict in the Archaeology of Living Traditions*, pp. 32–45, London: Unwin Hyman.

Sabloff, J. A. and Smith, R. E. (1969) 'The importance of both analytic and taxonomic classification in the Type-Variety System', *American Antiquity* 54: 278–85.

Sackett, J. (1982) 'Approaches to style in lithic archaeology', *Journal of Anthropological Archaeology* 1: 59–112.

Sackett, J. (1990) 'Style and ethnicity in archaeology: the case for isochrestism', in M. Conkey and C. Hastorf (eds), *The Uses of Style in Archaeology*, pp. 32–43, Cambridge: Cambridge University Press.

Sahlins, M. and Service, E. (1960) *Evolution and Culture*, Ann Arbor, MI: University of Michigan Press.

Saitta, D. (1992) 'Radical archaeology and middle range theory', *Antiquity* 66: 886–95.

Schieffelin, E. L. and Crittenden, R. (1991), *Like People You See in a Dream. First Contact in Six Papuan Societies*, Stanford, CA: Stanford University Press.

Schiffer, M. B. (1972) 'Behavioral Archaeology', *American Antiquity* 37: 156–65.

Schiffer, M. B. (1976) *Behavioral Archaeology*, New York: Academic Press.

Schiffer, M. B. (1987) *Formation Processes of the Archaeological Record*, Albuquerque, NM: University of New Mexico Press.

Schiffer, M. B. (1988) 'The structure of archaeological theory', *American Antiquity* 53: 461–85.

Schiffer, M. B. (1996) 'Some relationships between behavioral and evolutionary archaeology', *American Antiquity* 61: 643–62.

Schiffer, M. B. and Miller, A. (1999) *The Material Life of Human Beings*, London: Routledge.

Schiffer, M. B. and Skibo, J. M. (1997) 'The explanation of artifact variability', *American Antiquity* 62: 27–50.

Schmidt, P. R. and Patterson, T. C. (eds) (1995) *Making Alternative Histories. The Practice of Archaeology and History in Non-Western Settings*, Santa Fe, NM: School of American Research Press.

Schnapp, A. (1993) *The Discovery of the Past*, London: British Museum Press.

Schofield, A. J. (1991) *Interpreting Artefact Scatters. Contributions to Ploughzone Archaeology* (Oxbow Monograph 4), Oxford: Oxbow Books.

Schofield, J. (1977) 'Comments on units of archaeological stratification', *Norwegian Archaeological Review* 10: 101–2.

Semenov, S. A. (1964) *Prehistoric Technology*, London: Cary, Adams & Mackay.

Setzler, F. M. and Strong, W. D. (1937) 'Archaeology and relief', *American Antiquity* 1: 301–9.

Shanks, M. (1992a) *Experiencing Archaeology*, London: Routledge.

Shanks, M. (1992b) 'Style and the design of a perfume jar from an archaic Greek city state', *Journal of European Archaeology* 1: 77–106.

Shanks, M. (1997) 'Photography and archaeology', in B. L. Molyneaux (ed.), *The Cultural Life of Images. Visual Representation in Archaeology*, pp. 73–107, London: Routledge.

Shanks, M. and McGuire, R. (1996) 'The craft of archaeology', *American Antiquity* 61: 75–88.

Shanks, M. and Tilley, C. (1987a) *Social Theory and Archaeology*, Cambridge: Polity.

Shanks, M. and Tilley, C. (1987b) *Re-Constructing Archaeology*, Cambridge: Cambridge University Press.

Shanks, M. and Tilley, C. (1987c) 'Abstract and substantial time', *Archaeological Review from Cambridge* 6: 32–41.

Shanks M. and Tilley, C. (1989) 'Archaeology into the 1990s', *Norwegian Archaeological Review* 22: 1–12.

Shennan, S. (1978) 'Archaeological "culture": an empirical investigation', in I. Hodder (ed.), *The Spatial Organization of Culture*, pp. 113–39, London: Duckworth.

Shennan, S. (1988) *Quantitative Methods in Archaeology*, Edinburgh: Edinburgh University Press.

Shennan, S. (1989) 'Introduction: Archaeological approaches to cultural identity', in S. Shennan (ed.), *Archaeological Approaches to Cultural Identity*, pp. 1–32, London: Unwin Hyman (One World Archaeology 10).

Shennan, S. (1993) 'After social evolution: a new archaeological agenda?' in N. Yoffee and A. Sherratt (eds), *Archaeological Theory: Who Sets the Agenda?*, pp. 53–9, Cambridge: Cambridge University Press.

Shepard, A. O. (1956) *Ceramics for the Archaeologist*, Washington, DC: Carnegie Institution.

Skibo, J. M. (1992) *Pottery Function. A Use-Alteration Perspective*, New York: Plenum Press.

Snodgrass, A. (1991) 'Structural history and classical archaeology', in J. Bintliff (ed.), *The Annales School and Archaeology*, pp. 57–72, Leicester: Leicester University Press.

Sollas, W. J. (1911) *Ancient Hunters and their Modern Representatives*, London: Macmillan.

Sørensen, M. L. S. (1989) 'Looking at peripheries. The reproduction of material culture in late Bronze Age Scandinavia and England', in H.-A. Nordstrom and A. Knape (eds), *Bronze Age Studies*, pp. 63–76, Stockholm: Statens Historiska Museum.

Sørensen, M. L. S. (1997) 'Material culture and typology', *Current Swedish Archaeology* 5: 179–92.

Sparke, M. (1996) 'Displacing the field in fieldwork', in N. Duncan (ed.), *BodySpace*, pp. 212–33, London: Routledge.

Spaulding, A. C. (1953) 'Statistical techniques for the discovery of artifact types', *American Antiquity* 18: 305–13.

Spaulding, A. C. (1982) 'Structure in archaeological data: nominal variables', in R. Whallon and J. Brown (eds), *Essays in Archaeological Typology*, pp. 1–20, Evanston, IL: Center for American Archaeological Press.

Spector, J. (1991) 'What this awl means: toward a feminist archaeology', in J. Gero and M. Conkey (eds), *Engendering Archaeology. Women and Prehistory*, pp. 388–406, Oxford: Blackwell.

Spence, C. (1991) 'Recording the archaeology of London: the development and implementation of the DUA recording system', in E. C. Harris (ed.), *Practices of Archaeological Stratigraphy*, pp. 23–46, London: Academic Press.

Spencer, C. S. (1997) 'Evolutionary approaches in archaeology', *Journal of Archaeological Research* 5: 209–64.

Spier, L. (1917) *An Outline for a Chronology of Zuni Ruins*, Anthropological Papers of the American Museum of Natural History 18 New York.

Spriggs, M. (ed.) (1984a) *Marxist Perspectives in Archaeology*, Cambridge: Cambridge University Press.

Spriggs, M. (1984b) 'Another way of telling: Marxist perspectives in archaeology', in M. Spriggs (ed.), *Marxist Perspectives in Archaeology*, pp. 1–9, Cambridge: Cambridge University Press.

Stahl, A. B. (1993) 'Concepts of time and approaches to analogical reasoning in historical perspective', *American Antiquity* 58: 235–60.

Stein, J. K. (1987) 'Deposits for archaeologists', *Advances in Archaeological Method and Theory* 11: 337–95.

Stein, J. K. and Farrand, W. R. (1985) 'Context and geoarchaeology. An introduction', in J. K. Stein and W. R. Farrand (eds), *Archaeological Sediments in Context*, pp. 1–4, Orono, Maine: Center for the Study of Early Man.

Stern, R. (1990) *Hegel, Kant and the Structure of the Object*, London: Routledge.

Stevenson, J. (1883) 'Illustrated catalogue of the collections obtained from the Indians of New Mexico and Arizona in 1879', *Second Annual Report of the Bureau of Ethnology 1880–81*.

Steward, J. (1942) 'The direct historical approach to archaeology', *American Antiquity* 7: 337–433.

Steward, J. (1955) *Theory of Culture Change*, Urbana: University of Illinois Press.

Steward, J. and Setzler, F. (1938) 'Function and configuration in archaeology', *American Antiquity* 4: 4–10.

Stocking, G. W. (1983) 'The ethnographer's magic: fieldwork in British anthropology from Tylor to Malinowski', in G. W. Stocking (ed.), *Observers Observed. Essays on Ethnographic Fieldwork*, pp. 70–120, Wisconsin: University of Wisconsin Press.

Strathern, M. (1995) 'The nice thing about culture is that everyone has it', in M. Strathern (ed.), *Shifting Contexts. Transformation in Anthropological Knowledge*, pp. 153–76, London: Routledge.

Streuver, S. (1968a) 'Flotation techniques for the recovery of small-scale archaeological remains', *American Antiquity* 33: 353–62.

Streuver, S. (1968b) 'Problems, methods, and organization: a disparity in the growth of archaeology', in B. J. Meggers (ed.), *Anthropological Archaeology in the Americas*, pp. 131–51, Washington, DC: The Anthropological Society of Washington.

Sued Badillo, J. (1995) 'The theme of the indigenous in the national projects of the Hispanic Caribbean', in P. R. Schmidt and T. C. Patterson (eds), *Making*

Alternative Histories. The Practice of Archaeology and History in Non-Western Settings, pp. 25–46, Santa Fe, NM: School of American Research Press.

Sullivan, A. P. (ed.) (1998) *Surface Archaeology*, Albuquerque, NM: University of New Mexico Press.

Tarlow, S. (1999) *Bereavement and Commemoration. An Archaeology of Mortality*, Oxford: Blackwell.

Taylor, W. (1948) 'A study of archaeology', *Memoir Series of the American Anthropological Association*, no. 69 (vol. 50).

Teltser, P. A. (ed.) (1995) *Evolutionary Archaeology: Methodological Issues*, Tucson: University of Arizona Press.

Thomas, D. H. (1975) 'Nonsite sampling in archaeology: up the creek without a site?', in J. W. Mueller (ed.), *Sampling in Archaeology*, pp. 61–81, Tucson: University of Arizona Press.

Thomas, J. (1991) *Rethinking the Neolithic*, Cambridge: Cambridge University Press.

Thomas, J. and Tilley, C. (1992) 'TAG and "post-modernism": a reply to Bintliff', *Antiquity* 66: 106–14.

Thompson, M. W. (1977) *General Pitt Rivers*, Bradford-on-Avon: Moonraker Press.

Thompson, R. H. (1956) 'The subjective element in archaeological inference', *Southwestern Journal of Anthropology* 12: 327–32.

Tilley, C. (1989) 'Excavation as theatre', *Antiquity* 63: 275–80.

Tilley, C. (1993) 'Interpretation and a poetics of the past', in C. Tilley (ed.), *Interpretative Archaeology*, pp. 1–27, Oxford: Berg.

Tilley, C. (1994) *A Phenomenology of Landscape*, Oxford: Berg.

Trigger, B. (1968) 'The determinants of settlement patterns', in K. C. Chang (ed.), *Settlement Archaeology*, pp. 53–78, Palo Alto, CA: National Press.

Trigger, B. (1978) *Time and Traditions*, Edinburgh: Edinburgh University Press.

Trigger, B. (1984) 'Alternative archaeologies: nationalist, colonialist, imperialist', *Man* 19: 355–70.

Trigger, B. (1989) *A History of Archaeological Thought*, Cambridge: Cambridge University Press.

Tringham, R. (1991) 'Households with faces: the challenge of gender in prehistoric architectural remains', in J. Gero and M. Conkey (eds), *Engendering Archaeology*, pp. 93–131, Oxford: Blackwell.

Tschauner, H. (1996) 'Middle-range theory, behavioral archaeology, and post-empiricist philosophy of science in archaeology', *Journal of Archaeological Method and Theory* 3: 1–30.

Tyers, P. (1996) *Roman Pottery in Britain*, London: Batsford.

Tyler, E. J. (1973) *The Craft of the Clockmaker*, Ward Lock Ltd.

Tylor, E. B. (1871) *Primitive Culture*, London: John Murray.

Ucko, P. (1969) 'Ethnography and archaeological interpretation of funerary remains', *World Archaeology* 1: 262–80.

Uhle, M. (1902) 'Types of culture in Peru', *American Anthropologist* 4: 753–9.

Uhle, M. (1903) *Pachacamac*, Philadelphia: University of Pennsylvania Press.

Uhle, M. (1907) *The Emeryville Shellmound*, Berkeley, CA: University of California Publications in American Archaeology and Ethnology 7.

van der Leeuw, S. (1993) 'Giving the potter a choice', in P. Lemonnier (ed.), *Technological Choices. Transformations in Material Cultures since the Neolithic*, pp. 238–88, London: Routledge.

Vita-Finzi, C. and Higgs, E. (1970) 'Prehistoric economy in the Mount Carmel area of Palestine: site catchment analysis', *Proceedings of the Prehistoric Society* 36: 1–37.

Wagstaff, J. (ed.) (1987) *Landscape and Culture. Geographical and Archaeological Perspectives*, Oxford: Blackwell.

Watson, P. J. (1995) 'Archaeology, anthropology and the culture concept', *American Anthropologist* 97: 683–94.

Webb, W. S. and de Jarnette, D. L. (1942) *An Archaeological Survey of the Pickwick Basin in the Adjacent Portions of the States of Alabama, Mississippi and Tennessee*, Bureau of American Ethnology Bulletin 129, Washington, DC.

Webster, G. (1965) *Practical Archaeology*, London: Adam & Charles Black.

Wedel, W. R. (1938) *The Direct Historical Approach in Pawnee Archaeology* (Smithsonian Miscellaneous Collections, vol. 97, no. 7), Washington: Smithsonian.

Wedel, W. R. (1951) 'The use of earth-moving machinery in archaeological excavations', in J. B. Griffen (ed.), *Essays on Archaeological Methods*, Anthropological Papers of the Museum of Anthropology, University of Michigan no. 8: 17–33.

Weissner, P. (1983) 'Style and social information in Kalahari San projectile points', *American Antiquity* 48: 253–76.

Weissner, P. (1990) 'Is there a unity to style?', in M. Conkey and C. Hastorf (eds), *The Uses of Style in Archaeology*, pp. 105–12, Cambridge: Cambridge University Press.

Westman, A. (1994) *Site Manual*, London: MoLAS.

Whallon, R. (1973) 'Spatial analysis of occupation floors I: application of dimensional analysis of variance', *American Antiquity* 38: 320–8.

Whallon, R. (1982) 'Variables and dimensions: the critical step in quantitative typology', in R. Whallon and J. Brown (eds), *Essays in Archaeological Typology*, pp. 127–61, Evanston, IL: Center for American Archaeological Press.

Whallon, R. and Brown, J. (eds) (1982) *Essays in Archaeological Typology*, Evanston, IL: Center for American Archaeological Press.

Wheatley, D. (1993) 'Going over old ground: GIS, archaeological theory and the act of perception', in J. Andersen, T. Madsen and I. Scollar (eds), *Computing the Past*, pp. 133–50, Aarhus: Aarhus University Press.

Wheeler, R. E. M. (1922) 'The Segontium excavations 1922', *Archaeologia Cambrensis* LXXVII: 258–326.

Wheeler, R. E. M. (1927) 'History by excavation', *Journal of the Royal Society of Arts* LXXV: 812–35.

Wheeler, R. E. M. (1943) *Maiden Castle, Dorset*, Oxford: Research Report for the Committee of the Society of Antiquaries, London.

Wheeler, R. E. M. (1954) *Archaeology from the Earth*, Oxford: Clarendon Press.

Wheeler, R. E. M. (1958) *Still Digging*, London: Pan Books.

White, L. (1945) 'History, evolutionism and functionalism: three types of interpretation of culture', *Southwestern Journal of Anthropology* 1: 221–48.

Wiber, M. G. (1998) *Visual Images of Gender, 'Race' and Progress in Reconstructive Illustrations of Human Evolution*, Waterloo: Wilfred Laurier University Press.

Wilcox, D. (1981) *Snaketown Revisited*, Arizona State Museum Archaeology Series, no. 155.

Willey, G. R. (1953) *Prehistoric Settlement Patterns in the Viru Valley, Peru*, Bureau of American Ethnology Bulletin 155. Washington DC.

Willey, G. R. (1966–71) *An Introduction to American Archaeology*, Englewood Cliffs, NJ: Prentice-Hall.

Willey, G. R. (1968) 'Settlement archaeology: an appraisal', in K. C. Chang (ed.), *Settlement Archaeology*, pp. 208–26, Palo Alto, CA: National Press Books.

Willey, G. R. and Phillips, P. (1958) *Method and Theory in American Archaeology*, Chicago: University of Chicago Press.

Willey, G. R. and Sabloff, J. A. (1993) *A History of American Archaeology* (3rd edition), San Francisco: W.H. Freeman & Co.

Williams, D. (1973) 'Flotation at Siraf', *Antiquity* 47: 288–92.

Wilson, D. (1851) *The Archaeology and Prehistoric Annals of Scotland*, Edinburgh: Sutherland & Knox.

Wobst, M. (1977) 'Stylistic behaviour and information exchange', *University of Michigan, Museum of Anthropology Anthropological Papers* 61: 317–42.

Woolley, L. (1954 [1930]) *Digging up the Past*, Harmondsworth: Penguin.

Worsaae, J. J. A. (1849) *Primeval Antiquities of Denmark* (trans. W. J. Thoms), London: John Henry Parker.

Wylie, A. (1985) 'The reaction against analogy', *Advances in Archaeological Method and Theory* 8: 63–111.

Wylie, A. (1992) 'On "heavily decomposing red herrings": scientific method in archaeology and the ladening of evidence with theory', in L. Embree (ed.), *Metaarchaeology. Reflections by Archaeologists and Philosophers*, Boston Studies in the Philosophy of Science 147: 269–88.

Wylie, A. (1993) 'A proliferation of new archaeologies: "Beyond objectivism and relativism"', in N. Yoffee and A. Sherratt (eds), *Archaeological Theory: Who Sets the Agenda?*, pp. 20–6, Cambridge: Cambridge University Press.

Wylie, A. (1995) 'Alternative histories. Epistemic disunity and political integrity', in P. R. Schmidt and Patterson T. C. (eds), *Making Alternative Histories. The Practice of Archaeology and History in Non-Western Settings*, pp. 255–72, Santa Fe, NM: School of American Research Press.

Yates, T. (1991) 'Archaeology through the Looking-Glass', in I. Bapty and T. Yates (eds), *Archaeology after Structuralism*, pp. 154–202, London: Routledge.

Index